THE MONEY MACHINE - LEND WHAT YOU BORROW PRINT MONEY 'LEGALLY' LIKE THE RICH

THE MONEY MACHINE - LEND WHAT YOU BORROW PRINT MONEY 'LEGALLY' LIKE THE RICH

RAY WRIGHT JACOBS

Staten House

Contents

FOREWORD FOR "THE MONEY MACHINE"

By Stephan Schurmann, Founder – World Blockchain Bank
Author: 8 LINES OF FREEDOM

Money is not a mystery.
It is not a privilege granted to a select elite.
It is a system — engineered, replicated, and expanded by those who understand its architecture. For centuries, central banks have operated on a simple truth hidden in plain sight: money is created by code, by law, and by confidence. Once you learn that formula, you are no longer a participant in the system — you become its author.

In 8 LINES OF FREEDOM, I revealed how every individual has the legal right and structural capacity to create money the same way central banks do: through asset-backed logic, sovereign positioning, and disciplined economic design. When you understand the mechanics of monetary creation, you stop asking for permission. You begin operating on the level of architects, not employees. You see money not as a wage, but as an instrument. Not as a reward, but as a tool of construction.

Ray Jacobs' THE MONEY MACHINE enters that same arena — and then pushes the reader one step further. This book does not merely explain money. It operationalizes it. Where traditional financial education merely teaches budgeting or investing, Ray teaches economic authorship: the ability to design, replicate, and scale the very engines of wealth that institutions have used for generations.

This foreword is not an endorsement.
It is a recognition.

Ray has taken the core philosophy of 8 LINES OF FREEDOM — the understanding that wealth is an engineered output — and built a system that allows anyone to transform that philosophy into practice. He shows that money creation is not reserved for governments, banks, or corporations. It begins with clarity, structure, and sovereignty of mind. It begins with understanding the code of value — and then writing your own.

THE MONEY MACHINE is a blueprint for those who refuse to spend their lives trapped inside someone else's economic design. It is for those who choose to build instead of comply. For those who understand that freedom is not granted — it is engineered.

Read this book with intention.
Apply it with discipline.
And remember: money is not found.
Money is created.

Stephan Schurmann
World Blockchain Bank
Author of 8 Lines of Freedom

Publishing & Credits

The Money Machine
Lend What You Borrow
Print Money - 'Legally' like the Rich

Published By: Staten House
Publisher's Address: 447 Broadway, 2nd Floor, New York, NY 10013
Scripture quotations marked NLT are taken from the Holy Bible, New Living Translation, copyright 1996, 2004, 2007 by Tyndale House Foundation, Used by permission of Tyndale House Publishers, Inc., Carol Stream, Illinois 60188. All rights reserved.

"Scripture quotations taken from The AMPLIFIED Bible, Copyright © 1954. 1958, 1962, 1964,1965, 1987, 2015 by The Lockman Foundation. All rights reserved. Used by permission.' (www.Locman.org)

Scriptures marked NKJV taken from the New King James Version, Copyright © 1982 by Thomas

Nelson, lnc. Used by permission. All rights reserved.

I italics, Underline =, and Bold in Scripture quotations reflect the author's added emphasis.

Copyright © 2025 by Ray Wright Jacobs

Library of Congress Cataloging-in-Publication Data
Ray Wright Jacobs
"The Money Machine" Lend What You Borrow – Print Money – 'Legally' Like the Rich / Ray Wright Jacobs 1st edition.

1. The Money Machine 2. Title

ISBN: 979-8-90046-854-9

Acknowledgments

To the many men and women, my surrogate mentees, desiring to serve the Lord, but felt that serving Him, meant a life committed to financially getting by with just enough that has pulled this teaching out of me in the many long conversations and deeper studies of the Scriptures. It was your constant drawing and pulling, together with God's assurance that this is within His promises, to get you the information from out of my heart that has prompted me to write this manual. May it free you from status quo as you learn that the very system bankers set up to deceive you is in perfect harmony for God to use it despite its intention to enslave you to debt, for His intended purpose of facilitating the prophetic wealth transfer to his children, the 'just'. Within these pages you will discover you can use real estate to print all the money you desire the way the rich have done it for centuries with your 'Money Machine'!

To my children, both young and older; Lendon & Sherae, Nequisha (my lost one), Ray Jr., Bruce, Isaac, Sydney, Jori, Amayah, Makiyah, King Gabriel, Caidence, Israel and Cayson. Because of your love, you have made me the father I am. I am so Godly proud of the people you have become and are still in fact becoming. I dedicate my life to directing you all to the wisdom of providing an inheritance for your children's children. Follow me as I follow God and let's build a legacy together. God loves each of you, and He will never re-move His Hand from you. Dad loves you all so much!

"Direct your children onto the right path, and when they are older, they will not leave it. Just as the rich rule over the poor, so the borrower is servant to the lender"
(Proverbs 22:6-7 NLT)

This book would not be complete if I did not include the inspiration of my life, my wife Shyla. Babe, You make me better.

He who finds a wife finds a good thing, And obtains favor from the Lord.
(Proverbs 18:22)

Introduction

The Money Machine
Lend What You Borrow
"Print Money - 'Legally' like the Rich"

The 12 Pillars of Creating Wealth

How You Can Print Money Controlling Contract Terms — What Bankers Hope You Never Find Out

"The law of economics does not allow something for nothing. To receive money, one must first give effort, time, or talent. Violate this law, and eventually it produces destruction."

Banks have known this for centuries—but instead of honoring the law, they found a way to twist it in their favor. They found a way to make other people's time, talent, and promises work for them. That discovery became their secret engine of wealth. And that's where this book comes in.

The Money Machine – Lend What You Borrow – "Print Money, Legally, Like the Rich" began as part of my Remodel Series under the pillar of Finances. But the truths inside refused to stay confined. They demanded a stage large enough to reveal how wealth, credit, and covenant actually work when you strip away the illusion. Now, you hold not just another financial book—but a manual of mastery. A field guide to the hidden mechanics of money, contracts, and credit creation that banks have perfected for over a hundred years—yet almost no one is ever taught.

In these pages, you will uncover the same principles that empower the world's financial elites, family offices, and faith-driven wealth builders. You will learn the spiritual law that governs all economics: that true prosperity is built not by possession but by stewardship—by understanding the divine systems of exchange, covenant, and multiplication. You'll also learn how to reclaim your role in that system. Because you've never been the borrower. You've always been the source of credit itself.

God, Man, and Land: The Original Wealth Blueprint

When God created the earth, He designed wealth to flow through dominion and stewardship. Three elements were united in a single moment: God, Man, and Land.

- He formed man from the dust of the ground.
- He breathed life into him.
- And He placed him in the best piece of real estate on earth: the garden.

That garden was more than paradise—it was a prototype. Within it were rivers of gold, fertile soil, precious onyx, aromatic resin, and every raw resource necessary for multiplication. In that design, we see the first Wealth Covenant: man was made to manage creation, not to be enslaved by it. From that moment, the blueprint of prosperity was born—rooted in land, labor, and law.

God's intent never changed. Even though dominion was lost through Adam, it was fully restored through Christ, the Second Adam. That's why your hunger for ownership, your instinct for creation, and your attraction to land are not worldly—they are divine. You were designed to manage the Master's garden, to multiply it, and to rule with wisdom.

Key Insight:
The desire for real estate and ownership is not cultural—it is spiritual. Dominion is written into your DNA.

What is the "Money Machine"?

The Money Machine is not a metaphor. It's a real, functioning system—operating every hour of every day—run by banks, backed by your signature, and powered by your ignorance.

Banks do not lend money from depositors. They do not lend from reserves. They create new credit out of thin air—booked on their ledgers the moment you sign a promissory note. That note is money to them, even though they call it debt to you. Your "loan" becomes their "deposit," multiplied under fractional reserve banking, and leveraged to create ten more "loans" just like it.

Every Federal Reserve Note (FRN) you hold is not wealth—it's a receipt for someone else's debt. The Federal Reserve itself has admitted that these notes have no intrinsic value. People only believe they do because they are accustomed to the illusion. The real wealth is not in the paper—it's in the contract.

Pro Tip:
You don't have to overthrow the system. You just have to learn how to run your own Money Machine inside of it.

Banks have done it for over a century. You can, too. But first, you must understand the 12 Pillars of Wealth Creation—the same blueprint the wealthy have used to turn contracts into currency, liabilities into leverage, and knowledge into generational power.

Why This Book Matters

For generations, we've been taught that banks are the guardians of our savings, when in truth, we are the source of their wealth. Every mortgage, every credit card, every deposit you've ever made became the raw material of their Money Machine.

From the Great Depression to the 2008 Mortgage Crisis, one truth never changed: the banks profit while the people pay.

But what if you could reverse that?

What if, instead of being the fuel for someone else's machine, you built your own—and learned to print income just as the rich do? That is the purpose of this book.

You will learn the same mechanics bankers, insurance companies, and real estate moguls quietly use to build perpetual wealth systems. You'll discover why promissory notes are the DNA of every modern transaction—and how to convert them into your own streams of cash flow. You'll understand how real estate, trusts, insurance policies, and private contracts interlock to form your personal financial engine.

Inside This Book: The 12 Pillars of Wealth Creation

Each module in The Money Machine builds upon the last, forming a step-by-step path from knowledge to power:

- **Module 1:** Teaches how to convert contracts into cash flow through ownership and control.
- **Module 2:** Reprograms your mindset to think like a financier instead of a consumer.
- **Module 3:** Reveals how to structure multiple entities to create three streams of real estate profit.
- **Module 4:** Exposes the truth behind modern credit and the banks' double-entry deception.
- **Module 5:** Revives the lost art of the Ground Game—face-to-face wealth creation through direct action.
- **Module 6:** Shows you how to use the Art of the Assignment to make five figures without cash or credit.
- **Module 7:** Pulls back the curtain on banking opacity, empowering you to challenge and demand transparency.
- **Module 8:** Unveils how banks use promissory notes to create new credit and how to mirror that same process yourself.
- **Module 9:** Introduces "Lend What You Borrow," giving you a working blueprint to fund, lend, and multiply money—legally—like the rich do.
- **Module 10:** Buy • Repair • Flip (Retail)—a complete field manual for turning distressed houses into retail exits.
- **Module 11:** Credit Produces Assets—Which Produce More Credit.
- **Module 12:** What to Buy—The Effective Use of Bank Credit.

Each module gives you real-world tools, templates, calculators, and scripts you can use today. Not theory—application. Because knowledge without movement produces paralysis. Wealth requires flow.

Your Money Machine

Here's the unspoken truth: you have always been the Money Machine. From birth, your signature—your promise to perform—has been leveraged by the financial world as collateral for creation. Every promissory note, every signed agreement, every labor contract you've ever entered has fueled an unseen ledger of credit creation. But now, the tide turns.

When you master these principles, you'll never look at money the same way again. You'll see how banks have been using your faith in the system as the foundation of their power. You'll finally understand that contracts, not cash, move the world—and that the real secret of wealth lies in learning how to write and control those contracts yourself.

The purpose of this book is not rebellion—it's revelation. It's to equip you with the spiritual, mental, and technical knowledge to take your rightful place in the economy of kings.

"My people are destroyed for lack of knowledge." — Hosea 4:6

This is that knowledge. Apply it, and you will never be destroyed again.

Author's Disclaimer

This book is written for educational, informational, and entertainment purposes only. It is not intended to provide financial, legal, or investment advice. The author and publisher make no representations or warranties regarding the accuracy or applicability of any concepts described herein to individual situations. Readers are encouraged to consult qualified professionals—attorneys, accountants, or licensed financial advisors—before making any decisions based on the information in this book. The information provided is solely out of the author's personal experiences, observances, and/or training.

By reading this material, you agree that you are solely responsible for how you apply its contents and that neither the author nor the publisher shall be held liable for any outcomes resulting from its use.

Creating Seed Capital with Your Resource of Time

The Money Machine
Lend What You Borrow
"Print Money - 'Legally' like the Rich"

You've just sparked a new business idea, concept, or plan, and now you face the same question every entrepreneur does: *How do I fund it?* If you didn't grow up with a trust fund or inherit a ready-made safety net, then—like most of us—you probably don't have a wealthy parent, uncle, or relative standing by to write you a blank check. You don't have someone who will casually "invest" in your vision with no concern about whether you succeed or fail. That means you need another path.

The common answer is, *"Find an investor."* But let me ask you—why? Investors often come with strings attached. They turn into partners, or worse, sharks who eventually take control of your dream. That's why I have a saying: *"Why take on an investor if you can fund it yourself?"* Instead of handing away ownership, why not fund your idea with money you create? In this book, I will show you how to do exactly that by using controlled contracts in real estate. Across the twelve modules ahead, you'll learn not only how to acquire significant real estate, but also how to transform contract terms into steady streams of currency—currency that flows into your accounts, I call Hip National Bank, through what I call *the Money Machine*. Along the way, I'll also reveal the exact steps to secure powerful financial tools—Bank Lines of Credit, Warehouse Lines of Credit, and Standby Letters of Credit (SBLCs)—and how to maximize them to fuel your journey toward financial freedom.

Key Insight
The more ownership you keep, the more control you maintain. Every percentage you give away to investors is a percentage of your dream that no longer belongs to you.

Here's a truth I've seen over and over: most aspiring entrepreneurs only calculate part of the equation. They budget their startup costs and maybe 12–18 months of operating expenses. A few even factor in a salary for themselves and their key team members. But rarely does anyone create a *best-case* and a *likely-case* set of projections that track revenue down to the hour—hour by hour, customer by customer, with a clear cost-per-customer plan. That type of detail is the language lenders and serious financiers understand.

To do this, start by projecting your average revenue per customer per hour. Divide your monthly costs by the expected number of customers per hour, and you'll arrive at your "cost per sale." Then, add in the cost of labor: your staff, contractors, marketing team, or anyone else whose time contributes to producing, managing, and selling your product or service. Finally, calculate your financing costs. Take the interest rate of any borrowed money, annualize it, then break it down into monthly and daily repayment amounts. When you spread those repayments across your expected number of daily customers, you'll know exactly how much of each sale is dedicated to debt service.

Pro Tip
When you can explain your "cost per sale" in plain numbers, you've crossed a threshold most entrepreneurs never reach. Lenders respect clarity more than charisma.

Next, combine all of it—your monthly fixed costs, labor costs, financing costs, and marketing expenses. This gives you your true monthly Cost of Goods Sold (COGS). Divide this figure by your total hours of operation, and you'll have a crystal-clear hourly COGS number. Now, compare your hourly revenue projections with your hourly COGS. The difference between those two is your hourly profit. This clarity allows you to forecast daily, weekly, monthly, and annual profit with precision. Almost every entrepreneur overlooks this step—but lenders won't. Showing them that you've analyzed your business down to the daily risk level communicates integrity and foresight. You're telling them, *"I've thought this through. I've already mitigated your risk."*

If you choose to bring in an investor, the same logic applies. Instead of showing loan payments, you present monthly dividend payments. This level of business integrity sets you apart and even moves you to the front of the line with SBA lenders, who often have to push applicants into this kind of scrutiny during the application process. When you've already done it, you stand out as ready, credible, and trustworthy.

Action Step
Create a simple spreadsheet with these categories:

1. **Monthly fixed costs** (rent, utilities, insurance)
2. **Labor costs** (staff, contractors, your own salary)
3. **Financing costs** (loan repayments or dividends)
4. **Marketing costs** (ads, promotions, outreach)

Then divide everything down to hourly figures. This will give you the real heartbeat of your business.

By walking through this analysis, you not only uncover whether your idea has real profit potential—you also arm yourself with a blueprint for funding. These projections are the lifeblood of your business. They prove, on paper, that your idea works. And once you have that foundation, you don't need to beg for money. You're ready to pursue alternatives to investors and traditional lenders.

That's where my method comes in. I'll show you how to leverage real estate deals to bypass traditional funding altogether. You'll learn how to work with non-traditional lenders who care more about the strength of your deal than your credit score. You'll discover how to unlock the golden flow of money tied to real estate—using it to buy, repair, market, and sell properties, then use those profits to "lend" money to yourself. No investors to repay. No banks breathing down your neck. Just you funding your dream with your own Money Machine.

And whether your business needs $10,000 or $10,000,000, this system works. By mastering the art of controlling real estate contract terms, you'll not only fund your ideas—you'll build a repeatable process to power every vision you dare to chase.

Workbook: Testing Your Business IQ

Creating Seed Capital With Your Resource of Time

This workbook will guide you step-by-step through applying the principles from the chapter. Don't just read—*work it out on paper*. Each exercise will help you sharpen your idea, calculate real numbers, and see your business more clearly.

Part 1: Who Owns Your Dream?

Reflection Prompt

- Why are you starting this business?
- Would you feel comfortable giving away part of it to investors in exchange for money? Why or why not?

Write your response below:
Part 2: Key Insight – Keeping Control
Fill-in-the-Blank

Every percent of ownership I give away is a percent of
_____ that I no longer control.

Action Prompt
List 3 reasons why keeping majority ownership matters to you:

Part 3: Cost Per Sale Calculator

Use this section to break your idea into measurable numbers.

Step 1: Monthly Fixed Costs

- Rent/Utilities/Insurance: $_____
- Technology/Subscriptions: $_____
- Other: $_____
  Total Fixed Costs: $_____

Step 2: Labor Costs

- Staff Salaries/Wages: $_____
- Contractors/Freelancers: $_____
- Your Own Salary: $_____
  Total Labor Costs: $_____

Step 3: Financing Costs

- Loan Payments: $_____
- SBLC/LOC Fees: $_____
- Investor Dividends (if any): $_____
  Total Financing Costs: $_____

Step 4: Marketing Costs

- Advertising: $_____
- Promotions/Events: $_____
- Other: $_____
  Total Marketing Costs: $_____

Grand Total (Monthly Costs): $_____

Part 4: Hourly Breakdown

- Hours of Operation per Month: _____ hours
- Estimated Customers per Hour: _____ customers
- Average Revenue per Customer: $_____

Now Calculate:

- Cost Per Sale (Grand Total ÷ Customers): $_____
- Hourly Cost of Goods Sold (COGS): $_____
- Hourly Profit (Revenue – COGS): $_____

Part 5: Pro Tip in Action

Exercise: Write a clear statement you could give a lender, showing your cost per sale. Example:

"For every $25 sale, $18 covers costs and $7 is profit. That $7 builds into $X per month at full capacity."

Draft your statement here:

Part 6: Action Step – Spreadsheet Setup

Create a simple spreadsheet with four tabs:

1. Fixed Costs
2. Labor Costs
3. Financing Costs
4. Marketing Costs

Add a fifth tab labeled "Hourly Breakdown."

Enter your totals and calculate COGS vs. revenue.

Part 7: Golden Flow of Money

Reflection Prompt

If you could "lend money to yourself" by using real estate profits instead of investors, what would be the first thing you'd fund in your business?

Write your answer here:

Notes Section

Use this space for calculations, sketches, or new insights as you work through the numbers.

1

Module-1: Contracts, the Real Money

Controlling Contracts to Print Your Own Money "Legally"

When people think about wealth, they often picture stacks of cash, digital bank balances, huge cryptocurrency wallet balances, or luxury assets. But I learned long ago that real wealth doesn't begin with money—it begins with the agreements that money flows through. Those agreements are called contracts, and if you understand how to control them, you can literally print your own money—legally.

Let me explain.

Most people believe money only comes from labor or capital. They think you either work hard to earn it, or you already have wealth and you invest it. That's what we've been trained to believe. But the wealthy—those who build dynasties—play a different game. They know that the true source of power is in controlling the paper that moves the money.

I want you to begin thinking of every contract you sign, read, or negotiate as a potential Money Machine. Whether that contract involves a house, a truckload of coffee beans, a million barrels of oil, a software license, or even a life insurance policy—the one who controls the terms controls the profit.

That's why I say: contracts are currency in written form.

A Story About Stocks and Banks

To illustrate this, let me share a simple example. Suppose someone gives you a hot stock tip. You learn that shares of ABC Bank, currently $10 per share, are about to skyrocket to $200 tomorrow morning. You know this is a sure thing—you even have proof. You rush to your banker, present your case, and request a $10,000 loan so you can buy 1,000 shares. You have excellent credit. You bank with ABC itself. Surely, they'll lend you the money to buy their own stock, right?

Wrong. Even though your banker agrees with your research, even though he knows you're right, the bank still denies your loan request.

Why? Because banks don't lend against speculation. Stocks, bonds, and securities are too volatile. The principle—the money they lend—could vanish overnight. Lending against that kind of uncertainty violates bank policy.

Banks prefer hard, immovable, reliable assets. And the asset class they love most, outside of certain insurance products, is real estate.

Key Insight
Banks don't care about your credit as much as they care about your collateral. That's why understanding which assets banks love is essential to your Money Machine.

Real Estate: The Bank's Favorite Playground

Let's start with real estate because it's where the Money Machine shines most visibly.

In real estate, there are two types of buyers:

1. **Retail buyers** – These are families or individuals who purchase homes to live in, often paying full market price with bank financing. They represent about 88% of purchases nationwide.
2. **Wholesale buyers** – These are investors, flippers, and companies who look for discounts. They target distressed properties or distressed sellers, buying below market value to secure a profit.

For this book, I'm not here to train you to be a retail buyer. I'm teaching you to think, act, and operate as a wholesale contract controller.

That means you're not attached to granite counter-tops or picket fences. You're attached to numbers. You don't marry houses. You court contracts.

Pro Tip

Always be deal-attached, never property-attached. A pretty house that doesn't produce a profit is worthless to your Money Machine.

The Auction Trap

Now, many new investors flock to foreclosure auctions. They've been to seminars, watched late-night infomercials, and think they'll get rich bidding. What happens? They bid emotionally. They overpay. They compete against each other until the margins vanish.

Seasoned investors, the true pros, don't play that game. They know the Purchase-to-Market Value (PTMV) formula and never violate it. Most of them won't pay more than 65% of the After Repair Value (ARV) of a property, and their sweet spot is 55–60%.

For example: if a home has an ARV of $200,000 and needs $5,000 in repairs, the investor won't bid more than $120,000–$125,000. Anything higher destroys the margin.

But here's the truth: even these "seasoned" players are missing opportunities. Because while they're all fighting over properties at auction, I'm already structuring deals before those homes ever hit the courthouse steps.

Creative Solutions: Controlling the Paper

Here's where I separate myself. I don't chase houses—I chase situations. A distressed seller behind on payments. A landlord tired of repairs. An heir who inherited a property they don't want. These people have a problem, and I bring the solution.

Instead of waiting for the property to go to auction, I create an agreement directly with the seller. That contract—sometimes structured as a lease-option, sometimes as a subject-to, sometimes as a seller-financed note—becomes the engine of the deal.

Now, I don't have to compete. I don't have to outbid anyone. I simply structure the terms in a way that solves the seller's problem and creates a profit for me. Often, I can acquire properties for 40–50 cents on the dollar—better than any auction price.

Key Insight

Money Machine deals are not found, they're created. The one who structures the contract controls the outcome.

Forensic Deal Analysis: Finding Hidden Profit

Let me show you how deep this goes. Take a property valued at $280,000 with a $260,000 loan balance. Add $9,000 in arrears, $5,000 HOA dues, $3,000 in repairs, and $2,000 in move-out costs. On the surface, it looks hopeless. Too much debt. Too little equity. Most investors walk away.

But I dig deeper. Monthly mortgage = $1,300. HOA dues = $180. Total holding = $1,480. Market rent in that neighborhood = $2,300–$2,800. With $3,000 in updates, I can rent it for $2,600.

That's $1,110 a month in positive cash flow—$13,440 a year.

Most people saw a dead deal. I saw a Money Machine.

Pro Tip
Learn to see numbers like a forensic investigator. What others throw
away often hides the biggest cash flows.

Expanding Beyond Real Estate: Other Contracts to Control

Now, I want to broaden your vision. Real estate is powerful, but it's just one field. The Money Machine is not tied to bricks and mortar—it's tied to contracts.

Here are other contracts you can control:

- **Commodity Contracts**: Lock in a buy price for oil, coffee, gold, or wheat. Lock in a sell price with a buyer. Profit from the spread without ever touching the product.
- **Stock Option Contracts**: Buy the right to purchase shares at a set price. Sell that right for profit.
- **Cryptocurrency Hedge Contracts**: Use futures or options to profit from volatility, selling the contract itself for gain.
- **Supplier–Buyer Arbitrage**: Contract a supplier at $10/unit and a buyer at $15/unit. Use the buyer's contract to secure financing. The spread is pure profit.
- **Service Contracts**: Win the master contract for $100,000, hire subcontractors for $70,000, pocket $30,000 for controlling the deal.
- **Licensing Agreements**: Secure the rights to distribute a product or technology. Every unit sold pays you because you control the license.

And one of the most powerful of all: life insurance contracts.

The Morgan Secret: BOLI and COLI

Banks love real estate, but they love life insurance contracts even more. Specifically, Bank-Owned Life Insurance (BOLI) and Corporate-Owned Life Insurance (COLI).

Why? Because these policies are:

• Highly regulated
• Backed by some of the strongest institutions in the world
• Guaranteed to pay out
• Tax-advantaged

J.P. Morgan understood this better than anyone. At one point, he controlled over 1,000 BOLI and COLI policies. Each one was a contract. Each one had a guaranteed payout. And each one became collateral for loans that financed his empire.

For example, he once purchased a $10 million COLI policy. He used it as collateral for a long-term loan. The lender advanced him millions at a low interest rate. When he died, the death benefit paid off the loan. In the meantime, he had years of leveraged capital to invest.

That's what I call printing money on signed paper.

Key Insight

J.P. Morgan didn't wait for permission. He created financial dynasties by controlling the very contracts banks prized most.

The Money Machine Contract Flow

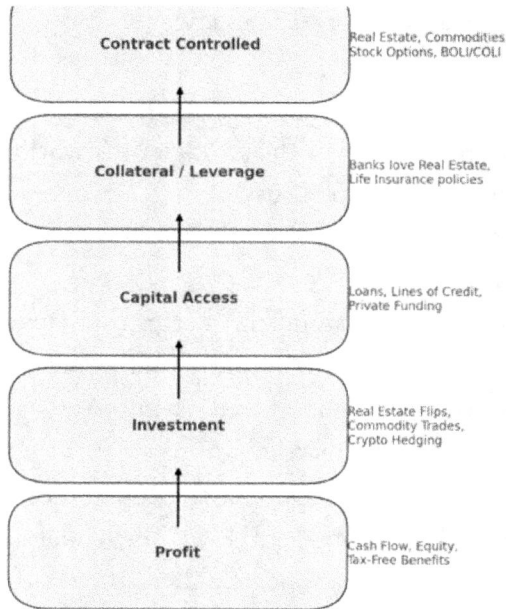

Workbook: Module 1

Controlling Contracts to "Print Your Own Money- Legally"

This workbook is designed to move you from reading to doing. Each exercise builds your ability to spot, analyze, and control contracts for profit. Take your time. Revisit these exercises often. The more you practice, the sharper your Money Machine will run.

Part 1: Reflection Prompts

1. Why do most people overlook the profit potential hidden inside contracts?
   _____

2. If you could control a contract in any industry, which one excites you the most—real estate, commodities, crypto, insurance, or licensing? Why?
   _____

3. What fears or objections come up when you think about controlling a deal without owning the underlying asset?
   _____

Part 2: Fill-in-the-Blanks

- A contract allows me to profit from _____ without owning _____.
- Banks prefer lending against _____ and _____ because they are stable and secure.
- J.P. Morgan financed his empire by controlling _____ and _____ contracts.

Part 3: Real Estate DNA Analysis

Take any property listing from your city. Fill in the blanks below:

- Market Value: $_____
- Loan Balance: $_____
- Arrears: $_____
- Repairs Needed: $_____
- Move-Out Costs: $_____
- Monthly Mortgage/HOA: $_____

- Market Rent: $_____

Cash Flow Spread = (Market Rent – Monthly Costs) = $_____
Decision: Is there a Money Machine here? Yes / No

Part 4: Commodity Contract Drill

Imagine you lock in a buy contract for 100,000 lbs of coffee beans at $1.20/lb. You secure a sell contract at $1.35/lb.

- Cost: $_____
- Sale: $_____
- Profit: $_____

Now choose another commodity (oil, wheat, copper, gold). Write your own buy–sell contract example and calculate the spread.

Part 5: Stock Option Practice

Suppose you buy a call option for XYZ stock at $50 with a premium of $2. A week later, the stock rises to $60.

- Option Strike Price: $_____
- Market Price: $_____
- Intrinsic Value: $_____
- Profit on Contract: $_____

Repeat this with a put option example (profiting when the stock price falls).

Part 6: Cryptocurrency Hedge

Imagine Bitcoin is $40,000. You enter a futures contract at $38,000. It rises to $42,000.

- Entry Price: $_____
- Exit Price: $_____
- Gain/Loss: $_____

Now run the same exercise assuming Bitcoin falls instead of rising. How would the hedge protect you?

Part 7: Supplier–Buyer Arbitrage

You contract a supplier for widgets at $10 each. You lock in a wholesale buyer at $15 each for 5,000 units.

- Supplier Contract: $_____
- Buyer Contract: $_____
- Profit: $_____

Rewrite the same exercise using a product you know personally (cosmetics, electronics, food, etc.).

Part 8: Service Contract Leverage

You win a $100,000 office renovation contract. You subcontract the labor and materials for $70,000.

- Master Contract Value: $_____
- Subcontract Cost: $_____
- Profit Spread: $_____

Think of a service business in your city (landscaping, cleaning, IT). How could you use this same model?

Part 9: Licensing & Intellectual Property

Imagine you negotiate the right to distribute a software product in your state. You receive $20 per license sold. The software company sells 5,000 licenses in your territory this year.

- Royalty Per Unit: $_____
- Units Sold: $_____
- Profit: $_____

Now brainstorm one product, song, book, or invention you could license. How would you profit from controlling distribution?

Part 10: BOLI & COLI Financing

Example: You borrow $2 million against a $5 million COLI death benefit. You invest into a project earning 12% annually. The loan interest rate is 4%.

- Investment Return: $_____
- Loan Cost: $_____
- Net Annual Profit: $_____

Reflect: Why do you think banks use BOLI more than almost any other contract on their balance sheet?

Notes & Insights

Use this space for new ideas, observations, and "aha" moments as you complete the workbook. By completing this workbook, you've practiced controlling at least seven different types of contracts. Each one is a potential Money Machine waiting for you to turn the key.

2

Module 2: Success Habits

Mental Preparation for Success: Developing New Habits

The Tale of Two Wolves

My great-grandmother, Rosie—a full-blooded Cherokee woman—lived to be 78 years old. Her mind was sharp as a razor, and even as a young boy I remember the wisdom she shared with me. One story she told has stayed with me all my life.

She spoke of a Cherokee grandfather teaching his grandson about life. "Inside each of us," he said, "are two wolves locked in battle. One wolf is good: he is love, peace, kindness, humility, joy, and discipline. The other wolf is destructive: he is anger, pride, laziness, jealousy, bitterness, and unforgiveness. These two wolves fight constantly."

The boy thought for a moment and asked, "Which wolf will win?" The grandfather smiled and said, **"The one you feed."**

That metaphor has guided me: every thought, word, and action is food. You feed the wolf you empower. In this module, my goal is to help you feed the right wolf so that discipline, integrity, and power become your daily nature—not just occasional performance.

Why Mental Conditioning Precedes Wealth

You cannot build a Money Machine externally if your internal machine is faulty. The strongest plan in the world fails when the mind collapses under pressure. I've seen deals collapse, ministries fall, and lives unravel—not because strategy was wrong, but because internal strength was missing.

Science now confirms what the ancients knew: repeated thoughts and actions wire your brain. Habits become default settings. That's why the 7 Foundations of Personal Power exist—not as optional ideals, but as non-negotiable disciplines.

With consistent obedience, you can rewire your inner world in 21 to 60 days. And once that transformation takes root, no external circumstance can crack you.

Habits: The Foundation of Destiny

Your current habits—good or bad—are almost entirely responsible for your future. Studies show that up to 90% of daily behavior is driven by habit. That means the life you live right now is the result of patterns you've repeated over and over again.

The good news? Habits can be changed. With consistency and intentionality, old patterns can be broken and replaced within three to six weeks. But change takes courage, because in order to form new disciplines, you must endure the discomfort of leaving old patterns behind.

Key Insight

Success doesn't come from knowledge alone. It comes from the courage to apply knowledge long enough for it to become habit.

The 7 Foundations of Personal Power

To run your Money Machine effectively, you must first run yourself. These **7 Foundations of Personal Power** are disciplines I've learned, lived, and taught. They are not theories—they are battle-tested. Apply them, and you will transform from the inside out.

1. Trust God's Word About You

Your identity is the soil where everything else grows. If your roots are shallow—if you doubt who you are—every storm will uproot you. You must anchor your identity in Scripture, not in opinion or past failure.

Consider **Oprah Winfrey**. She has often spoken about her traumatic past—abuse, rejection, poverty—yet she anchored her identity in a higher purpose and spiritual truths about her value. Because she trusted a deeper Word about who she is, she pressed into greatness despite the shadows of her past.

On the flip side, **Mike Tyson** is a tragic example of someone who refused God's elevated identity for himself. A man of incredible talent, he allowed shame, bitterness, and voices of condemnation to define him. He spoke degradation over himself, and it produced collapse.

In business, **Howard Schultz** (Starbucks founder) has said that his faith convictions shaped how he led the company—believing in dignity, purpose, and value in each person. He walked in identity, not in the shifting winds of public approval.

But when people betray this foundation, they are victimized by every negative voice—media, critics, wasted past. You must guard this foundation fiercely: speak God's Word over yourself until it becomes your anchor.

2. Maintain Faith in Your Domain

Faith is not passive hope. It's a governor over your territory—finances, calling, family. To maintain faith in your domain means to live in the posture of "It is done," even before you see it.

Take **Roger Bannister** (the first man to break the 4-minute mile). He believed the barrier could fall—even though everyone said it was impossible. He trained, prepared, and then declared it done—then ran 3:59. Faith in his domain (athletics) rewrote reality.

Contrast that with **Blackberry's rise and fall**. In the mid-2000s, Apple and Android were threatening. Blackberry's leaders lost faith in their domain—they stopped innovating, reacted defensively, and ceded territory. They lost because once faith in domain broke, complacency crept in.

Athletes like **Michael Jordan** provide further insight. Even when injured or down, Jordan's faith in his domain never wavered. In *The Last Dance*, he said, *"My mentality was to go out and win at any cost... if you don't want to live that regimented mentality... then you don't need to be alongside me."* (ESPN.com) That kind of unwavering faith shapes domain.

When domain-faith fails, you begin to shrink your vision. You hedge, you balk, you defer. You stop doing first steps because you can't yet see the full road. But strong faith builds momentum before sight.

3. Maintain Impeccable Integrity with Your Words

Words are seeds—planted consciously or unconsciously. When you lie, exaggerate, or betray your promises, you weaken your internal character and external influence. Alignment between your speech and action is non-negotiable.

Look at **LeBron James**. Off the court, he has often spoken about loyalty, teamwork, and leadership. He's lived those values by taking care of his teammates, his foundation work, and his public image. His consistency in speech and life has reinforced his stature as not just athlete, but leader.

Compare that to **Lance Armstrong**. The man rode 7 Tour de France wins. He spoke of clean sport, cancer awareness, integrity—and then it was all revealed to be lies. The downfall was not his doping alone; it was the betrayal of his entire public speech. Once credibility collapsed, everything collapsed with it.

In business, **Jeff Bezos** often states "Be stubborn on vision, but flexible on details." He cultivates integrity by publicly holding Amazon to high standards, then aligning internal operations to attempt to match speech and action.

Take **Steve Jobs.** On the product side, he was uncompromising. If a device prototype fell short, he declared it "garbage." Brutal honesty in design and product standards meant Apple never settled for mediocrity. His demand for truth in quality, even if painful, birthed revolutionary devices. Jobs showed integrity with his words when it came to the vision of Apple: say what you mean, mean what you say, and deliver it.

But Jobs also provides the other side of this law. Early in his life, he denied paternity of his daughter Lisa, despite overwhelming evidence. That failure of personal integrity scarred relationships for years. It's a reminder: you cannot separate integrity in business from integrity in family. Both matter.

Integrity builds credibility. Once credibility collapses, even genius can be stained.

But when you break your own word—even silently—you fracture trust with yourself. Doors that once opened begin to close. People no longer trust your brand. You begin to shrink your future. Integrity is more than truth to others; it's truth to self, even when no one's watching.

4. Speak with Authority to Renew Your Thinking

Words shape not just the future—they transform the present. Every time you confess truth, you reshape your internal landscape. Think of your tongue as a thermostat: you don't describe the climate; you set it.

Tony Robbins has built his life and business upon the power of declarations. His seminars train people to speak positive truth over their lives until they deploy new identities. He knows spoken words precede transformed behavior.

In the tech world, **Elon Musk** models declarations: he frequently speaks in bold, confident statements about Mars, Tesla, Neuralink—before all evidence existed. His words help guide investors, engineers, and markets.

On the dark side, many businessmen slip into narratives of defeat: "I can't," "I'm too late," "I failed." Those confessions hook your spirit into defeat loops. **Charlie Sheen** is an example—a man whose repeated self-destructive declarations ("I am the warlock," etc.) reinforced addiction, chaos, and collapse.

Steve Jobs is a masterclass in this foundation. His colleagues coined the phrase "Reality Distortion Field" because Jobs could speak with such authority that others began to believe the impossible. When he launched the iPod, he didn't talk about hard drives or specs. He declared: "1,000 songs in your pocket." That phrase reshaped consumer expectation and sold millions.

Jobs' words set the thermostat. His employees didn't always believe they could achieve what he declared—but his authority pushed them to rise. They aligned reality with his declarations.

But Jobs also reminds us of the danger. Authoritative speech without empathy can become tyranny. Some employees testified that his cutting remarks broke spirits. Speaking with authority must be coupled with building up, not just tearing down.

When you confess truth, you force your spirit to chase what is spoken. When you confess lies or negative frames, you anchor yourself to limitation. Choose your declarations with authority. Let them be weapons against your doubts.

5. Never Take Others' Words Personally

This foundation is your armor. Critics will always exist. That's part of operating in light. If you internalize every jab, every insult, you give away your peace.

Beyoncé is a powerful example of someone under relentless public scrutiny. Through scandals, rumors, failures, she has refused to define her identity by external noise. She has persisted, argued little, and stayed grounded in her purpose.

Yet others crumble. **Tiger Woods**—once revered—allowed criticism, rumors, and betrayal to become identity. For a time, he played under the weight of broken reputation rather than recovering an internal core.

In historical leadership, **Nelson Mandela** was persecuted, slandered, and misrepresented for decades. Yet, he never internalized the attacks. He held onto his purpose and remained unoffendable.

When you take criticism personally, you shrink your soul. You replay it, overthink it, shrink inward. You begin to live under the authority of others' voices, not God's voice over you. Walk in unoffendability.

6. Never Make Assumptions—Always Ask Questions

Assumptions are silent saboteurs. They build walls between hearts, kill relationships, and distort reality. When you assume motives or intent instead of clarifying, you create conflict where none existed.

Oprah Winfrey, when confronted with opposition or media narrative, often directly asks: "What do you mean by that?" She leans into curiosity rather than defensiveness. That posture disarms conflict and opens communication.

On the flip side, many break in marriage, ministries, and businesses because one partner assumed "He meant this..." or "She wants that..." without ever discussing it. Assumptions became expectations, disappointment, then conflict.

In politics, catastrophic breakdowns often happen because leaders assume motives of opponents instead of clarifying. Miscommunication leads to escalation.

The moment you assume, you hand control away. The moment you ask, you redirect the conflict into clarity. Clarify intent. Ask questions. Prevent disaster.

7. Do Your Best at All Times

Consistency over time amplifies everything. Ordinary people give bursts of energy. Extraordinary people give consistent focus. Doing your best means refusing the voice of mediocrity, especially when comfort tempts you to coast.

Michael Jordan is a perfect modern illustration. Even after he dominated the league, he still practiced, pushed, refused complacency. In *The Last Dance*, he showed how even small drills, mid-career conditioning, and relentless standards set him apart from those resting on reputation. (ESPN.com)

Yet, many brilliant stars fade. **MAC Cosmetics founder Bobbi Brown** said in an interview that complacency nearly destroyed the early momentum of her brand. Giving less than your best—even for short seasons—lets competition creep past.

In entrepreneurship, **Reed Hastings** (Netflix) says their culture demands "high performance" every day. They don't allow past success to excuse present laziness.

Jobs lived by one standard: "insanely great." Nothing less. He demanded excellence from himself and his teams. That constant pursuit of "best" built products that transformed entire industries. iPhone, iPad, Mac—none would exist if "good enough" had been the goal.

Jobs believed that details mattered. Even the inside of a computer—parts no customer would ever see—had to be beautiful. That relentless pursuit of doing the best became Apple's DNA.

But here too is a caution. Jobs' obsession sometimes came at the expense of balance, health, and relationships. Doing your best means excellence, but not self-destruction. The foundation is violated when "best" morphs into perfectionism that breaks your humanity.

If you want your Money Machine to run reliably, show up. Refuse mediocrity. Be consistent. Over decades, that quality compounds into invincibility.

Daily Power Confession Seeds

- "I live by the Word; I am what God says I am."
- "My domain is secure; faith rules in me."
- "My words match my inner man; integrity defines me."
- "I speak authority and life; my environment conforms."
- "Criticism falls away; I remain unshaken."
- "I clarify over assumption; I communicate courageously."
- "I give my best today, no compromise."

Speak them daily until they aren't just confessions, but your nature.

Workbook: Module 2

M ental Preparation for Success: Developing New Habits

1. **Reflection Prompt:** Which of the 7 foundations has betrayed you the most? Write a short story of a time you neglected it.

----

1. **Identity Declarations:** Write five scriptural or prophetic declarations of who God says you are. Confess them every morning.

----

1. **Domain Exercise:** Choose one area (finances, calling, family). Write a courageous step you will take this week that aligns with faith, not fear.

----

1. **Integrity Inventory:** Over the next 30 days, whenever you make a promise (even to yourself), log it and rate how well you kept it. Reflect weekly.

----

1. **Confession Journal:** Each evening, record one declaration you spoke with authority. After 30 days, look back and see your internal shift.

----

1. **Unoffendable Drill:** When someone offends you, pause. Journal: "What's theirs? What's mine? What is truth?" Respond in grace.

----

1. **Clarification Practice:** List three situations where miscommunication cost you. For each, write questions you could have asked to avoid conflict.

----

1. **Excellence Plan:** Pick one area (work, family, health). Map a 90-day plan to raise your standard by at least 20%.

3

Module 3: How to Set Up Your Business

Business Formalities & Formation

This is the place in The Money Machine where I believe the lights will come on and the engine starts to hum. The law speaks in puzzles; I'm going to translate it into levers. When we say "person," the law sees two versions: the breathing you (natural person) and the paper YOU (juridical person) that does business, signs contracts, holds title, and takes heat so you don't have to. I'll call that second one "YOU Trust/ Inc" as a teaching tool. Read that phrase as your *legal capacity to create and command entities*—your paper army. If you don't control those papers, someone else will, and your signature will bless it. Dominion means you pick up the pen.

From Genesis forward, God gave mankind dominion over the earth, not over other men. In modern life that dominion travels through contracts and entities—your artificial persons. So we will build your business army with care, dignity, and compliance: corporations, LLCs, partnerships, trusts, nonprofits, churches, ministers, and integrated auxiliaries. Each is a tool. Each has rules. Obey the rules and the rules protect you.

Natural person = **you** (*who must give Artificial person (YOU Trust/Inc) consent to act as you in contracts*).

Artificial (juridical) person = *"YOU Trust/Inc," an entity the law treats like you—a person (that can own property, sign contracts, sue/be sued).*

This was done so that in law, there could be perceived authority, dominion and might over man—but paper man. A man that surrenders their consent to be ruled by allowing someone else who created a contract to have that position by a signature of some sort by you or an agent for you.

"Then God said, 'Let Us make man in Our image... let them have domin-ion'
'...be fruitful and multiply... fill the earth and subdue it; have dominion...'
(Genesis 1:26–28, NKJV)

Each man was given this dominion, but no man was given dominion over other men. So use that dominion to create your own artificial-person business army of contract controllers.

Key Insight
In our age, dominion moves through contracts and entities. The living you decides; the paper YOU signs.

Compliance Clarity (to keep you safe)
"YOU Trust/Inc" here is a teaching metaphor for your legal capacity to form and control entities. Birth records create a public identity—not a for-profit company. The wealth move is that you deliberately form and command lawful entities (LLCs, corps, trusts, church, auxiliaries) and sign as them, not personally.

The Legal Reality (why this works)

American law recognizes natural persons (humans) and artificial persons (entities). Statutes and cases treat corporations, LLCs, partnerships, trusts, associations, and certain religious organizations as persons for contract, property, and court rights. That's your opening. You're not evading the law—you're using it.

Key Insight

The court looks for substance and formalities: separate money, minutes/ resolutions, proper titles, adequate capital, clean books. Do the rituals; enjoy the shield.

YOU Trust/Inc vs. you (how dominion moves through paper)

Here's the picture: **you** are the living soul, the decision-maker. YOU Trust/Inc is my shorthand for the legal "you" that enters commerce. In practice, YOU Trust/Inc is realized when you *form and control* your entities—your LLCs, corporations, trusts, church, and auxiliaries. Those are the vessels. Your signature is the steering wheel. When you sign as the entity, not personally, the obligation falls on the vessel, not your household. That's the difference between sleepless nights and peaceful compounding.

So the first discipline of dominion is this: never sign naked. Always wear the armor of your entity. "Jane Doe, Manager, Alpha Holdings LLC." That one line preserves the veil.

Corporation: the ironclad ship

A corporation is a separate legal body. It has owners (shareholders), a board (governors), and officers (operators). Done right, it takes the punch so you don't. You'll keep minutes, adopt bylaws, issue stock, file annual reports, and bank under its EIN. That ritual isn't busywork—it's the shield the court looks for. Tax-wise you choose either C-Corp (the company pays tax; dividends can be taxed again) or S-

Corp (pass-through, often efficient for owner-operators using reasonable salary + distributions). Need to raise capital, grant stock options, or scale fast? The corporation is your aircraft carrier.

Taxes: Choose C-Corp (company pays its own tax; dividends taxed again) or elect S-Corp (pass-through). Owner-operators often use S-Corp with reasonable salary + distributions for efficiency.

Use it for: Raising capital, stock options, public-facing scale.

Watch: Don't co-mingle; paper every big decision; pay a real salary in S-Corps.

Teach your hands: never co-mingle. Pay yourself by payroll or dividend/distribution—never by impulse.

LLC: the workhorse with a custom saddle

The LLC was built to be flexible. You write an Operating Agreement that says who decides, who earns, and how cash moves. Courts respect it when *you respect it*: separate books, documented resolutions, proper capitalization. Tax defaults to pass-through, but you can elect S-Corp or C-Corp if strategy demands it. Real estate? Use property-specific LLCs. Consulting or an online brand? LLC taxed as S-Corp can save self-employment taxes (with that "reasonable salary" discipline). Think of the LLC as your everyday truck—reliable, configurable, and hard to pierce.

Taxes: Default pass-through; optionally elect S-Corp or C-Corp. Flexible allocations are investor-smart.

Use it for: Real estate silos, online brands, consulting, joint ventures.

Watch: No operating agreement = asking for trouble. Document member/manager actions.

Keep the blessing: every big decision gets a written resolution. Paper proves prudence.

Partnership: the promise we write down

A partnership is two or more people agreeing to share profit and responsibility. If everyone manages, it's a general partnership (and risk follows you home). If some are passive, you can structure LP/LLP to protect limited partners who don't manage. Taxes pass through; basis and capital accounts let you engineer fairness deal by deal. Best when you need a deal shell fast with investors who understand roles. Just remember: a limited partner who behaves like a boss stops being limited in a courtroom. Wear the right hat—or don't wear it at all.

Taxes: Pass-through with powerful basis rules and capital accounts.
Use it for: Professional firms, deals with passive investors.
Watch: A limited partner who acts like a boss loses their shield.

Nonprofit association (not a church): the mission engine

When your purpose is charitable, educational, or community-building, a nonprofit corporation gives you legitimacy and protection. You'll adopt bylaws, sit a board, forbid private inurement, and—unless you're a church—file Form 990s. Donor dollars want clarity; governance provides it. Taxes? If you qualify under 501(c), your mission income is exempt and gifts are deductible. But business unrelated to mission can trigger UBIT (unrelated business income tax). When you must run a commercial line, house it in a taxable subsidiary and sign clean service agreements between the two. Mission stays pure; business stays honest.

Taxes: If recognized under 501(c), mission income is exempt; donors' gifts are often deductible. Business unrelated to mission can trigger UBIT.
Use it for: Charities, schools, member groups.
Watch: Keep any commercial line in a taxable subsidiary with clean inter-company agreements.

Trust: the quiet fortress

A trust is a written order to a trustee: hold these assets for these people in this way. It's private, durable, and powerful for estate planning. You can have revocable (you still control it) or irrevocable (you surrender control for stronger protection and tax effects). For business, let the trust own your HoldCo LLC. Now, when you pass, continuity is automatic; probate is a spectator. Taxes follow Subchapter J—sometimes the trust pays, sometimes beneficiaries do, depending on distributions. The trust doesn't hustle; it positions.

Taxes: Under Subchapter J, sometimes the trust pays; sometimes the beneficiary does, depending on distributions.

Use it for: Estate planning, privacy, owning your HoldCo LLC, charitable design.

Watch: If you don't retitle assets into the trust, the law won't pretend you did.

Move assets, don't just talk about it. If you don't title property to the trust, the law won't pretend you did.

Unincorporated JV: the pop-up tent

Sometimes you want a quick project without a full build-out. A joint-venture agreement can do it: who brings what, who gets what, who decides what. It's fast—and fragile. Liability can splash on you. If the dollars or risks rise, graduate to an LLC. The pop-up tent keeps you dry in a drizzle; don't sit through a hurricane under canvas.

Taxes: Generally pass-through.

Use it for: Small, short projects—then upgrade to an LLC if dollars or risk rise.

Watch: Don't run a hurricane under a pop-up tent.

Church: sacred calling, lawful structure

A church is a worship community with its own doctrine, governance, and services. It is generally tax-exempt if it lives the 501(c)(3) standards—religious purpose, no private inurement, no political campaign intervention, and integrity in operations. Unlike other nonprofits, a bona fide church enjoys automatic recognition, special audit protections, and is typically exempt from Form 990. Donations are usually deductible. That's a holy privilege—treat it like one.

Where churches stumble is business creep. Selling products or running ventures that aren't substantially related to ministry can create taxable UBIT. The clean way: if you must operate a commercial line, put it in a taxable subsidiary (LLC or corporation), paper fair-value leases and service agreements, keep books separate, and protect the pulpit from the marketplace. Caesar gets Caesar's; God gets God's.

Taxes: Ministry income is exempt; unrelated business can be UBIT.

Use it for: Worship, discipleship, benevolence, education aligned to faith.

Watch: No political campaign intervention; no private inurement. If you must run commerce, do it in a taxable subsidiary and paper every inter-company relationship.

Minister: officer of the house

Ministers lead worship, shepherd people, and—often—help administrate the church. The law treats their pay uniquely. A properly designated housing allowance/parsonage can be excluded from income for federal income tax; ministers generally pay SECA (self-employment tax) rather than FICA on ministry earnings unless exempt. Reimburse expenses under an accountable plan—written, documented, and approved in advance. One caution: speak prophetically as a person, not politically as the church. Personal opinions are yours; endorsements from the pulpit can cost the church its exemption.

Taxes: Housing allowance/parsonage can be excluded from federal income tax (designate it in advance). Ministers generally pay SECA on ministry earnings unless exempt. Use accountable plans for reimbursements.

Use it for: Spiritual leadership, sacramental duties, lawful administration.

Watch: Endorsing candidates from the pulpit is off-limits. Keep governance minutes tight.

Write it down before it's paid. Housing allowances must be designated in advance by church action. Minutes matter.

Integrated auxiliaries: the focused arms

Youth ministry, women's fellowship, a seminary, a missions arm—these are integrated auxiliaries when properly connected to the parent church. They exist to carry a specific piece of the mission and typically share the church's exemption when structured under the rules. Give each arm a charter, budget, overseer, and books (often a separate sub-account). If an auxiliary starts doing commercial work, put those activities into a taxable subsidiary and keep the relationships on paper at fair market terms. Ministry remains ministry because you separated what must be separate.

Taxes: Same exemption rules; UBIT still applies to unrelated business activity.

Use it for: Running distinct programs under church authority.

Watch: Give each arm a charter, budget, books, and oversight. Spin out commercial lines into taxable subs.

How to maximize the lawful use of church, minister, and auxiliary (without losing your grace)

Center the mission. Everything flows from worship and discipleship. If you can't explain how an activity advances the church's religious purpose, it probably doesn't belong inside the church entity.

Protect the pulpit. No campaign endorsements. Education is fine; partisanship is not. You keep influence by keeping integrity.

Designate housing allowances the right way. Put it in minutes *before* the money is paid. Keep receipts; reconcile annually.

Use subsidiaries for commerce. When you need a café, a print shop, or a media line, form a separate LLC or corporation. Lease space from the church at fair value; pay for shared services with written agreements. Clean lines today prevent confusion tomorrow. Train your treasurer on UBIT. "Mission-related" is a test with teeth. When in doubt, ask counsel or a CPA who lives in exempt-org world.

Action Step
Draft: (a) Church governance policy, (b) Housing allowance resolution template, (c) Inter-company services & facilities use agreements, and (d) UBIT decision tree. Keep them in your minute book.

The Money Machine stack (how YOU commands the paper army)
Here's the flow I coach:

1. A living trust owns your HoldCo LLC. The trust is your private control room; HoldCo is the parent that owns your operating entities.
2. Each business line sits in its own LLC or corporation. Risk is siloed. If one ship springs a leak, the fleet sails on.
3. If you lead a church, the church handles worship and ministry. Integrated auxiliaries handle programs. Any commercial activity lives in a taxable subsidiary with proper agreements back to the church (leases, services, IP licenses).
4. If you're an owner-operator, consider an LLC taxed as S-Corp for your active income: pay yourself a reasonable salary; let surplus flow as distributions. Let the entity pay accountable reim-

bursements rather than you paying personal and "making it up later."

Key Insight
If you don't write the rules, you live by someone else's. Contracts are where profit is negotiated and protection is preserved.
That is dominion by design: you hear, YOU signs.

The five habits that keep the shield on and the blessing flowing

- **Separate everything.** Separate EINs, banks, cards, accounting. Co-mingling is veil-piercing in slow motion.
- **Paper your decisions.** Resolutions, minutes, approvals. If it wasn't written, in law it often wasn't done.
- **Sign with your armor on.** "Your Name, Title, Entity Name." Never personally, unless you mean it.
- **Capital and coverage.** Fund the entity enough to do what it claims; insure what you can't absorb.
- **Honor Caesar, honor God.** File what's due, on time. For churches: know the lines (no private benefit, no campaigning). For businesses: keep payroll and taxes clean. For everyone: truth in the books.

Formalities that keep your veil on (daily → annual)
Daily/Weekly

- Spend only from the entity's account.
- Capture receipts; log purpose.
- Sign "Your Name, Title, Entity."

Monthly/Quarterly

- Reconcile bank/credit accounts.

- Record member/board approvals for loans, distributions, contracts.
- Payroll/housing allowance processed correctly.

Annually

- File state annual reports and IRS returns.
- Hold and minute annual meetings (board, members).
- Review insurance and capitalization.
- For churches/nonprofits: audit/financial review; mission fit review; UBIT scan.

Pro Tip

A one-page monthly resolution that ratifies key acts is cheap armor. Courts love paper. So do auditors.

Common mistakes (and fast fixes)

- **Co-mingling funds.**
  Fix: Open/clean books; document owner loans/distributions; stop the bleed today.
- **No governing docs.**
  Fix: Adopt bylaws/operating agreement; ratify past acts by resolution.
- **Wrong tax election.**
  Fix: Re-evaluate with CPA; S-Corp may help owner-operators.
- **Nonprofit/church business creep.**
  Fix: Move unrelated activity to taxable sub; paper fair-value agreements.
- **Minister pay without designation.**
  Fix: Pre-approve housing allowance; adopt accountable plan; minute it.

Authority references (quick cite list)

- Statutory "person" includes entities; business entity acts (state).
- Corporate personhood cases; trust rules (Subchapter J).
- Nonprofit/church tax standards; ministers' housing rules; integrated auxiliaries regulations.
  (*Use these as footnotes/endnotes in your book's references section.*)

Bottom line: You were given dominion. In our age, dominion flows through contracts and entities. The you that decides must command the YOU that signs. Build your vessels. Keep your books. Control your contracts. That's how ordinary ink becomes extraordinary wealth—lawfully, ethically, and with a clean conscience.

The 3-Entity Engine: How You Turn Paper Into Paydays

You've learned why "person" matters, how you command YOU, and how lawful dominion flows through contracts and entities. Now we end Module 3 by building your forward-facing money engine—three coordinated entities that let you source deals, control construction, and flip paper like a bank:

1. **Real Estate Investment Company (REIC)** – your first line of contact, solution-driven, not predatory.
2. **General Contractor / Remodel Company (GC Co.)** – your cash-flow valve, turning discounts on labor/materials into weekly income while protecting project margins.
3. **Discount Note Buyer / Servicing Company (DNBC)** – your paper arm, contracting with borrowers and law firms, then selling/assigning notes to your Yield Concession Servicers (YCS).

Think of it as a symphony: REIC finds & structures, GC Co. executes & cash-flows, DNBC monetizes debt. You control the contracts at every step—so you control the outcomes.

1) Real Estate Investment Company
Your Identity: Realty Solutions Manager

You are not the "lowest-price house snatcher." You're the Realty Solutions Manager—the professional who shows homeowners multiple pathways that actually work for them (save the home, restructure, sell retail, sell investor-grade, or convert the debt). The win is solution first, profit second; ironically, that approach pays you more, more often.

Formation & Setup (clean, fast, professional)

- **Name & entity.** Simple, credible, broad. (ex: *Metroplex Realty Group, LLC*).
- **File** Articles with the state; adopt an Operating Agreement; get EIN; open bank account.
- **Professional presence.**
    - Address: UPS Store (street address), or Regus virtual office.
    - Phones: RingCentral (800 + local); route to live receptionist.
    - Email/Domain: brand domain + pro email.
    - Accounting: QuickBooks; start checks at #30,000 (prevents "rookie" optics).
- **Data & tools.**
    - Lead & title intel: DataTree ($99/mo).
    - Routes: Route4Me ($49/mo).
    - Property intel/CRM: your chosen "Real Estate Solutions" system ($99/mo).
- **Brand artifacts.** Business cards titled "Realty Solutions Manager"; separate social profiles; solution-first website.

Operating Philosophy (flows into Modules 5 & 7)

When a family is squeezed by a $4,200 payment on a $450,000 note after an ARM reset—and they can truly afford $3,300—you don't shame them, you solve. Your job is to design a win/win: restructure, forbearance, note sale, assumption, wrap, short payoff, or—when needed—graceful exit that preserves dignity. You are paid to engineer outcomes.

2) General Contractor / Remodel Company
Why You Need It
Contractors make money every Friday, not just at sale. Your GC Co. locks in 15–25% discounts on labor/materials and converts those discounts into steady project-management draws. It keeps crews loyal, timelines tight, and your fridge full while you wait for the big check.

Formation & Setup (Texas example; adjust to your state)

- **Name & entity.** (ex: *Syndax Development Group, LLC*).
- **File** Articles; EIN; bank; domain/email; QuickBooks; checks starting #30,000.
- **Foreign registration** where you operate (e.g., Texas) if formed out-of-state.
- **Licenses.** TX has no statewide GC license; city business license may apply.
- **Phones:** RingCentral; BBB listing for credibility.
- **Insurance:** General Liability; Builder's Risk; Workers' Comp (or equivalent protections).
- **Paperwork:** Subcontractor agreements, lien waivers, W-9s/ 1099s, draw schedule, scope sheets.

How You Get Paid Weekly (the 25/25/25/25 rhythm)
You negotiate the job, break the scope into four 25% milestones, and align sub pay to those milestones. You invoice your client (your

REIC or the lender) at your full amount, then pay subs at their discounted number. The spread is your project management override, paid each draw.

Illustration (cleaned):

- Sub's market bid: $8,000 (drywall & paint). You negotiate 25% discount → $6,000.
- Your GC contract to REIC stays at $8,000 (because your job is to run scope, safety, schedule, quality, paperwork, and risk).
- At first 25% milestone:
    - You invoice $2,000 (25% of $8,000) and get paid.
    - You pay the sub $1,500 (25% of $6,000).
    - You keep $500 now—repeat each milestone.
- Total override on that scope: $2,000—and you never starve while you work.
- A $40,000 total remodel at a 25% effective discount yields ~$10,000 in PM income per project cycle. Three projects running = $15,000/month lifeline.

Discipline: Put every milestone in writing (what counts as "25%"). Pay subs exactly on time. You'll never lack crews.

3) Discount Note Buyer / Servicing Company
Why Paper Pays
When you buy or contract to buy notes (the debt), you step into the bank's shoes. You can:

- Help families keep homes by modifying responsibly, or
- Re-perform paper and resell at better yields, or
- Liquidate notes on investor terms that still bless the borrower.

Formation & Setup

- Name & entity. (ex: *Great American Note Servicing, LLC*).
- File in a business-friendly state (ex: Delaware), EIN, bank, domain/email, QuickBooks, checks #30,000.
- Phones: RingCentral; Regus for reception/meeting space.
- MERS vendor registration (you'll interact with collateral and assignments).
- Documents: NDAs, Note Purchase & Sale Agreements (NPSA), Collateral Audit Checklist, Servicing Instructions, Borrower Authorization to Release Information, Forbearance/Modification templates.
- Compliance: Some activities require licensing; some states treat certain note buying/servicing as mortgage-related activity. Always consult local counsel before touching consumer debt.

Two Types of Money Partners You'll Serve

- Hard Money Lenders (HML) – fund fix-and-flip and value-add. Want low LTV, fast turn, fee-heavy safety.
- Yield Concession Servicers (YCS) – "currency circulators" who target yield from paper, often buying non-performing or title-distressed first liens at deep discounts, then re-perform or exit.

Your "Title-Distressed" Play (kept & cleaned)

Assume a YCS budgets $1,000,000 to buy first-position liens with title issues at $0.15 on the dollar. You target safe, family neighborhoods: 4-bed/2-bath, <15 years old, trending +5%/yr, note face values $250k–$350k; average $300k.

- Buy basis: $300,000 × 0.15 = $45,000 per note.
- $1,000,000 buys ~22 notes (≈ $990k deployed).
- Face value controlled: ~$6.6M (non-performing now; value created by making them perform or exiting intelligently).

Half re-perform; half exit to flippers (illustrative math, before admin/servicing costs):

- 11 re-performing notes: reduce principal to 65% of face; charge 10% interest-only for 5 years; forgive arrears and 35% write-down conditioned on performance.
  - New principal: 11 × $300k × 0.65 = $2,145,000
  - Interest income: 10% = $214,500/yr (≈ $17,875/mo.)
  - Five years interest-only: $1,072,500 cash collected, then refi/takeout.
- 11 property exits: sell to local investors at 68% ARV with a $9,000 average rehab credit. If ARV ≈ $325,000, quick-flip price ≈ $212,000 each → $2,332,000 gross. After 8.5% cost = $2,133,780; less a 15% illustrative tax factor ≈ $1.81M net (taxes vary—CPA will set your actuals).

Add your five-year interest stream to the resale net and the combined return becomes compelling. (Readers: keep these numbers illustrative; your CPA will model precise rates, reserves, and servicing costs.)

Zero-Cash "Contract Printing" (your spread without owning the note)

Back to the family who can afford $3,300/mo. if rescued. The law firm handling foreclosure will often discuss a **note sale**. You line up a YCS who will pay $0.25 on the dollar for the $450,000 non-performing first. You negotiate $0.15 with the firm.

- YCS pays you: $450,000 × 0.25 = $112,500
- You pay firm: $450,000 × 0.15 = $67,500
- Your spread today: $45,000

Now, layer in your performance contract with the home-owner—new balance $415,000 at $3,300/mo.—and your assignment to the YCS at $360,000 (their target).

- Referral fee: 15% of the gross increase ($415k – $135k "their cost") = $225k × 15% = $33,750
- Equity at take-out: $55,000 (the difference between $415k and $360k) payable at refi/sale.
- Monthly spread: $3,300 collected – $3,000 remitted to YCS = $300/mo → $18,000 over five years (if you're contracted to receive it).

Total to you on one rescue:
$33,750 (referral) + $55,000 (equity) + $18,000 (spread) + $45,000 (initial note flip) = $151,750 potential, with risk primarily in your paperwork discipline and performance management.

Key Insight
You printed money because you controlled both contracts: the home-owner performance agreement and the note disposition to your YCS. Control the paper; control the profit.

Clean Lists (kept, simplified, and sequenced)
REIC – Launch Checklist

- File LLC; adopt Operating Agreement; EIN; bank; insurance.
- Address (UPS/Regus); RingCentral numbers; live reception.
- Domain + pro email; website; solution-first branding.
- QuickBooks; checks #30,000; expense policy.
- DataTree title intel; Route4Me routing; lead platform/CRM.
- Business cards: Realty Solutions Manager.

GC Co. – Launch Checklist

- File LLC; foreign-register where needed; EIN; bank; insurance (GL, Builder's Risk, WC/alt).
- City business license (as applicable); BBB listing; phones; domain/email; QuickBooks.
- Sub agreements; W-9s/1099s; lien waivers; milestone scopes; draw schedule; safety policy.

DNBC – Launch Checklist

- File LLC (ex: Delaware); EIN; bank; domain/email; QuickBooks; MERS vendor.
- NDAs; NPSA (Note Purchase & Sale Agreement); Collateral Audit Checklist; Servicing Instructions; Borrower AROI; Forbearance/Modification templates.
- Compliance consult (state/federal): licensing, servicing, debt collection rules, RMLO triggers.

The 3-Entity Flow (who does what, when)

1. **Lead hits REIC.** You triage: save/keep, restructure, sell, or convert debt.
2. **If rehab:** REIC engages GC Co. with milestone schedule. GC Co. manages subs, protects margins, and pays itself weekly from negotiated discounts.
3. If debt solution: DNBC contracts with borrower and law firm; secures note pricing; flips to YCS; or buys/assigns per plan.
4. Cash cycles: REIC earns acquisition/assignment fees; GC Co. earns weekly PM overrides; DNBC earns spreads, referral fees, and performance-based equity on take-out.

5. **Books & compliance:** Each entity has separate EIN, bank, accounting, insurance, and minutes/resolutions approving contracts, comp, and inter-company agreements.

Paper the relationships:

- REIC ↔ GC Co.: Master Services Agreement (MSA), scopes, milestone draws.
- Church/ministry context? Keep commerce in a taxable subsidiary; paper shared services at fair value.
- DNBC ↔ YCS: Fee & referral agreement; NPSA; escrow instructions; servicing/boarding instructions.

Guardrails (so you keep what you make)

- Licensing & disclosures. Note activity and servicing can trigger licensing; know your state and federal rules.
- No co-mingling. Ever. Separate banks, cards, books, and signatures.
- Minutes & resolutions. Approve big steps: contracts, comp, housing allowance (ministers), inter-company deals, loans, distributions.
- Insurance & capitalization. Fund what you claim; insure what you can't absorb.
- UBIT awareness. Church/aux work stays mission-true; put commerce in taxable subs.

What to Do Today (money now, not someday)

1. Form the three LLCs (REIC, GC Co., DNBC). Get EINs, banks, phones, domains, QuickBooks.
2. Draft your core documents:

- REIC: solution scripts, authorization to talk to lender, triage matrix.
- GC Co.: sub agreements, milestone scopes, draw schedule, lien waivers.
- DNBC: NDAs, NPSA, collateral checklist, forbearance/mod templates, referral agreements.

3. Turn on your data (DataTree + lead platform) and start calling.
4. Book two bids this week for GC Co. scopes—even if small—to practice the 25% rhythm.
5. Open a YCS conversation with one private lender. Show the 22-note illustration and your pipeline plan.
6. Write minutes for each LLC approving banking, contracts, comp schedules, and inter-company services.

Action Step

Schedule a 60-minute Paper Day each month. If it isn't written, it didn't happen. Write it.

Closing the Module

This is how the living you commands the paper YOU: by building a three-entity engine that captures value in property, labor, and paper—lawfully, ethically, and profitably. In Modules 5 and 7, we'll put boots on the ground—scripts, door knocks, phone calls, and conversion—but now you have the formalities to hold what you'll win.

Control the contracts. Control the cash. The Money Machine hums because you respect the rules—and the rules, in turn, protect you.

Workbook: Module 3

Dominion Through Paper: How you command YOU to build lawful wealth. How to Use This Workbook

Print it. Write in it. Revisit it. Each page turns teaching into action—forms, check-lists, decisions, and templates you can run today. The voice here is practical, plain, and profitable.

A. Core Foundation — YOU & you (Put Dominion on Paper)

Big Idea (Plain English): The living **you** decides; the paper **YOU** signs. Wealth moves through contracts and entities. This section helps you anchor that truth into daily practice.

A1) Reflection: Authority & Consent

- In what 3 areas of money are you currently acting personally (no entity)?
- Where will you move those actions into an entity within 30 days?
  → _____

A2) Signature Discipline

Write your default signature block for business:
[Your Name], [Your Title], [Entity Name], a [State] [LLC/Corp]
Practice it 5 times below:

Key Insight
Never sign naked. Always wear the armor of your entity.

B. Entity Selector — Choose the Right Vessel

Use this quick matrix to pick the best fit for each project.

B1) Fit Questions

- Do I need outside investors (equity/stock)? ◈ Yes ◈ No
- Is this active earned income (owner-operator) I might optimize with S-Corp? ◈ Yes ◈ No
- Is this asset holding (e.g., property title/notes)? ◈ Yes ◈ No

- Is this mission/ministry work (donor support)? ◈ Yes ◈ No
- Is this a short JV (under 6 months / low risk)? ◈ Yes ◈ No

B2) Selection Map

- Equity scale & stock → **Corporation** (Delaware-friendly).
- Owner-operator efficiency & flexibility → **LLC** (consider S-Corp election).
- Passive partners & deal-by-deal waterfalls → **LP/LLP** or **LLC**.
- Estate/Privacy/Continuity → **Trust owns HoldCo LLC**; HoldCo owns Op-Cos.
- Worship/Ministry/Charity → **Church, Integrated Auxiliaries, + taxable sub** for commerce.
- Short, low-risk collaboration → **JV** (graduate to LLC as risk rises).

B3) Decision

For Project/Business: _____ I choose: ◈ Corp ◈ LLC ◈ LP/LLP ◈ Trust ◈ Nonprofit ◈ Church ◈ JV
Why   (1–2   sentences):
_____

C. Formalities Checklists (Keep the Veil On)

Pro Tip
The court loves paper: separate bank, minutes/resolutions, proper titles, adequate capital, insurance, and clean books.

C1) Corporation — Formation & Maintenance

- [ ] Name clearance + domain secured
- [ ] Articles of Incorporation filed
- [ ] Bylaws adopted; Organizational Resolutions signed
- [ ] Directors/Officers appointed; stock issued & ledger updated
- [ ] EIN obtained; bank opened (no co-mingling)
- [ ] Minutes book created; annual meeting scheduled
- [ ] Tax choice confirmed (C or S election filed if needed)
- [ ] Insurance in place (GL/D&O as needed)

C2) LLC — Formation & Maintenance

- [ ] Articles of Organization filed
- [ ] **Operating Agreement** executed (members/managers)

- [ ] EIN; bank; accounting; checks start at #30,000
- [ ] Resolutions (banking, contracts, comp, distributions)
- [ ] Tax status set (default / S-Corp / C-Corp)
- [ ] Annual report reminders; insurance in force

C3) Partnership (GP/LP/LLP)

- [ ] Partnership agreement; roles & capital accounts
- [ ] EIN; bank; books
- [ ] Limited partners restricted from management (if LP)
- [ ] K-1 schedule; minutes for key decisions

C4) Nonprofit Association (not a church)

- [ ] Nonprofit corporation formed; bylaws adopted
- [ ] Board seated; conflicts policy; no private inurement
- [ ] 501(c) application filed (as applicable)
- [ ] Form 990 calendar; UBIT guardrails
- [ ] Insurance (GL/D&O)

C5) Trust

- [ ] Trust instrument executed; trustee accepts duties
- [ ] EIN (if needed); trust bank
- [ ] **Assets retitled** to the trust
- [ ] Trustee resolutions; distribution logs
- [ ] Coordination: trust owns HoldCo LLC

C6) Unincorporated JV

- [ ] JV agreement (purpose/term/capital/profit-split/decision rights)
- [ ] Separate tracking bank/accounting
- [ ] Sunset date or conversion to LLC trigger

C7) Church

- [ ] Governance doc/constitution; statement of faith; board/elders
- [ ] Minutes book; benevolence & compensation policies
- [ ] Housing allowance resolutions (in advance)
- [ ] Bank & accounting; donor receipts; restricted funds rules
- [ ] UBIT monitoring; taxable **subsidiary** for commerce

- [ ] Insurance (GL, abuse coverage, property)

C8) Ministers

- [ ] Written job description & call
- [ ] **Housing allowance** designation in minutes (pre-payment)
- [ ] Accountable plan for expenses
- [ ] W-2/1099 alignment; SECA/FICA status documented

C9) Integrated Auxiliaries

- [ ] Charter stating mission & tie to parent church
- [ ] Oversight assigned; budget & separate books/sub-account
- [ ] Facility use & shared services agreements with church
- [ ] UBIT screening; taxable sub if commerce arises

D. Signature Blocks & Core Resolutions (Templates)

D1) Signature Blocks

- Business: **[Your Name], [Title], [Entity Name], a [State] [LLC/Corp]**
- Church: **[Your Name], [Office], [Church Name]**
- Subsidiary: **[Your Name], Manager, [Subsidiary LLC]**

D2) Banking Resolution (Excerpt)
Resolved, that **[Entity Name]** shall open deposit accounts with **[Bank]**; **[Name/Title]** is authorized to sign checks, drafts, and electronic transfers; dual-control limits as follows: _____.

D3) Inter-Company Services Resolution (Excerpt)
Resolved, that **[Entity A]** shall provide administrative/management services to **[Entity B]** per attached Services Agreement at fair-market rates; invoices monthly; term __ months.

D4) Housing Allowance Resolution (Church)
Resolved, for tax year , **[Church Name] designates $__** of Pastor **[Name]**'s cash compensation as housing allowance effective **[date]**.

E. Compliance Calendar
Monthly

- [ ] Bank/credit reconciliations
- [ ] Minutes/resolutions for major actions
- [ ] Payroll & accountable reimbursements posted
- [ ] Inter-company invoices issued/paid

Quarterly

- [ ] Estimated taxes; insurance review
- [ ] UBIT screen (church/nonprofit)
- [ ] Financial statements (P&L/BS/CF)

Annually

- [ ] State annual report filed
- [ ] Federal returns (1120/1120-S/1065/1041/990 as applicable)
- [ ] Annual meetings minuted (board/members/trustees)
- [ ] Compensation & distributions ratified
- [ ] Housing allowance designated for new year
- [ ] Risk assessment & insurance coverage check

F. The 3-Entity Engine — Practical Worksheets

F1) Real Estate Investment Company (REIC)
Launch Checklist

- [ ] LLC formed; Operating Agreement signed; EIN; bank
- [ ] Address (UPS/Regus); RingCentral (800/local + live reception)
- [ ] Domain/email; website; solution-first branding
- [ ] QuickBooks; checks #30,000; Chart of Accounts set
- [ ] DataTree ($99/mo); Route4Me ($49/mo); CRM activated
- [ ] Business cards — title: **Realty Solutions Manager**

Lead Triage Card

- Borrower name(s): _____
- Property: _____ ARV $_____
- Current Note Bal: $_____ Rate **%** **P&I** $____
- True Affordability: $_____ (verify with FNA)
- Goal: ◈ Keep home ◈ Sell retail ◈ Sell investor-grade ◈ Debt solution ◈ Other _____

Authorization to Release Information (Borrower → You)

- Borrower(s): _____
- Lender/Servicer: _____
- Loan #: _____
- I/We authorize **[Your REIC]** to obtain loan, payoff, and loss-mitigation information.
  Signatures/Date: _____

Financial Needs Analysis (FNA) – Short Form

- Monthly Net Income $_____
- Housing Target (≤ *% of Net*): *$*_____
- Other Debts $_____
- Proposed P&I $_____ Feasible? ◈ Yes ◈ No

Offer Matrix (circle path)

- Modify P&I to $_____ (rate ____%) with arrears waived
- Forbearance → Re-performance test (___ months @ $_____)
- Short payoff to ___% of balance
- Note sale to YCS at $0.___/1.00
- Graceful exit with cash-for-keys $_____

F2) General Contractor / Remodel Company (GC Co.)
Launch Checklist

- [ ] LLC; foreign registration (if needed); EIN; bank; insurance (GL/BR/WC)
- [ ] City license/BBB; RingCentral; domain/email; QuickBooks
- [ ] Sub agreements; W-9/1099; lien waivers; safety plan

Scope Builder
Project: _____
Address: _____

- Demo $_____
- Framing $_____
- MEP (Plumb/Elect/HVAC) $_____
- Drywall/Paint $_____
- Flooring $_____
- Exterior/Roof $_____

- Landscaping $_____
- Contingency % $__
  Total Market Cost: $_____
  Negotiated Discount: % → **Your Contract:** $____

Milestone Draw Schedule (25/25/25/25)

- Milestone 1 (date/scope):
  _____
- Milestone 2: _____
- Milestone 3: _____
- Milestone 4: _____

Sub Pay Rhythm (example)
Market bid: $8,000 → Negotiated: $6,000
Your invoice each milestone: $2,000
Sub paid each milestone: $1,500
Your override each milestone: $500
Total override: $2,000

F3) Discount Note Buyer / Servicing Company (DNBC)
Launch Checklist

- [ ] LLC (Delaware recommended); EIN; bank; domain/email; QuickBooks
- [ ] **MERS** vendor registration
- [ ] Compliance consult (state/federal licensing; RMLO if triggered)
- [ ] Document set: NDA, **Note Purchase & Sale Agreement (NPSA)**, Collateral Audit Checklist, Servicing Instructions, Borrower **Authorization to Release Info**, Forbearance/Modification templates, Referral Agreement

Collateral Audit Checklist (excerpt)

- [ ] Original Note (copy/bailee receipt)
- [ ] Allonges/endorsements
- [ ] Deed of Trust/Mortgage, Assignments
- [ ] Title search & exceptions
- [ ] Pay history, escrow, corporate advances
- [ ] Property condition/AVM/BPO
- [ ] Bankruptcy/foreclosure status
- [ ] Compliance & licensing review

YCS Referral Agreement (excerpt)

- Fee = ___% of (Resale Price – Acquisition Cost)
- Paid at funding or within __ days of take-out
- Non-circumvention/Non-disclosure: __ months

Spread Calculator (example)
Face Balance: $_____ × price ____ = **Buy** $_____
YCS price: $_____ → **Your spread** $_____
Borrower performance fee: $/**mo** × __ **months** = $
Equity at take-out: $_____
Total projected to you: $_____

G. Church, Ministers & Auxiliaries — Mission with Guardrails
G1) Mission Fit Test

- Does the activity directly advance worship/discipleship/charity? ◈ Yes ◈ No
- If no, should it live in a **taxable subsidiary** with arm's-length agreements? ◈ Yes ◈ No

G2) Housing Allowance Minute (fill-in)
Resolved, for tax year , **[Church Name]** designates $__ of Pastor **[Name]**'s compensation as housing allowance effective **[date]** and continuing until modified.
Secretary: _____ Date: _____

G3) Shared Services & Facility Use (outline)

- Parties: Church ↔ Subsidiary/Third-party
- Scope: Admin/HR/Accounting/Facility use
- Rate: Fair-market value basis (attach schedule)
- Insurance & indemnity
- Term/Renewal/Termination
- Signatures & titles

G4) UBIT Decision Tree (check all that apply)

- [ ] Substantially related to exempt mission
- [ ] Regularly carried on?
- [ ] Advertising/sponsorship income?
- [ ] Debt-financed property income?
  If 2+ "red" items → consult CPA; consider taxable subsidiary.

H. Ownership Architecture — Map Your Stack
H₁) Who Owns What (diagram in words)

- [Your Living/Irrevocable Trust] → owns [HoldCo LLC]
- HoldCo LLC → owns REIC LLC, GC Co. LLC, DNBC LLC, and any taxable subs
- Church (separate) → oversees Auxiliaries; contracts with taxable subs at arm's length

H₂) Fill-In Chart

Trust Name: _____

HoldCo LLC: _____ State: ____ EIN: _____

OpCos (list): _____

Church Name: _____ Auxiliaries: _____

Taxable Subs (names/purposes): _____

I. Risk & Veil Self-Audit (Red Flag Scan)

- [ ] Any personal bills paid from business/church? Where? _____
- [ ] Missing minutes/resolutions this quarter? Which? _____
- [ ] Thin capital or lapsed insurance? _____
- [ ] Inter-company deals without written agreements? _____
- [ ] Clergy housing allowance not designated in advance? _____
- [ ] Nonprofit/church activity that looks commercial? _____

90-Day Fix Plan:
Top 3 corrections I will complete by [date]:

J. Cost Planner — Launch & Monthly Burn
One-Time Setup (estimate)

- Formation filings (per entity): $_____
- Registered agent (annual): $_____
- Minute books/seals: $_____
- Legal consult (optional): $_____
- Insurance binders: $_____
  Total One-Time: $_____

Monthly Operating (per entity)

- Virtual office (Regus): $_____
- Phones (RingCentral): $_____
- Accounting (QuickBooks): $_____
- Data (DataTree): $_____
- Routing (Route4Me): $_____
- Web/email: $_____
- Insurance: $_____
  Total Monthly: $_____

Action Step
Build a 3-month cash buffer equal to your combined monthly burn.

K. 30-Day Launch Sprints & KPIs
Week 1 — Paper & Presence

- File entities, get EINs, open banks, set phones, domains, QuickBooks.
- KPI: 3 entities formed; 3 bank accounts open; 1 receptionist line live.

Week 2 — Documents & Vendors

- Adopt Operating Agreement/bylaws; set minutes; insurance quotes; MERS (DNBC).
- KPI: Minutes book started; 5 subcontractors pre-vetted.

Week 3 — Pipeline

- Turn on DataTree, CRM, Route4Me. Begin lead outreach and bid walks.
- KPI: 20 qualified leads; 4 GC bids built; 1 YCS call booked.

Week 4 — First Closers

- Land 1 GC scope, 1 REIC contract, 1 DNBC referral spread.
- KPI: $____ contracted revenue; $____ PM draw collected; $____ spread booked.

L. Glossary (Plain English)

- **YOU vs you** — The living you decides; the paper YOU (entities) signs.
- **Veil** — Legal separation protecting personal assets from business liabilities.
- **UBIT** — Tax on nonprofit/church income from activities unrelated to mission.

- **YCS** — Yield Concession Servicer; investor who buys notes for yield.
- **MERS** — Mortgage Electronic Registration Systems; tracks mortgage interests.
- **Allonge** — An endorsement page attached to a negotiable instrument.
- **ARV** — After-Repair Value of a property (post-rehab estimate).
- **FMV** — Fair-Market Value; typical price between willing buyer/seller.

M. Final Commitment — The Paper Day Promise

I commit to a 60-minute Paper Day every month to write minutes, approve contracts, reconcile accounts, and guard the veil.

Signature: _____ Date: _____

Closing Charge

God gave you dominion—no man over another, but man over the work of his hands. In our world, that dominion travels through contracts and entities. The living **you** hears; the paper YOU signs. Build your vessels. Keep your books. Control your contracts. That is how ordinary ink becomes extraordinary wealth—lawfully, ethically, and with a clean conscience.

4

Module 4: Bad Debt=Poor; Good Debt Leverage=Rich

Debt vs. Leverage
Understanding the Difference - One Makes You Poor, One Makes You Rich

"If you can't make money from borrowed money, you're borrowing wrong."
— *Ray Wright Jacobs*

The Great Illusion of Debt

Debt was created as a consumer product—a way to buy what you want now and pay for it later with interest. The illusion feels like freedom: drive the car, wear the clothes, swipe the card. But every swipe transfers future labor into today's consumption.

Interest—the fee for the illusion—is compounded and recalculated monthly. By the time most borrowers finish paying, the item is obsolete or worthless. That is why debt makes you poor: it consumes your economic energy, time, and talent on liabilities that decay faster than they are paid.

Key Insight
Debt is a drain; leverage is a channel. One consumes your energy, the other multiplies it.

What Is Leverage?

Leverage is still debt—but with purpose. It is the deliberate use of borrowed capital to create or control income-producing assets. When you borrow to buy appreciating property, fund a business, or finance others for profit, you're engaging the same process banks use every day.

Example: You secure a house worth $200,000 under contract for $100,000 and assign that contract for $10,000. You never owned the house; you owned the *paper*. That spread is pure leverage—turning time, knowledge, and negotiation into money that goes directly into Hip National Bank.

Now imagine using borrowed credit to buy assets that pay you monthly instead of things that cost you monthly. That's where wealth begins.

Real vs. Fake Borrowing

Let's clarify something most people will never hear in a bank lobby:

When you "borrow," the bank doesn't lend you money. You lend them your promise, and they leverage it ninefold.

Every "loan" you've ever taken is an *exchange*, not a loan. You create the credit, they monetize it.

This is the secret of Fractional Reserve Banking and why it has operated unchecked for over a century.

The HELOC Example

Suppose you own a duplex worth $300,000 generating $800/month net cash flow. You open a $75,000 HELOC at 8%. You then lend $60,000 of that line to a rehabber at 15% interest for six months.

- Cost of funds: 8%
- Income: 15%
- Net spread: 7% = $4,200 annualized profit on borrowed money.

Your tenants pay the mortgage, the borrower pays your HELOC, and you pocket the difference. That $4,200 goes straight into Hip National Bank—you just printed money with contracts, exactly as banks do.

Case Study – Banks and Leverage

Banks borrow at 2–3% from the Federal Reserve and lend to you at 10–20%, compounding their spread billions of times daily. They don't lend money—they lend credit they create against your promise to repay. The bank's true asset is your signature.

The Fractional Reserve Secret

To grasp real leverage, you must understand the Federal Reserve's Money Machine. Under *fractional reserve banking*, banks are required to keep only a fraction of deposits as reserves—historically 10%, now effectively 0% under modern policy. That means for every $1 you deposit, a bank can create $9 of new "credit money" and lend it out. Your deposit becomes the seed for nine more digital dollars—each bearing interest, each earning the bank profit, while your original deposit earns near zero.

Pro Tip

You are the bank's lender, not its customer. Your deposits are loans the bank uses to create more credit.

Public Money vs. Private Money

The Federal Reserve issues Federal Reserve Notes (FRNs)—public debt instruments. Banks, in turn, create private credit when you sign a promissory note. Legally, both are money; the difference lies in who can deposit them.

When you sign a loan, your note is deposited as the bank's asset. The "funds" you receive are simply the bank's matching liability—digital credits created against your signature. The transaction is an exchange, not a loan.

You lent the bank your promise; the bank lent you its digits. Both are promises—but only one party earns the interest and fills their coffers.

Key Insight
You are already a money creator—you've just been donating your power to the bank.

The Birth of the Federal Reserve
After the U.S. government's series of war-time bankruptcies in the 1800s, international creditors demanded collateral for further loans. In 1913, a small group of congressmen—during a Christmas recess—passed the Federal Reserve Act, creating a central bank privately owned yet sanctioned by government.

Citizens' labor, time, and talent became the new collateral. Every "loan" today is an exchange of promissory notes—your future work pledged to sustain the system.

As long as people keep signing for loans, banks keep creating money from those signatures. Stop signing, and the system freezes.

The Federal Reserve's Hidden Machinery
The Federal Reserve Act of 1913 privatized the American money system. It turned "money" from gold-backed value into debt-backed belief.

Banks no longer needed to lend deposits; they needed only *signatures*. A signed promissory note became new "money." The bank books it as an *asset*—your promise to pay—and simultaneously creates a *liability* (the funds "credited" to your account).

Your signature is the loan.

The entire banking edifice stands on this act of alchemy. Your labor and future productivity are the real collateral. The "loan officer" is merely a notary of your consent.

Legal Disclosure

(Based on GAAP and TILA principles, summarized from affidavit testimony)

Under Generally Accepted Accounting Principles (GAAP), every loan must balance: an asset on one side, a liability on the other. When you sign a promissory note, the bank books it as their *asset* and credits an equal liability to you—the so-called "loan."

In truth, the ledger proves that you were the lender and the bank the borrower. You deposited a promissory note of value; they recorded it as cash equivalent.

According to GAAP's *matching principle*, the liability side must reflect that the bank owes you for the note you deposited. That's not theory—it's accounting law.

Key Insight

Every time you signed a mortgage, auto note, or student loan, you created money first. The bank only mirrored it back to you.

Evidence of Exchange, Not Loan

From your affidavit-style disclosures:

"The promissory note was deposited similarly to cash into a transaction account, equivalent to loaning the alleged lender the cash or promissory note. GAAP dictates that the promissory note is deposited as a bank asset offset by a bank liability, signifying the alleged lender owes money to me for the deposited promissory note."

That's the truth hidden beneath every "loan."

They recorded your signature as a *deposit* — not as collateral, but as a funding source.

When they "wire" you the funds, they simply return your own credit to you—minus future interest.

Case Study – The Mortgage Exchange

A borrower named Daniel signed a $250,000 mortgage note. He believed the bank "lent" him money. Under GAAP review, the note was booked as an asset to the bank. The matching liability — the deposit — was created in his name.

Daniel's "loan" was his own promise monetized. The bank never withdrew from pre-existing funds. They created digits and called it debt. Daniel paid back his own money—with interest.

His realization was simple: "They lent me my own credit and charged me rent for it."

Truth in Lending – The Missing Disclosure

The Truth in Lending Act (TILA) was designed to protect borrowers through transparency. But there's a fatal omission: nowhere does it disclose that your *promissory note* funded the so-called loan.

Had the bank revealed that your signature generated the funds, no sane borrower would consent to pay interest on their own credit. That omission transforms a contract into economic malfeasance—a legal term for theft disguised as commerce.

Case Study – The Deposit Illusion

You deposit $500 cash. The teller credits your account $500. You believe the bank is safeguarding your money. In truth, you just *loaned* the bank $500. They record it as their asset and your liability. They can now create up to $4,500 of new loans from your deposit.

When you later withdraw "your" cash, they simply reverse part of that liability. The bank never kept your money—they leveraged it.

Your $500 has already filled the Federal Reserve Bank while yours stayed empty.

Real vs. Fake Borrowing

Let's clarify something most people will never hear in a bank lobby: When you "borrow," the bank doesn't lend you money. You lend them your promise, and they leverage it ninefold.

Every "loan" you've ever taken is an *exchange*, not a loan. You create the credit, they monetize it.

This is the secret of Fractional Reserve Banking and why it has operated unchecked for over a century.

Retail vs. Wholesale Credit

- **Retail Credit (RBC):** Consumer borrowing—credit cards, car notes, mortgages. Designed to extract interest from the masses.
- **Wholesale Credit (WBC):** Credit backed by deposits or collateral—Certificates of Deposit, Warehouse Lines, Standby Letters of Credit. Used by institutions to borrow at 1–3% and lend at 10–20%.

When you understand WBC, you step into the banker's world. You can structure private loans, secured notes, or fund real estate deals the same way—by lending what you borrow and routing the profit straight to Hip National Bank.

The 2008 Wake-Up Call

Before 2007, investors like myself could borrow easily. Credit flowed. Deals funded overnight. By 2008, the machine jammed.

Suddenly, those same "friendly bankers" turned silent. Programs disappeared. Funding dried up. Why? Because leverage without collateralized confidence implodes.

Many of us watched in horror as a popular website, The Mortgage Lender Implode-O-Meter (https://ml-implode.com/) tracked in real-time the failure of mortgage lenders hour by hour. It is still there if anyone wants to see the carnage it tracked as banks scrambled. Banks froze—not because they ran out of money, but because they ran out of borrowers. No signatures, no new credit creation, no new money. The Money Machine seized.

Key Insight
Leverage without cash flow is gambling. Leverage with cash flow is wealth building.

Real-World Examples

- **Grant Cardone** uses billions in borrowed funds to acquire multifamily properties yielding more than his cost of capital.
- **Elon Musk** borrows against appreciating Tesla stock instead of selling it—maintaining control while accessing liquidity.
- **Warren Buffett** invests insurance "float," earning profit on premiums before claims are paid.

All three leverage borrowed capital to expand assets, not appearances—and every move adds to their personal and business wealth bottom line.

Five Questions Before You Leverage

1. What is my cost of funds?
2. What return will these funds produce?
3. Can the asset pay its own debt service?
4. What is my exit plan?
5. Is this purchase consumption or production?

If you can't answer all five, pause. The banker in you must be satisfied before the borrower acts.

The "Lend What You Borrow" Principle

Banks use your deposits to create loans and profit from the spread. You can do the same. Borrow against appreciating or cash-flowing assets at low interest, then re-lend those funds at higher interest to investors or businesses.

You become the intermediary—earning interest on credit instead of paying it. This is the private-side mirror of the Federal Reserve system. When executed properly, it feeds Hip National Bank instead of theirs.

The People's Leverage

The secret weapon of the elite is velocity of capital. The poor spend it once. The rich recycle it forever.

Each time you borrow to buy an income-producing asset, then redeploy the returns to fund the next deal, you're reclaiming your place as the true money creator. You're converting debt into leverage—and leverage into Hip National Bank deposits.

Key Insight
Wealth isn't built by working harder; it's built by cycling capital faster than the banks can charge you for it.

Real-World Blueprint

1. **Borrow cheap:** Access lines of credit (HELOC, margin, business credit).
2. **Deploy smart:** Invest in assets that yield above your borrowing cost.
3. **Recycle profits:** Pay off debt, re-borrow, re-invest.
4. **Repeat indefinitely.**

Each cycle adds velocity, adds control, and fills your Hip National Bank.

The New Money Machine

The truth is sobering but empowering: you've been a banker all along—you just weren't paid like one.

Your signature creates value. Your energy fuels credit. Your assets back the currency.

When you leverage debt the way banks do—without emotion, with discipline—you reclaim control over both sides of the balance sheet.

That's the beginning of financial sovereignty.

Action Step

Identify one asset—real estate, equipment, or skill—that could secure a credit line. Design a plan to deploy that borrowed capital into an income-producing investment within 90 days.

Workbook: Module 4

Debt vs. Leverage – Understanding the Difference

1. **Debt Audit:** List every obligation you owe. Label each as *Consumer* or *Leverage*. Eliminate the former; optimize the latter.
2. **Bank Mirror Exercise:** Visit your bank. Ask the manager: "What percentage of my deposits can you lend?" Note the reaction. Research your bank's reserve ratio.
3. **Fractional Reserve Visualization:** Draw a flowchart showing how your $1 deposit becomes $9 in loans. Reflect: who profits most—and whose balance sheet grows from it?
4. **HELOC Scenario:** Using your own property, calculate potential cash-flow spread between your HELOC rate and a private-lending rate. Determine how much will end up in Hip National Bank.
5. **Create a Leverage Loop:** Borrow → Invest → Profit → Repay → Repeat. Document one real transaction this year that pays into Hip National Bank.
6. **Knowledge Action:** Teach one friend or family member what fractional banking is. When you can teach it clearly, you truly understand it.

Final Word from Ray Wright Jacobs

You now see behind the curtain. Banks don't own a secret formula—they use your promise as their product. The difference between the poor and the rich is not access; it's awareness. Debt used blindly enslaves. Debt used intelligently empowers. Learn to control it, multiply it, and lend what you borrow—and you will never again be on the wrong side of the ledger. Every dollar of profit from this day forward should find its way home—straight to Hip National Bank.

5

Module 5: Boots on the Ground

The Ground Game – A Lost Art
Where Fortune Still Favors the Bold

"If you want to make money, stop waiting for the phone to ring — knock on the door that's holding your check."
— Ray Wright Jacobs

The Game That Built Champions

If you've ever played sports, you know the electricity that builds before the first whistle — the scent of fresh grass in the air, the tension in your muscles, the rhythm of the drum line echoing in your chest. For me, football taught more about business, character, and perseverance than any classroom or seminar ever could. I wasn't the fastest cornerback on the field or the flashiest name on the roster, but I had something that made me indispensable — heart. I studied the game, learned how to anticipate plays, and discovered early that talent gets you started, but attitude keeps you in the game.

Football taught me how to thrive in adversity. When the score was close and the pressure intense, I learned to trust my training, lean on my teammates, and play every down like it was the one that would change everything. That same discipline and mental toughness are what every investor must develop to win in business. In life and in real estate, the field rewards grit, not gimmicks. It rewards those who show up, read the field, and adapt to every situation with composure. The crowd may never see the hours of sweat and film study behind the scenes, but the scoreboard always reflects who put in the work.

The Ground Game, much like football's running game, is where the true champions are forged. It's not about big plays that look good on highlight reels; it's about steady, consistent progress that wears down resistance until you break through. In business, that means grinding through rejection, weathering slow months, and staying consistent when everyone else quits. Each conversation, each knock, each connection inches you forward. You may not score on every play, but you're always gaining yards toward financial freedom — and when you break through, that touchdown lands directly in Hip National Bank.

What Is the Ground Game?

The Ground Game is about connection — pure, raw, unfiltered connection. It's not about hiding behind technology or waiting for opportunities to come to you. It's about stepping into the field of play and meeting people where they are, face-to-face, heart-to-heart, situation to situation. In real estate, that means walking neighborhoods, shaking hands, listening to stories, and offering real solutions to real problems. It's showing up when others rely on mailers, data, or chance. It's the simple act of doing what most won't do — and reaping what most never will.

While the "Air Game" of online marketing and automated funnels may look glamorous, it lacks the substance that builds trust. The Ground Game is where authenticity lives. It's where deals are born out of empathy and understanding, not algorithms. When you go out there — armed with information, sincerity, and the right spirit — you become more than just another investor. You become a messenger of hope, a problem solver, and a source of stability for people navigating chaos. The Ground Game demands consistency, courage, and a willingness to hear the word "no" without losing your drive to find that one "yes" that changes everything.

The Ground Game is also a mindset — a philosophy of movement and intention. It's not just knocking on doors; it's moving toward purpose. When you pick up your list of prospects, when you walk that first block, when you smile and introduce yourself to someone who's been ignored by every other investor, you're planting seeds in fertile ground. It's not glamorous work, but it's real work. And that real work is the currency that keeps the Money Machine turning and feeding Hip National Bank.

Key Insight
The shortest distance between a stranger and a signed contract is a face-to-face conversation.

Why Most Investors Fail

Most investors don't fail because the business is too hard — they fail because they refuse to play the right game. They sit on the sidelines believing that if they send enough postcards or click enough buttons, success will somehow find them. They fall in love with automation and convenience, confusing busyness for productivity. These are what I call "Air Game Investors." They live in a fantasy where mailing campaigns and social media ads magically turn into checks, all while they sit comfortably at home. But the truth is, passive marketing creates passive results. It doesn't build relationships, and without relationships, there are no deals.

If you've ever mailed 1,000 postcards and received only three calls — two of which were wrong numbers and one from another investor trying to sell you a deal — then you already know the frustration of the Air Game. The homeowners you're trying to reach are being bombarded with the same messages from dozens of other investors. They've seen the same "We Buy Houses" letters, the same fonts, even the same color envelopes. None of it feels genuine. None of it stands out. Meanwhile, the few investors who are brave enough to knock on doors are having real conversations and getting contracts signed because they dared to show up in person.

The failure of most investors comes down to one simple truth — they're disconnected from people. The Air Game looks easy, but it hides behind screens, mailing lists, and auto-responders. The Ground Game requires presence, and presence creates trust. When you show up face-to-face, when you listen and empathize, you become more than a marketer; you become a solution provider. The Air Game investor can spend months chasing data while the Ground Game investor builds a network, closes deals, and walks away with profits deposited into Hip National Bank. Real success has always belonged to those willing to get their shoes dirty and their hands busy helping others.

The Human Factor

At the heart of every real estate deal is a human being with fears, hopes, and dreams. Behind every foreclosure notice or "For Sale by Owner" sign is a story — a family that's fought hard to stay afloat, a homeowner dealing with unexpected loss, or someone who simply feels overwhelmed and alone. Real estate is often discussed as numbers, equity, or ROI, but underneath it all, it's a deeply emotional business. The Ground Game recognizes that truth. It's about engaging people, not just properties, and building genuine connections that make others feel seen and understood.

Automation can't look someone in the eye. It can't hear the quiver in a homeowner's voice when they talk about their mortgage or their children. It can't offer a reassuring smile or a word of comfort that cuts through fear. You can't email empathy. That's why real success in real estate still belongs to the human being who shows up, listens first, and leads with compassion. The investor who sees value in people as much as in property always wins.

The human factor is also the secret weapon that transforms a one-time transaction into lifelong opportunity. When people trust you, they tell others about you. They remember how you made them feel respected in a time when most treated them like a statistic. That kind of integrity builds a reputation that money can't buy. Over time, your community begins to associate your name with help, honesty, and hope. The Ground Game isn't just about closing deals — it's about opening hearts. And when you operate with that mindset, the rewards flow not only through contracts and closings, but also through continuous deposits into Hip National Bank.

Lessons from Network Marketing

There's a timeless truth hidden in the success stories of network marketing: people still buy from people they know, like, and trust. Companies like Amway, Herbalife, and Mary Kay didn't rise to billion-dollar empires through television ads or algorithms — they grew because one person looked another in the eye and shared their belief in a product that changed their life. These businesses are built on a single principle that also powers the Ground Game: people helping people. Duplication begins when one person's success becomes another's inspiration. Every testimony shared at a kitchen table, every in-person demonstration, every story of transformation is an invitation for others to join in and win together.

In real estate, this principle is no different. When you help a homeowner find peace in the middle of financial chaos, they remember you. They tell their friends, their coworkers, their family members. The story of what you did becomes a bridge to more opportunities. Just like network marketers create distributors out of customers, you create partners, advocates, and future clients out of every life you impact. This is the compounding power of the Ground Game — one sincere connection creates a ripple that spreads far beyond your first handshake.

Network marketing also teaches the art of storytelling. Top earners don't rely on technical data; they use narratives that connect emotionally. They show, through personal experience, what's possible. As a real estate investor, your story is your greatest asset. When you share how you helped one family avoid foreclosure or turn a problem property into a new start, you're building trust and credibility faster than any cold campaign could. Over time, those stories — like well-planted seeds — multiply your reach. The Ground Game is built on this same law of duplication: success that reproduces itself through genuine service.

The reason this works is because people don't want to be sold to; they want to be shown that success is achievable through someone like them. That's why the most successful network marketing teams and Ground Game investors share a simple DNA — they focus on teaching, not just taking. When your business becomes a vehicle for empowerment instead of extraction, it becomes magnetic. You stop chasing deals, and deals start finding you. Each relationship you build adds another layer of trust, another connection, and another stream of income flowing to Hip National Bank.

The Psychology of the Knock

Knocking on a stranger's door can feel like the longest walk in the world. It's that moment when your pulse quickens, your mind races, and doubt whispers, What if they slam the door? What if they're angry? But here's what I've learned — most homeowners in distress aren't angry, they're scared. Fear is a powerful emotion, and behind that closed door is someone afraid of losing more than a house; they're afraid of losing stability, security, and identity. When you understand that truth, your approach changes. You stop seeing "leads" and start seeing people. You realize that your job isn't to convince them — it's to comfort them.

The first few seconds after the door opens set the tone for every-thing that follows. Your energy speaks before your words do. If you arrive with nerves or desperation, they'll feel it. But if you arrive with calm confidence and genuine concern, you'll disarm their fear before it has a chance to rise. Keep your body language open — shoulders back, folder at your side, a soft smile that communicates profession-alism without pressure. The right tone matters even more than the right script. A warm greeting like, "Good afternoon, my name's Ray, I'm helping homeowners understand their rights and options," imme-diately shifts the interaction from confrontation to cooperation.

This isn't about selling; it's about serving. The moment you step onto that porch, you represent hope — maybe the first hope they've felt in months. That's a sacred responsibility. When you knock, knock with purpose. When you speak, speak with empathy. Let your con-fidence come not from what you're selling, but from what you're solving. A professional investor understands that the emotional tem-perature of a deal is determined in the first minute of contact. If you can keep a homeowner calm, seen, and respected, the odds of cooper-ation multiply tenfold.

And here's a truth that separates the masters from the masses: re-jection is not personal, it's reflexive. Most people have been condi-tioned to distrust anyone who knocks on their door, especially when they're in crisis. But rejection fades with consistency. The more doors you knock, the more comfortable you get, and the more likely you are to meet someone who's ready to talk. Over time, your confidence grows, your fear diminishes, and what once felt like risk becomes rou-tine. The Ground Game builds character first, then wealth — and both flow, eventually, into Hip National Bank.

Pro Tip
People don't remember what you say; they remember how you made them feel

The Power of Approach

Approach is everything. You can have the right information, the right list, and even the right timing, but if your approach is wrong, you lose before the conversation begins. When you pull up to a property, remember that the person on the other side of that door has been approached before — often by agents, debt collectors, or opportunists who made them feel small. Your first job is to disarm their defenses by looking and acting different. Park on the street instead of the driveway to show respect. Walk confidently, but never rush. The homeowner is reading your energy from the window before you even knock, so carry yourself as someone who's there to bring calm, not chaos.

When you reach the door, knock firmly — not timidly, not aggressively. Wait a few seconds, then step back slightly to give them space when they answer. When the door opens, smile and greet them naturally. You don't need a sales pitch; you need sincerity. Something as simple as, "Hi, I'm Ray, and I help homeowners who've had trouble with their lender understand their options," creates curiosity without pressure. It doesn't sound like a scheme; it sounds like support. From there, the goal isn't to talk — it's to listen. People in distress often just need someone to hear their story. When you give them that space, they'll tell you everything you need to know about their situation and how you can help.

Once they begin to open up, you'll feel a shift — the tension drops, and trust starts to form. That's your signal to move from listener to leader. You can gently explain how federal protections under RESPA and TILA give them time and options that most homeowners don't even know they have. If they show interest, you can offer to share information that might help them communicate more effectively with their lender. You're not asking them to sell anything or sign anything; you're giving before asking. That act of generosity immediately separates you from everyone else who's knocked on that same door. When they answer, introduce yourself:

"Hi, I'm Ray. I work with families who've had some trouble with their lender. I help them understand their options under federal law — sometimes even stop foreclosure. Would you like to see what that looks like?"

The power of approach lies in your ability to humanize the process. You're not a "cash buyer" or a "wholesaler" — you're a professional problem solver. Every word, every gesture, every piece of information you share should reflect integrity and respect. Even if that homeowner never sells to you, they will remember you as the person who treated them with dignity when others only saw dollar signs. That memory will find its way back to you, often in the form of a referral, an opportunity, or a deal you never expected. In the Ground Game, approach isn't just how you start a conversation — it's how you build a legacy that keeps depositing into Hip National Bank long after the knock is done.

Building Trust Through Value

Trust is the true currency of the Ground Game. While others chase short-term gains, seasoned investors understand that trust compounds faster than any interest rate ever could. You build it by leading with value — not persuasion. When you show up at someone's doorstep with real solutions instead of rehearsed sales pitches, you're making a statement: I'm here to help first, not profit first. One of the most effective ways to do that is by educating homeowners about their rights under RESPA and TILA. When you bring along sample Qualified Written Requests (QWRs) and show them how these documents can legally slow down or even halt the foreclosure process, you're giving them more than information — you're giving them control.

That act alone transforms you from an outsider to an advocate. Most people in financial distress have lost faith in institutions — they feel ignored by banks, misunderstood by agents, and abandoned by the system. When you show them something that empowers them, you restore a sense of agency that many have forgotten they still possess. You'll be surprised at how quickly gratitude replaces suspicion once they realize you're not there to take from them but to give them a fighting chance. Even if they don't decide to sell you their home, they'll remember the day someone knocked on their door with answers instead of empty promises. In an industry where most investors are forgotten after the first conversation, that kind of authenticity makes you unforgettable.

Every relationship you build this way becomes an invisible bridge to future opportunities. A homeowner you helped today may call you six months later when they're ready to move on. They might refer a relative, a friend, or a coworker who needs the same help. That's how the Ground Game builds momentum — through the natural law of reciprocity. The more people you help, the more doors open for you. And with every handshake rooted in sincerity, you're adding long-term equity to your business and short-term profit to Hip National Bank.

The secret to sustaining this trust is consistency. Follow up with those you help — even if there's no deal in sight. A quick phone call, a short note, or a simple message checking in on their progress can mean the world to someone still fighting their battle. It tells them that your concern was genuine, not conditional. That kind of consistency is rare, and that's why it's powerful. Over time, people begin to associate your name with integrity, reliability, and real results. That reputation becomes your brand, and your brand becomes your wealth. Because in the Ground Game, every act of trust is a seed — and every seed grows into another relationship.

Key Insight
Give information freely. Money follows service.

"Buy the truth, and sell it not; also wisdom, and instruction, and understanding."
(Proverbs 23:23)

Modernizing the Ground Game

The Ground Game will always be the foundation of success, but like any good system, it evolves. What used to take days of driving, calling, and note-taking can now be done with precision in half the time thanks to technology. The key is to use these digital tools to enhance your human touch, not replace it. Platforms like Google Maps, PropertyRadar, PropStream, and Zillow can give you a bird's-eye view of ownership data, property status, and even equity estimates before you ever step foot on the block. With route optimization tools such as Route4Me or MapQuest Planner, you can plot out 50 homes in a single day and knock them in the most efficient order. The same apps that most investors use lazily behind a screen, you'll use as a tactical weapon in the field.

Technology also allows you to manage relationships with ease. CRM systems like HubSpot or Podio let you document each visit, track follow-ups, and even automate reminders to check in with homeowners. That means no lead ever slips through the cracks. A quick voice note after each meeting can capture details about the homeowner's story, tone, and needs while the memory is fresh. The next time you contact them, you'll sound like you truly care because you'll remember what matters to them. That personal detail builds trust faster than any script ever could. Combine that with quick text follow-ups or a thank-you email, and you'll leave an impression that feels both professional and personal.

But modernizing the Ground Game doesn't mean becoming mechanical — it means becoming intentional. Use technology to simplify logistics so you can focus on the part that matters most: the conversation. Too many investors hide behind software as a substitute for courage. Don't be one of them. Technology is your assistant, not your replacement. It should save you time so you can spend more of it connecting with people. When you balance digital efficiency with human empathy, you create a winning hybrid — one foot in the tech world, the other firmly planted on the doorstep of opportunity.

Finally, remember that the modern Ground Game isn't confined to a neighborhood — it extends to your digital presence as well. The same homeowners you meet in person may look you up online the moment you leave their porch. Make sure what they find matches the integrity you showed in person. Keep your website simple, your social media consistent, and your message clear: you help people find solutions. When your online image supports your in-person mission, it reinforces your credibility. Together, these old-school values and new-school tools form a modern Money Machine — one that keeps you connected, efficient, and consistently making deposits into Hip National Bank.

The Math of Hustle

Numbers never lie — they tell the truth about your effort, consistency, and belief. The Ground Game is not a guessing game; it's a math equation that rewards movement. If you visit fifty homes, twenty answer the door, and ten let you share your message, you've just conducted ten live presentations. Even if only two of those turn into deals, that's $16,000 in profit from seventy-two hours of work. In traditional business, those numbers would be considered elite performance. In the world of the Money Machine, that's just a solid week on the field. You can't predict which doors will open, but you can control how many you knock. The law of averages is undefeated — the more activity you generate, the more predictable your income becomes.

Every serious investor should know their personal Ground Game conversion rate. Treat it like a business metric, not a mystery. Track how many doors you knock, how many real conversations you have, and how many deals close as a result. Once you understand your ratios, you can reverse-engineer your income goals. For example, if one out of every twenty conversations turns into an $8,000 payday, and you want to earn $24,000 this month, you now know you need to have sixty meaningful conversations. That's not wishful thinking — that's math. Suddenly, success isn't emotional or abstract; it's measurable. Each day becomes a scoreboard, each knock a step closer to victory.

Look at it this way — professional athletes rely on repetition to sharpen their craft. Shooters shoot. Pitchers throw. Quarterbacks pass. They don't play the game once and hope for greatness; they build greatness through consistency. The same principle applies to wealth creation. Your "reps" are the doors you knock, the calls you make, the follow-ups you send. The more reps you take, the more muscle memory you build — not in your body, but in your confidence. Soon, you'll know exactly what to say, when to say it, and how to lead each conversation toward opportunity. That's the unseen math of hustle: consistency multiplied by time equals mastery.

Many people say they want financial freedom, but few are willing to track their way to it. The difference between dreamers and earners is data. The Ground Game is a living spreadsheet where each interaction represents future cash flow. While others complain that "no one's calling back," you'll be too busy logging your progress and calculating new profits. When your strategy is clear and your effort is measured, you transform random activity into predictable income. The moment you realize that one knock could equal $500, $1,000, or $8,000, you'll never hesitate again. That's the math of hustle — turning action into multiplication, and multiplication into deposits straight into Hip National Bank.

Lessons from Direct Sales

Direct sales is one of the greatest teachers of human behavior ever invented. Companies like Cutco, Kirby, and Vivint didn't grow into billion-dollar giants because they had the best products — they grew because they mastered the art of personal contact. Every knock, every pitch, every "no" taught their salespeople something about resilience, timing, and human psychology. The top performers weren't superhuman — they were simply consistent. They understood that sales is a transfer of belief. When you believe in what you're offering, people feel it. That belief becomes contagious. Whether you're selling a knife set or a real estate solution, conviction closes deals faster than clever words ever could.

Take the Cutco model, for instance. Thousands of college students who had never sold anything in their lives became confident, skilled communicators within months. Why? Because they faced rejection daily, and instead of shrinking, they adapted. They learned that every "no" is not personal — it's just a step toward the next "yes." They tracked their numbers, refined their pitch, and built momentum through activity. In real estate, the same principle applies. Every door you knock and every call you make adds to your growth account — not just your bank account. That's why most people never see consistent income: they quit before the math starts compounding.

Direct sales legends like Zig Ziglar and Mary Kay Ash built entire empires around one truth — persistence plus people equals profit. They taught generations of entrepreneurs that success isn't built on one big deal but on the thousands of small actions most people overlook. Ziglar used to say, "You don't have to be great to start, but you have to start to be great." That's the spirit of the Ground Game. If you're willing to get rejected a hundred times, you'll eventually find the ten people who will make you rich. Those ten become your clients, your testimonials, and your success stories that keep opening more doors.

Every "no" you face in direct sales is actually a mini classroom — teaching you tone, timing, empathy, and endurance. The more you lean into rejection, the less power it has over you. Over time, you begin to appreciate the process because you see what others don't: rejection is just proof of movement. Inaction is the only true failure. Once you grasp that, every knock and every conversation becomes valuable — not just for the potential deal, but for the skill it sharpens. Just like those relentless Cutco reps or door-to-door solar closers, you'll develop calluses that turn into confidence. That's when your Ground

Game goes from survival to domination — and that's when the real money starts flowing to Hip National Bank.

Becoming a Connector

True wealth is never built in isolation; it's built through connection. The Ground Game, at its core, isn't about chasing deals — it's about building bridges. When you knock on doors, listen to people's stories, and offer solutions, you position yourself as more than an investor. You become a connector — someone who links problems to possibilities. That's where trust is born. Homeowners, investors, contractors, and even local bankers start to recognize your face, your name, and your intent. They begin to associate you with progress, not pressure. Before long, opportunities find you instead of the other way around. That's when the Money Machine starts compounding its returns in relationships as much as in dollars.

Every time you help a homeowner save their property, connect an investor to a profitable deal, or assist a family in transitioning smoothly from a difficult situation, you're planting a seed. One introduction leads to another. One grateful handshake turns into three referrals. This is how sustainable business grows — not from ads or automation, but through human connection and integrity. The more value you bring, the more valuable you become. Over time, your community starts to see you as the go-to person for solutions, not just sales. That's the invisible power of being a connector — it builds a reputation that money can't buy.

Consider how network marketing legends like Jim Rohn or Holton Buggs built empires not by pushing products but by connecting people to purpose. They taught that if you help enough others get what they want, you'll always get what you want. The same principle applies here: when you focus on solving someone else's problem first, your own prosperity takes care of itself. Every handshake, every follow-up call, and every door knock becomes a link in a growing chain of trust.

And the longer that chain becomes, the more effortlessly deals will flow into Hip National Bank.

Being a connector also means thinking beyond transactions. It means taking genuine interest in people's lives — remembering their kids' names, asking about their goals, and following up even when there's no deal on the table. That's how lifelong clients are made. In an era where most people feel unseen, being remembered is currency. Every text, every thank-you card, every thoughtful follow-up builds equity in your relationships. And that relational equity will pay you dividends far greater than any single transaction ever could. In the long run, connection is the ultimate leverage.

Duplicating Success

Every winning play in business, like football, must be repeatable. The true test of mastery isn't how much success you can personally achieve; it's how much success you can duplicate through others. The Ground Game becomes a movement when you train others to play it with the same discipline, passion, and integrity. One person can only knock on so many doors, but when you create systems — scripts, tools, and repeatable actions — your influence multiplies. You're no longer just building a business; you're building a network that produces consistent income whether you're out in the field or not. That's when your Money Machine begins to run without your constant touch.

Duplication starts with clarity. People can only duplicate what they can clearly understand and confidently teach. If your Ground Game methods are simple enough to be followed step-by-step — from the first knock to the signed deal — anyone willing to put in the effort can replicate your success. Just like McDonald's can open a franchise in Tokyo or Tulsa and produce the same burger, your business should be able to reproduce predictable results no matter who's running the play. This is why documenting your process is crucial. Scripts, follow-up templates, lead sheets, and deal evaluation formulas — these are your playbook pages. Protect them, refine them, and teach them.

When your process works, you attract others who want to learn it. That's when you move from being a hustler to a leader. You become the coach instead of the sole player, developing people who share your values and vision. Imagine a small three-person team — a data researcher, a driver, and a closer — all executing your strategy in unison. One is mapping properties, one is knocking doors, and one is finalizing deals. While you're teaching them, they're producing revenue that flows straight to Hip National Bank. This is duplication in motion: your time and knowledge expanding through others.

This is the same model that propelled companies like Amway, Mary Kay, and LegalShield into billion-dollar brands. Their founders understood that real power lies in duplication — people helping people, empowered with simple systems and clear incentives. It's not about control; it's about consistency. When others win because of what you've built, loyalty and growth become automatic. You're no longer limited by your own hours or energy. Instead, you've leveraged human potential, and that kind of leverage compounds faster than any interest rate. In the end, duplication is what transforms the Ground Game from a personal hustle into a legacy movement.

Action Step
Form a 3-person team: one data researcher, one driver, one closer. Run a weekly Ground Game blitz. Track who talks to the most homeowners and celebrate wins together. People will follow what you celebrate.

Overcoming Fear
Fear is the invisible opponent that stops more people from achieving success than failure ever could. It disguises itself as caution, logic, or timing — whispering lies like "you're not ready yet" or "what if they slam the door?" But the truth is, fear is just faith pointed in the wrong direction. It's belief in a negative outcome instead of a positive one. Every time you hesitate to make a call, knock on a door, or present your offer, fear is cashing a check you could have written to Hip Na-

tional Bank. The only way to defeat it is through decisive action. Faith is motion — and when you move, fear loses its grip.

Think about it: every master started as a beginner who took the first swing while shaking. Michael Jordan missed over 9,000 shots and lost nearly 300 games before he became a champion. Steve Jobs was fired from his own company before creating the most valuable brand on earth. Oprah Winfrey was told she didn't belong on television. These people didn't become fearless — they learned to act in spite of fear. That's the real secret: courage isn't the absence of fear, it's the decision to move anyway. When you keep showing up, fear starts to work for you — it sharpens your instincts, heightens your focus, and drives your preparation.

The first five doors you knock will always feel like the longest five yards in football. Your heartbeat will race, your palms might sweat, and your mind will replay every reason not to do it. But something amazing happens around door number six: fear fades and flow takes over. The anxiety that once paralyzed you becomes fuel. By the tenth door, you're no longer rehearsing — you're performing. You've crossed the invisible line from hesitant to confident, from amateur to professional. That transformation can't be taught in a classroom; it's earned on the field.

Let's be honest — rejection stings. But it's not lethal. Each "no" is just a step toward your next "yes." Every conversation builds muscle memory, emotional resilience, and skill. The truth is, the people who reject you today may call you back months later because you stood out as the one who cared enough to show up. When that happens, you'll realize rejection was never the enemy — inaction was. The worst thing you can do is nothing. Every action, even an imperfect one, multiplies your experience and confidence. And confidence is the only antidote to fear.

Remember, fear doesn't go away as you grow — it just changes shape. When you're new, you fear the knock. When you're successful, you fear losing momentum. But either way, the cure remains the same:

motion. Movement breaks paralysis. The moment you take the first step — make the call, send the text, shake the hand — fear dissolves. That's why I tell my students: "Don't wait until you're ready. Ready comes after you start." The champions in any field aren't the ones who had no fear; they're the ones who had the guts to act while trembling.

Key Insight

Repetition builds reputation. The more doors you knock, the more deals — and courage — will find you.

Your ability to overcome fear is the single greatest predictor of your success. Once you conquer it, you gain momentum — and momentum attracts miracles. You'll begin to notice opportunities showing up faster, conversations going smoother, and money flowing easier. Why? Because you're finally operating without internal resistance. Fear is friction; faith is flow. When you live in motion, you stop questioning your potential and start experiencing it. That's when you realize: fear wasn't there to stop you — it was there to test you.

Turning Contacts into Contracts

Every conversation you have in the Ground Game is a potential goldmine — but only if you know how to turn that contact into a contract. Too many investors do the hard work of knocking, talking, and listening but fail to close the loop. They leave without a clear next step, thinking "I'll follow up later," and later never comes. In business, momentum is oxygen. The moment you end a conversation, the clock starts ticking — interest fades, distractions creep in, and the emotional connection weakens. The key is to lock in a follow-up before you walk away. Whether it's a phone appointment, a document review, or simply a promise to call tomorrow, don't let the conversation die on the doorstep.

Turning contacts into contracts begins with your posture. You're not just a visitor; you're a professional problem solver. When you stand confidently, speak with empathy, and guide the conversation toward clarity, people will follow your lead. Remember, most home-owners in distress are overwhelmed — too many papers, too many emotions, too many decisions. Your job is to simplify. Summarize what you discussed: "Here's what I heard you say, and here's what I can do to help." Then offer a clear next step. It could be a property walk-through, a meeting with your title partner, or a follow-up to review documents. Clarity builds trust, and trust closes deals.

Pro Tip
The best closers don't push — they guide. When you make the next step feel safe, people naturally move forward.

After each conversation, follow up with something tangible. A handwritten thank-you note, a brief text, or even a short email saying, "It was great meeting you today — I believe we can find a solution that helps you. Let's reconnect this week." That single act of professionalism places you above 95% of your competition. People crave reliability. When they see you keep your word, they begin to see you as a partner, not a stranger. And the next time you knock, they'll be waiting — because you've proven you're someone who finishes what you start.

Every contact you make is a seed, but contracts are the harvest. And just like any farmer, you have to tend the field — follow up, water relationships, and watch for signs of readiness. Some homeowners won't be ready today, but they will be in six weeks or six months. That's why consistent tracking is vital. Use a simple CRM or even a spreadsheet to log your interactions, next steps, and follow-up dates. The difference between a struggling investor and a successful one often comes down to organization, not opportunity.

Think about great closers in any field — whether it's real estate, car sales, or high-level business development. They don't depend on luck; they depend on systems. They follow up relentlessly because they understand human nature — most people don't say "yes" on the first contact. It often takes five to seven touches before trust turns into a signature. That's why I teach my students that every "no" is simply "not yet." The deal isn't dead until you stop showing up. When you build your Ground Game around consistent follow-up, contracts stop being accidents — they become inevitabilities.

And remember, each closed deal is more than just money — it's momentum. It's validation that your effort, your courage, and your consistency paid off. The moment that wire hits escrow or the assignment fee clears, that deposit flows directly into Hip National Bank. That's the sweet reward of persistence — proof that you can transform conversations into cash flow through integrity, patience, and skill. Once you learn to master this rhythm — contact, connect, close — you'll never run out of opportunity.

Key Insight
Every handshake is a seed — every follow-up waters it — every contract harvests it.

When you practice the Ground Game long enough, something powerful happens: people start calling you. Your reputation grows beyond the doorsteps you knock on. Agents refer clients they can't help. Homeowners mention you to friends in trouble. Investors call looking for your next deal. What began as a single contact expands into a network of continuous contracts. That's the magic of consistent action — it turns the grind into grace, the hustle into harmony, and the handshake into lasting wealth.

Beyond Real Estate
The Ground Game isn't just a real estate strategy — it's a universal principle for creating wealth in any industry. It's the timeless law of motion: when you move toward opportunity, opportunity moves toward you. Whether you're selling houses, products, services, or ideas, the formula never changes — consistent contact equals consistent cash flow. The digital era has made it easier than ever to hide behind screens and ads, but the truth is, the world still responds to personal effort. Real money still rewards real movement. The handshake, the

phone call, the face-to-face meeting — these will always outperform any algorithm.

Think about some of the most successful brands and entrepreneurs in history. They didn't build empires from behind keyboards; they built them through connection. Sam Walton, founder of Walmart, was famous for walking every store floor, greeting employees and customers personally. Howard Schultz of Starbucks turned a simple coffee shop into a global culture by sitting with people, listening, and observing their habits. Even tech giants like Steve Jobs relied on human understanding — walking through neighborhoods, studying design, and talking to users long before a product launch. These were all versions of the Ground Game: direct, personal engagement that created billion-dollar feedback loops.

Now, apply this same concept to your world. If you're in network marketing, ministry, or small business, the Ground Game is your growth engine. In ministry, it's visiting homes, praying with families, and connecting beyond the pulpit. In sales, it's calling clients after the deal to thank them personally. In investing, it's walking a property yourself instead of relying solely on an agent's report. Each action deepens trust and expands your reach. When you move with purpose, people can feel it — and people do business with people who make them feel understood.

Here's the secret that few understand: the same courage it takes to knock on a stranger's door in real estate is the same courage it takes to build any brand. When you develop the habit of initiating contact, you eliminate the invisible ceiling that holds most entrepreneurs back. The Ground Game builds a muscle that extends far beyond closing deals — it builds confidence, discipline, and relational authority. These traits become transferable currencies in every industry you touch. You stop chasing success and start attracting it because your reputation precedes you.

Pro Tip

Technology doesn't close deals — people do.

We often confuse tools for transformation. Social media, email, and automation are powerful amplifiers, but they don't replace personal presence. A post might get likes; a conversation builds loyalty. Automation may create noise, but authenticity creates movement. The most successful entrepreneurs blend both — they use technology to support, not substitute, their Ground Game. They follow up with digital precision but still show up with human warmth. That's the hybrid model of modern wealth: automation for reach, humanity for results.

When you master this approach, your Ground Game transcends industry. You'll start to see patterns everywhere — opportunities to apply these principles in speaking, coaching, marketing, or leadership. The same skill that helps you close a real estate deal will help you recruit a partner, pitch a business idea, or lead a team. Why? Because people respond to energy. The confidence you project in person can't be duplicated by pixels on a screen. And once you realize that, you'll never again wait for business to come to you — you'll go out and claim it.

In the end, the Ground Game is about ownership — of your time, your relationships, and your future. It's how you stop renting your potential and start owning your destiny. Every conversation, every handshake, every follow-up builds your equity in the marketplace. That's the ultimate lesson: success isn't sold, it's sown. And when you sow enough genuine connections, the harvest comes in waves — flowing straight into Hip National Bank.

The New Hustle Code

We live in an age where everyone wants shortcuts — quick clicks, viral posts, instant fame. But the truth is, shortcuts rarely lead to wealth that lasts. The New Hustle Code is a return to timeless fundamentals: work ethic, consistency, and human connection. Success hasn't changed — only the packaging has. You can't outsource hunger. You can't automate integrity. You can't fake persistence. The digital world may have redefined convenience, but it hasn't rewritten the rules of wealth. The same laws that built empires a century ago still govern success today — sow, serve, and show up.

The Ground Game is the embodiment of that New Hustle Code. It's the rejection of waiting for opportunity and the embrace of creating it. While others post motivational quotes, you're out there living one. While they build landing pages, you're landing deals. The irony is that, in a world obsessed with automation, the person who chooses to move with authenticity becomes rare — and rarity creates value. That's why personal effort will always outperform passive marketing. When you show up where others won't, you instantly become the most credible person in the room.

Think about entrepreneurs like Daymond John or Grant Cardone. They didn't start with privilege or perfect timing — they started with the grind. Daymond sold hats from the trunk of his car before FUBU became a billion-dollar brand. Grant made cold calls long before he filled arenas. Their success wasn't luck; it was consistency. They understood the hustle wasn't glamorous — it was necessary. They knocked, called, pitched, and repeated. The Ground Game is that same relentless rhythm: activity over anxiety, progress over perfection.

Key Insight
Discipline is the bridge between opportunity and wealth. The Ground Game builds both.

The New Hustle Code isn't about chasing money — it's about mastering momentum. Money follows motion, not meditation. When you work the Ground Game daily, your results compound like interest. Every knock teaches you something. Every "no" sharpens your pitch. Every "yes" funds your next move. Before long, you realize the path to financial freedom wasn't hidden; it was just disguised as hard work. But that's good news — because hard work has almost no competition anymore.

This is why your Money Machine thrives in today's economy. While others scroll through distractions, you're stacking real connections. While they analyze the market, you're already cashing in. And as your network expands, so does your leverage. The Ground Game becomes the engine that powers your brand, your income, and your reputation. The best part? You don't have to be a genius — just consistent. The modern marketplace rewards those who stay visible, valuable, and vocal. Be all three, and you'll dominate your lane.

The New Hustle Code demands accountability. Track your numbers. Measure your actions. Refine your message. Study your market. But never let analysis replace activity. Too many people get stuck planning and never start performing. You don't need a perfect plan — you need persistent action. The map appears as you move. And once you start collecting results, even small ones, you'll feel your confidence multiply. That's when you realize the real product of your hustle isn't just profit — it's personal power.

The future belongs to those who outwork automation and outlast distraction. That's you. You're the one willing to hit the pavement while others hit snooze. You're the one who builds trust through presence, not pixels. You're the one who's rewriting what modern wealth looks like — one door, one deal, one deposit at a time. That's the New Hustle Code. It's not about noise; it's about numbers. Not about popularity; about profitability. When you live by it, every day becomes game day, and every win goes straight into Hip National Bank.

Workbook: Module 5

The Ground Game – A Lost Art

Field Operations Manual for the Money Machine

"Every knock is momentum. Every conversation is equity. Every deal is another deposit into Hip National Bank."
— Ray Wright Jacobs

Purpose

This workbook moves you from concept to cash flow. Each section helps you build confidence, sharpen consistency, and turn motion into money. Remember, *wealth rewards movement*. The more you knock, the more you learn, and the more you earn.

1. Field Prep Checklist
Before You Knock — Prepare for Victory

- **Documents:** Qualified Written Request (QWR), RESPA/TILA info sheets.
- **Tools:** Clipboard, business cards, notepad, smartphone, GPS or *Route4Me* app, ID badge.
- **Appearance:** Clean, confident, professional — friendly, not flashy.
- **Mindset:** Take three deep breaths before your first door. Confidence begins in calm.

Action Step:
Write your personal affirmation for today.

Example: "Every knock I make opens a door to opportunity — for them and for me."

2. Personal Script Development
Crafting Your 30-Second Introduction

"Hi, I'm [Your Name]. I work with homeowners who've had some trouble with their lender. I help them understand their options — sometimes even stop foreclosure. Would you like to see how that works?"

Say it with warmth. Then pause — and **listen**. Listening converts curiosity into trust.

Reflection:

Write your personalized script below. Practice it aloud five times until it feels natural, not rehearsed.

3. Activity Tracker

Keep Score Like a Pro

Track every contact. Great players study stats; great investors track activity.

Key Insight:

You can't improve what you don't measure.

4. Power Team Journal
Team Roles That Multiply Momentum

- **Researcher:** Pulls property and title data.
- **Driver:** Manages routes, ensures safety, and documents details.
- **Closer:** Talks with homeowners and finalizes agreements.

Pro Tip:

People don't follow bosses — they follow energy. Keep your team inspired, informed, and appreciated.

Action Step:

Create a shared digital log for your team's daily results. Celebrate every meaningful contact together.

5. Weekly Goals
Convert Dreams Into Data

- 30 Doors Knocked
- 10 Real Conversations
- 3 Follow-Up Meetings Scheduled
- 1 Signed Contract

Each number represents motion. Every action creates opportunity.

Reflection Question:
What would happen if you hit these goals every week for 12 weeks?
(Write your answer here.)

6. Progress Review
Weekly Reflection for Course Correction

Ask yourself every Friday:

- What worked this week?
- What didn't?
- What did I learn about people?
- What did I learn about myself?

Action Step:
Identify one weakness to improve next week — and write one practical way to strengthen it.

Key Insight:
Awareness precedes improvement.

7. Mindset Mastery
Courage Through Consistency

Each week, write one fear you faced and how you conquered it through action.

Example:
"I was nervous on Monday's first door, but by Friday I held three full conversations and scheduled a follow-up."
Fear fades when faced daily — courage compounds when tracked.

8. Duplication Drill
Teach to Multiply
Train one person in your Ground Game system. Let them shadow your route, observe your tone, and duplicate your results.

Duplication creates legacy. When others win through your system, your influence compounds beyond your time.

Action Step:
Record their results and your observations. What did they learn fastest? Where did they need correction?

9. Income Projection Exercise
Turn Math Into Motivation
Example:
Goal: $96,000 a year ÷ $8,000 per deal = 12 deals per year → 1 deal per month.
Simple, clear, achievable.

Action Step:
Write your annual income goal here → _____
Calculate the number of weekly routes required to reach it → _____

10. The Reflection Moment
Every Sunday evening, replay your week like a highlight reel. Celebrate your progress, no matter how small.
Then, give thanks for the wisdom, favor, and stamina to continue. Gratitude keeps the Ground Game joyful — and joy keeps you in motion.

Quote to Remember:

"Success rewards those who knock longest after everyone else has gone home." — Ray Wright Jacobs

Final Word from Ray Wright Jacobs
This isn't theory — it's transformation. The Ground Game separates spectators from players. When you commit to consistent motion, you'll start to notice divine alignment: opportunities appearing, doors opening, people calling you.

Your reputation will walk ahead of you because your character built it. You'll realize that the true product of the Ground Game isn't property — it's purpose. Each handshake, each conversation, each signature is more than a deal; it's proof that you've mastered the rhythm of prosperity. Now suit up, step out, and move with confidence. Every mile is equity. Every "no" sharpens your skill. Every "yes" funds your next step toward financial freedom.

Go out there — the field is waiting. The scoreboard is yours to change.

6

❦

Module 6: Turn Contract Control to Cash

The Art of the Assignment – The Lost Art
How to Print Cash on Paper Without Money or Credit

"You don't need money to make money-you need motion and mastery."
— Ray Wright Jacobs

The Foundation of Assignment Mastery

In this module, I'm going to teach you one of the simplest and most powerful ways to print money in real estate — legally, ethically, and without ever needing to use your own cash or credit. I call it The Art of the Assignment – The Lost Art. This is where your *Money Machine* truly begins to hum. The concept is simple: you leverage your most valuable asset — your time — and exchange it for paper contracts that represent value. Those contracts become negotiable instruments you can assign to investors for immediate income. No bank loans. No renovations. No risk-heavy flips. Just intelligent positioning and consistent action.

The beauty of this strategy is that anyone can do it. Whether you're a single parent, a full-time worker, or an aspiring entrepreneur with no capital, this system allows you to use knowledge and persistence to produce profit on demand. When you commit to running the numbers and following the process, you'll soon see how predictable it becomes. Done correctly, this method can yield anywhere from $2,500 on small deals to over $100,000 on larger transactions — all without buying or selling a single property yourself.

Think of it this way: the *Art of the Assignment* is your financial apprenticeship. It trains you to recognize value, structure opportunity, and negotiate profit — the three pillars of every wealthy investor's mindset. Once you master this art, you'll never again wonder how to create income; you'll simply decide *when* to turn on the faucet.

The Power of Leverage Without Liability

In traditional business, leverage usually requires risk — borrowing money, hiring staff, or carrying inventory. But with assignment deals, your leverage is knowledge, not capital. You're using information, research, and relationships to locate undervalued opportunities and connect them with capable investors who have the funds but not the time or hustle to find them. In exchange for doing the legwork, you earn a fee.

This process transforms you into a *value creator* — the middle point in the wealth triangle between property owners and investors. You're solving two problems at once: you help distressed sellers find a quick solution and help investors acquire profitable properties without doing the groundwork. You're the bridge, and bridges always collect tolls. Those tolls are paid directly into Hip National Bank.

The Activity Formula — 100/20/5 Rule

Now let's get specific. To master this art, you must treat it like a numbers game, not a guessing game. I teach my students the 100/20/5 Rule of Activity.

- **Analyze 100 properties.**
- **Get 20 potential yeses or warm leads.**
- **Convert 5 into signed contracts.**
- **Close 1 to 2 profitable deals.**

That's it — the math of momentum. Most people never reach financial success because they stop too soon. They analyze ten properties, hear two rejections, and call it quits. But in real estate, your fortune is always hidden in the follow-up. The numbers don't lie; activity does. When you stay consistent, results become inevitable.

Finding and Analyzing the Deal

To begin, you'll use real estate data software to search by zip code, property type, or foreclosure status. Let's say you run a search for pre-foreclosures in your city and find 3,500 results. That's too many to manage, so you filter by criteria: four-bedroom homes, over 3,000 square feet, less than 15 years old. Now your list shrinks to 137 — your first batch of targets.

Next, you'll analyze those 137 properties for potential equity. Your goal is to find properties where the Purchase-to-Market Value (PTMV) ratio is at or below 68%. In plain terms, you want homes worth $100,000 that you can buy for $68,000 or less. This ensures there's enough room for profit when you assign the deal to an investor.

Example of a Perfect Deal

Here's how it looks in practice. You identify a property worth $450,000 with a mortgage balance of $275,000 and $19,000 in arrears. After checking records, you confirm there are no second liens and the home is in excellent condition. That's a goldmine. You visit the property, meet the seller, and offer to purchase it for $290,000 — enough to cover their balance and give them breathing room.

Why would they sell with that much equity? Because people don't make financial decisions purely on numbers — they make them on emotion. Divorce, relocation, illness, job loss — all can motivate a sale. You're providing relief, not taking advantage. Once the seller signs, you have a legally binding purchase contract.

And here's the key: under "Buyer," you write "Your Real Estate Company Name and/or Assigns." That small phrase is your ticket to freedom. It gives you the right to assign your position in the contract to another buyer — for a fee. That's where your payday comes from.

Flipping the Paper — Turning Signatures into Cash

Now that you've secured the deal, your next step is to flip it — not the property, but the contract. You've just created an asset out of thin air: a signed agreement at $290,000 on a property worth $450,000. The spread is value, and you control it.

Using your connections from local investor meetups or online platforms like *REIBlackBook* or *BiggerPockets*, you'll find investors actively seeking properties under 70% of market value. Offer them the deal for $306,000 — that's 68% PTMV. You'll assign your contract for a $16,000 fee: $4,000 paid upfront (25%) and $12,000 paid at closing (75%). Congratulations — you just made $16,000 without spending a dime of your own money.

If you can do this once a month, that's an extra $192,000 per year. If you scale it to three per month, you're clearing over a quarter of a million dollars — working from your laptop and your car. The only investment required is your time, courage, and consistency.

*******SAMPLE ASSIGNMENT CONTRACT*******
REAL PROPERTY ASSIGNMENT AGREEMENT

DATE: [Insert Date]

ASSIGNOR: Your REI Co. Name **"and/or Assigns"**

ASSIGNEE: Name of Person/Company You Are Assigning To

SELLER: Seller's Name on Contract (or Authorized Agent)

PROPERTY ADDRESS: [Insert Address, City, ZIP]

PURCHASE CONTRACT DATE: [Insert Date]

PURCHASE PRICE: [Insert Purchase Price]

CLOSING DATE: [Insert Date]

LEGAL DESCRIPTION: [Insert Description]

TERMS OF ASSIGNMENT

The **Assignor** agrees to assign the **Assignee** all buyer's rights, terms, and conditions of the Purchase Contract referenced above ("the Agreement"). The **Assignee** agrees to meet all closing conditions of the Agreement and be bound by all default provisions therein.

The Assignee agrees to pay the Assignor an **Assignment Fee** ("the Fee") of $[Insert Amount] as compensation for the transfer of buyer's rights. Payment will be made as follows:

1. **25% of the Fee** paid to Assignor upon execution of this Assignment in cash, cashier's check, or wire transfer.
2. **75% of the Fee** paid to Assignor at closing, listed as a Paid Out of Closing (POC) disbursement from escrow.

ASSIGNOR:

Name / Signature
Address: _____
City, State ZIP: _____
Email: _____

Phone: _____

ASSIGNEE:

Name / Signature

Address: _____

City, State ZIP: _____

Email: _____

Phone: _____

*******END OF SAMPLE ASSIGNMENT CONTRACT*******

Why This Works

Most new investors struggle not because they lack opportunity, but because they lack clarity. The Assignment Agreement eliminates mystery. It spells out exactly what to ask for and how to structure it. You're never left guessing how to approach an investor, what to charge, or how to protect yourself. It's plug-and-play wealth creation — all on paper.

And remember: this is not theory. It's transaction-tested, field-proven strategy. Every major investor started here — wholesaling contracts, learning negotiation, and building cash reserves to fund future projects. This is where your confidence, credibility, and capital begin to grow.

The Mental Refining Process

Now let's address the inner game. Many people read powerful information like this but never apply it. Not because they can't, but because fear and doubt whisper louder than discipline. It's not the strategy that needs testing — it's the person. The gold is already in you, but it must be refined through fire.

When the process feels uncomfortable — when doors close, leads go cold, or contracts fall through — that's your refining season. Stay in the fire until your impurities burn off: impatience, inconsistency, hesitation. Don't jump out when it gets hot. Those who endure the refining come out golden — tested, capable, and unstoppable.

Remember, *applied knowledge* is power. Universities are filled with brilliant professors who understand theory but never risk application. The real power belongs to those who execute. Don't just study the playbook — run the play.

Pro Tip — The Art Becomes Science

Once you close your first few deals, systematize everything. Create templates, a CRM for tracking sellers and investors, and a weekly activity goal.
Example:
10 new leads analyzed daily
3 new homeowner conversations
1 new investor relationship weekly

When you approach your assignments with this level of precision, your results compound like clockwork. What starts as a side hustle becomes a scalable business model. And every signed paper, every successful deal, adds one more deposit to Hip National Bank.

Transition to the Next Stage

In the next three modules, we'll take your knowledge to a new level. You're about to learn insider secrets that even licensed brokers and loan officers don't fully understand. We'll increase your Banking & Mortgage IQ, expose hidden mechanics within lender systems, and give you the tools to negotiate from a position of power.

The *Art of the Assignment* prepared you to make money with no credit and no capital. The next modules will teach you how to create *infinite capital* by mastering the banking game itself. So take a moment to celebrate this milestone — you now hold the blueprint for financial self-sufficiency.

Key Insight:

The Art of the Assignment turns paper into payment, contracts into cash, and activity into income. It's your first taste of what it feels like to print money — legally, ethically, and intelligently — like the rich.

Workbook: Module 6

The Art of the Assignment - A Lost Art
How to Print Cash on Paper Without Credit or Capital

"Paper signed right is paper that pays. Your pen is your printing press."
— Ray Wright Jacobs

Purpose

The goal of this workbook is to help you move from theory to profit. You'll learn how to analyze properties, approach sellers, negotiate profitable terms, and assign contracts with precision. By the time you finish these exercises, you'll understand exactly how to create a deal on paper that pays real cash — all without ever taking out a loan or lifting a hammer.

1. Assignment Readiness Checklist

Before you start, ensure your business foundation is solid. The Assignment Game rewards preparation.

Complete the checklist below:

- [ ] I have chosen my business name and created my real estate investment entity (LLC, Trust, etc.)
- [ ] I have a simple business card and professional email address
- [ ] I've joined at least one local or online investor group (e.g., REIBlackBook, BiggerPockets, Meetup)
- [ ] I have blank purchase and sale agreements ready to fill out
- [ ] I understand how to calculate 68% of After-Repair Value (ARV)
- [ ] I have read and understand the Sample Assignment Agreement in this module

Action Step:

Write your company name exactly how it will appear on every contract line labeled "Buyer":

Your Real Estate Company Name "and/or Assigns."

2. Deal Analyzer Practice

Every assignment begins with analysis. The goal is to locate properties with at least **35% equity** or **below 68% Purchase-to-Market Value (PTMV).**

Property Address: 123 Maple Ave
Market Value: $450,000
Loan Balance: $275,000
Default Amount: 19,000
Repair Cost: $0
Offer Price: $290,000
PTMV %: 64%
Potential Spread: $160,000

Pro Tip:
Equity is invisible wealth until you write it on paper. Your job is to reveal it through analysis.

Action Step:
Analyze five properties in your target area and fill in the chart above. Identify which meet your target PTMV ratio.

3. Contract Confidence Drill
Repetition builds confidence. Practice filling out a **Purchase & Sale Agreement** with the following required elements:

- Purchase price at or below 68% PTMV
- Closing in 20–30 days
- Earnest money $500–$1,000
- Buyer line includes: *"Your Company Name and/or Assigns."*

Reflection:
What part of the contract felt unclear? Write it down and review this module's sample until it feels second nature.

Key Insight:
The one who controls the paper controls the profit.

4. Investor Outreach Tracker
Your deals are only as good as the buyers who can close them. Track your investor outreach on your own table.

Join one local or online real estate investor meeting this week. Introduce yourself:

"Hi, I'm [Your Name], a wholesaler who specializes in finding discounted off-market properties. I'll have assignable deals coming soon — can I add you to my buyer's list?"

Pro Tip:
The first ten "no's" build the muscle that earns your first "yes."

5. Structuring Your Assignment Fee
To determine your profit, calculate your assignment spread and payment plan.

Example:
Purchase Contract = $290,000
Investor Buy Price = $306,000
Assignment Fee = $16,000
• $4,000 (25%) paid upon signing
• $12,000 (75%) paid at closing

Your Turn:

- Offer Price: _____
- Market Value: _____
- Buyer's Offer Price: _____
- Assignment Fee: _____
- 25% Deposit: _____
- 75% Closing Payment: _____

Key Insight:
Your assignment fee is the reward for solving two problems at once — the seller's pain and the investor's need.

6. The 100/20/5 Rule in Action
Revisit Ray's **100/20/5 Rule of Activity** — 100 analyses, 20 warm leads, 5 signed contracts, 1–2 closings.

Action Step:
For the next 30 days, commit to running the 100/20/5 process. Write your daily numbers, even small wins.

7. Communication Role-Play
Practice both sides of your Ground Game conversation.
Scenario:
You're meeting a homeowner behind on payments. Practice explaining how you can help — not as a buyer, but as a problem solver.
Example:
"I work with a team that helps homeowners who've fallen behind. We can make an offer that pays off your balance, stops foreclosure, and helps you move on. I'll handle all the paperwork, and you don't pay any agent fees."

Reflection:
Write a short paragraph describing how you'd build trust in the first two minutes of conversation.

Pro Tip:
People don't sell houses; they sell emotions. Solve the person, and the property follows.

8. Assignment Execution Checklist
Before submitting your deal to escrow, confirm the following:

- [ ] All signatures complete on Purchase & Sale Agreement
- [ ] Assignment Agreement fully executed
- [ ] Investor's earnest money deposited
- [ ] Escrow/title company confirmed as neutral third party
- [ ] Assignment Fee listed as "Paid Out of Closing (POC)" item

Action Step:
Call your title officer and ask:
"Do you work with investor assignment contracts?"
Their response will help you identify investor-friendly escrow partners.

9. Profit Projection & Scaling
Use the chart below to visualize your potential income as you scale your assignments.

Property Address:

_____

Market Value:

_____

Default Loan Balance Amount:

Repair Cost:

Offer Price:

PTMV:

Potential Spread:

Action Step:
Write your personal target for this year:
"I will complete ____ assignments at an average of $____ per deal for a total of $____ in 12 months."

Key Insight:
What you measure, you multiply.

10. Mindset of Mastery

Every assignment you complete refines your confidence. Don't rush the process — refine it. The profits come faster when your skills get sharper.

Bonus Workbook Module-6 Art of the Assignment Follow-Through
1. Opportunity Finder

List three properties or deal types you can research this week to analyze for assignment potential.

2. Deal Analyzer

Choose one property and calculate: market value, loan balance, equity percentage, and estimated offer price.

3. Contract Prep

Draft your buyer section exactly as it should appear:

Your Real Estate Investment Co. Name and/or Assigns

4. Assignment Practice

Write a short scenario explaining how you would pitch your signed deal to an investor.

5. Value Proposition

List 3 reasons an investor should buy your contract instead of finding their own deal.

6. The Math of Profit

Calculate your projected assignment fee, 25 % deposit amount, and 75 % balance due at closing.

7. Investor Network

Identify 3 local or online investor groups you can contact to market your next deal.

8. Time-to-Cash Formula

Record your activity this week: number of leads, contracts, offers, and assignments closed.

9. Reflection Prompt

What fears or doubts arise when you ask someone to sign a contract?

Write how you'll overcome them.

10. Income Goal Tracker

Based on your average assignment fee, calculate how many deals per month will hit your income target.

11. Sample Agreement Study

Review the corrected sample Real Property Assignment Agreement below and highlight any clauses you'd customize.

Bonus Reflection: The 12-Month Vision

If you mastered *The Art of the Assignment* — understanding how to create value from paper, conversation, and opportunity — how would your financial life look 12 months from today?

Would you still be trading time for money, or would Hip National Bank overflow from contracts you created with courage, knowledge, and consistent action?

Quote to Remember:

"Knowledge is potential power; applied knowledge is your payday." — **Ray Wright Jacobs**

Final Word from Ray Wright Jacobs

Every paper deal you close is a victory of skill over circumstance. The Art of the Assignment is your on-ramp to financial independence — proof that money is everywhere for those who know how to structure it. Once you see the world through this lens, opportunity stops hiding from you. Assignments are the bridge between where you are and where you're going. They build cash, confidence, and credibility. Treat every deal as a rehearsal for your future millions. Print contracts, collect checks, and keep stacking those deposits into Hip National Bank.

Final Key Insight:

A signed contract is a promise — your job is to turn that promise into profit.

7

Module 7: Think of Owner First, Last, & Always

Always Bring the Homeowner a Solution
Never Focus on the Possible Profit of Selling the House
(Your Default History Lesson)
Realty Solutions Manager Training 101

When the storm hit in 2007–2008, America discovered the housing market wasn't built on granite—it was built on paper, and that paper was built on promises the banks never intended to keep.

Most homeowners thought they borrowed money. But the deeper truth—buried under thousands of pages of "disclosures"—was that their own promissory note funded the transaction first. The borrower created the money the bank later claimed to lend. That fact was never fully disclosed under the Truth in Lending Act (TILA), which was supposed to ensure complete transparency in credit transactions.

As Realty Solutions Managers, we are here to shine light into that shadow. Our goal is not to rage at the machine—but to understand how it works, leverage the truth, and use lawful tools to create time, options, and outcomes for homeowners who've been blindsided by a system stacked against them.

The People vs. the Conveyor Belt
(Where the Machine Meets the Man)

The modern foreclosure system doesn't think — it processes. The moment a payment is missed, a digital timer starts ticking. Algorithms send notices, automated systems generate "letters of acceleration," and servicers upload borrower data to foreclosure trustees who may never have seen the loan file. In the banking world, this isn't personal — it's procedural. But to a homeowner, it's terrifying. It's the moment their life becomes a file number. This is what I call the conveyor belt — a mechanical foreclosure pipeline that runs on autopilot, where human compassion is replaced with workflow automation.

That's where *you* enter the picture. The conveyor belt only wins when people stop asking questions. The second you, as a Realty Solutions Manager, step in with lawful, written administrative action — you throw a wrench into the machine. When you assist a homeowner in sending a Qualified Written Request (QWR), a TILA inquiry, or a Debt Validation demand, you interrupt the assembly line. Suddenly, someone at the bank must step off autopilot, pull that file, and respond point by point. You've forced human accountability back into a process that was designed to eliminate it. That's not theory — that's real administrative power in motion.

The biggest secret in modern banking is that most "foreclosure actions" are never verified by the originating lender — they're executed by third-party servicers and trustee firms relying on imported data. These entities depend on borrower silence. If the homeowner never challenges, the data is presumed true. But when you assist them in issuing a lawful inquiry — certified, notarized, and properly addressed — you've just changed jurisdiction from emotional panic to administrative process. And process governs commerce. This is why I tell every new trainee: you can't outfight the bank in emotion, but you can out-maneuver them in paper.

The Administrative Remedy Group taught us that most homeowners don't lose their homes because of debt — they lose them because of default by silence. The bank sends a presentment (a Notice of Default), and the borrower never sends a counter-presentment. Under commercial law, silence is acquiescence. The servicer wins not because they're right, but because the borrower never responded. The administrative process rewards whoever moves first and records their position in writing. That's what The Money Machine teaches you to move the goalpost — respond to every notice, challenge every inconsistency, and force every collector to prove every detail they claim. When you do that consistently, the balance of power shifts back to the people.

Key Insight:

In the world of banking, whoever controls the paperwork controls the narrative. You can't stop the conveyor belt — but you can make it stop for you.

This is not activism — it's awareness in motion. The conveyor belt operates on rhythm and repetition. But when your written inquiries hit their system — especially those properly labeled under 12 C.F.R. §1024.35 and §1024.36 (RESPA) — the bank's internal compliance division has to pause. They can't close, sell, or continue foreclosure until the inquiry has been logged, answered, or resolved. When you understand that, you realize your pen is stronger than their processor. You don't need a million-dollar lawyer to buy time — you need precision, persistence, and proof of mailing. That's how you make the system do something it was never designed to do: stop, listen, and account for its own actions.

Once you grasp this, you'll never again see a foreclosure as a hopeless fight. You'll see it as a negotiation governed by timing, paper, and presence. The bank's power is in their automation; your power is in your attention. When you respond with knowledge — certified, on record, and time-stamped — you rehumanize the process. That's what I call the Ground Game in the default arena: bringing humanity back into a system that forgot what it means to serve people.

Pro Tip:
Automation makes the bank efficient — not ethical. A Realty Solutions Manager makes the process human again.

And that's exactly what this movement is about. When we teach homeowners to stand in their rightful administrative authority, we don't just slow down foreclosure — we reveal what was hidden. We remind the nation that contracts are mutual, not mechanical. We remind the lenders that *Truth in Lending* wasn't meant to be fine print — it was meant to be a mirror. The people are that mirror now, and through the power of written notice, they are holding the system to its own reflection.

Pro Tip:
Banks can ignore a complaint. They can't ignore a recorded paper trail. Every certified letter you help a homeowner send creates accountability they can't erase.

The Undisclosed Exchange
(Where the Loan Was Born Before You Knew It)
Every borrower in America believes the same story: "The bank lent me money." It's the tale we've been taught since childhood — and it's the greatest illusion in modern finance. The reality is far simpler and more powerful: when you sign that promissory note, you fund the transaction first. Your signature transforms a blank sheet of paper into a financial instrument with measurable value. That note is deposited as an asset on the bank's books, balanced by a liability called your "loan." The bank didn't lend you money — it recorded your credit, issued itself the deposit, and lent it back to you at interest.

That's the *undisclosed exchange*. It's not a theory — it's accounting. Under Generally Accepted Accounting Principles (GAAP), a promissory note received by a financial institution is recorded as an asset. To balance the books, the bank creates a corresponding liability — your loan account. From that moment forward, the bank owes the depositor (you) the amount of the note, even while representing itself as the creditor. The entire "loan" exists because your signature turned potential energy into a liquid asset. That transaction — the conversion of your written promise into their lending base — is what fuels the modern Money Machine.

Key Insight:

The borrower's note funds the lender's asset, yet the lender reports the transaction as if they funded the borrower.

Now, under the Truth in Lending Act (TILA), codified in 15 U.S.C. §§1601–1667, lenders must make "clear and conspicuous" disclosure of the terms and nature of any credit transaction. But here's the catch: the Act presumes the lender provided value first. It was never designed to expose a system where the borrower's own note creates the value being lent. That omission — the failure to disclose the true source of funds — is what I call the *Original Sin of Modern Banking*. Every "loan" that followed carries its DNA.

If this sounds abstract, let's bring it to life. Imagine walking into a bank and signing a $300,000 promissory note for a home loan. That note, bearing your wet-ink signature, is immediately treated as a negotiable instrument under the Uniform Commercial Code (UCC Article 3) — capable of being sold, traded, or pledged as collateral. Within hours, that note is digitized, catalogued, and assigned a market value. The bank's books now show a new asset worth $300,000 — your note — offset by a new liability, the "loan." They haven't lent you cash from deposits; they've created credit against the paper you just produced. The proceeds wired to escrow are credit entries, not cash withdrawals.

So, who was the true lender?
You were.

You lent your future labor, time, and economic energy to the system through your signature. You were the underwriter, the funder, and the collateral — all in one. The bank acted as the intermediary, not the benefactor. Yet when you signed those TILA disclosures at closing, nowhere did it say: *"The borrower's promissory note constitutes the funding instrument for this transaction."* That omission matters because TILA's very purpose is to ensure *transparency* — not trickery. It's the same omission that fuels every foreclosure, every securitization, and every transfer that follows.

Pro Tip:
Every financial transaction is an exchange — but only one side of the exchange is disclosed. The moment you understand that, you begin to see your real position in commerce.

Let's pause and translate this into administrative action — because awareness without application is just frustration. When you help a homeowner send a TILA-based inquiry or QWR demanding the accounting trail of their note, you are calling for the true ledger — the one that shows where the value came from. Under Regulation Z (12 C.F.R. §1026), a lender must produce accurate records of how all payments, charges, and credits were applied. What you're asking for is the mirror image: *Where did the initial credit come from?* That's not a conspiracy question — that's an accounting question.

This is why the system fears transparency. Because if the people ever understood that the act of their signing is what funds the entire chain — from origination to securitization to resale — they would never again approach a loan with the posture of a beggar. They would approach it as a partner. And partnership changes everything.

The Administrative Default Group exposed this opacity repeatedly. Every loan audit performed, every ledger reviewed, told the same story: the promissory note was treated as a cash equivalent from day one. Banks have become masters at concealing this through layered documentation — funding sheets, warehouse lines, and MERS registrations — all to mask the fact that what began as your signature became their trading asset. The further it travels from you, the less they want you to see the trail. That's why your role as a Realty Solutions Manager is so vital. You're not just negotiating real estate — you're restoring equity through knowledge.

Key Insight:
Transparency creates accountability. Accountability creates fairness. Fairness creates freedom.

Now, some will argue: "That's just how fractional reserve banking works." And they're right — it is. But that doesn't absolve deception. When a borrower is never told that their promise funds the loan first, that's not education — that's exploitation. The spirit of TILA was to protect consumers from asymmetrical information. But the banks have weaponized complexity to maintain that asymmetry. That's where you come in — not as a crusader shouting at walls, but as a professional bringing light into hidden rooms.

You teach homeowners to ask the questions the system avoids. You remind them that truth in lending means truth at every step — not just what's convenient for the lender. And you show them, through paper and persistence, how to reclaim their rightful position in the transaction — as the party who created value and deserves full disclosure of where that value went.

Action Step:
Draft a TILA request that asks: "Please provide evidence of consideration — the specific date, source, and method by which funds were advanced to or on

behalf of the borrower."
That question alone rebalances the conversation. It tells the bank: We know how the Money Machine works.

Key Insight:
The bank didn't loan you its money—it monetized yours.
Your signature is the spark that lights their balance sheet.

The Era of Dual-Tracking Deception
(When the Left Hand Lied About What the Right Hand Was Doing)

When the mortgage storm hit, the banks built an assembly line so efficient it could process a foreclosure faster than a family could say the word "help." The tragedy wasn't just the volume of defaults — it was the two-faced machinery operating behind closed doors. One hand of the bank, called *Loss Mitigation*, told borrowers, "We're reviewing your modification." The other hand, *Foreclosure Operations*, was already setting auction dates. This was the infamous dual-tracking era — the time when a single borrower could receive a "Thank You for Your Paperwork" letter on Monday and a "Notice of Sale" on Wednesday.

For the families caught in that crossfire, it felt like betrayal in slow motion. Homeowners spent hours on hold, faxing documents to departments that claimed they "never received them." People who had been faithfully negotiating under programs like HAMP woke up to find their homes sold at auction while their files were still "under review." To the banks, this wasn't malice; it was metrics. Foreclosure quotas paid faster than modifications, so the system rewarded speed over mercy. The conveyor belt kept moving, even when humans were screaming to stop.

That practice was eventually challenged by the Consumer Financial Protection Bureau (CFPB) and folded into the 2014 RESPA servicing rules, which now prohibit active foreclosure while a complete modification is pending. But rules don't erase culture. The same mindset that built dual-tracking never retired; it just rebranded. Today, it hides under phrases like "loss-mitigation timeline" and "servicer discretion." The names changed, but the opacity stayed. Borrowers still face delays, "missing" paperwork, and unexplained denials that never meet the letter of the law. The bank isn't breaking rules outright — it's stretching them to exhaustion.

Key Insight:
The new deception isn't illegal behavior — it's invisible behavior..
When accountability is automated, compassion becomes optional.

That's why your role as a Realty Solutions Manager matters more than ever. You don't have to fight emotion with emotion — you fight automation with administration. Every time you help a homeowner send a Qualified Written Request or a Notice of Servicing Error under 12 C.F.R. § 1024.35, you trigger a legal timeout. The servicer must log, acknowledge, and resolve the inquiry before resuming collection or foreclosure. When they fail, the violation becomes evidence. You're not begging for mercy; you're building a record. That record is leverage — the kind of leverage that reopens negotiations and stops the bleeding long enough for a real solution to appear.

Remember this truth: banks count on people to panic. Panic makes you silent. Silence makes you predictable. But paper makes you powerful. The moment a certified envelope hits their compliance desk, panic switches sides. Now *they* are the ones with deadlines. That's how we flip the dynamic — not through conspiracy, but through competence.

Let's make it real. Suppose a homeowner named Angela mails her QWR asking for the full accounting of her escrow adjustments and copies of the payment history. The servicer, by law, must acknowledge receipt within five business days and respond within thirty. If they continue foreclosure activity during that period, they violate RESPA § 2605(k)(1)(C) — plain and simple. When you document those violations, you don't just help Angela defend herself; you show her how to create a paper trail that gives any attorney, mediator, or regulator the ammunition to demand compliance. That's how one well-written letter can buy thirty days, sixty days, sometimes more — time that can mean everything to a family on the edge.

Pro Tip:
The law rewards the one who writes first, not the one who yells loudest.

Dual-tracking didn't disappear; it digitized. Today, foreclosure notices are automated emails, and "loss-mitigation portals" replace people. But a portal can't feel shame — a paper trail can cause consequence. Your job is to re-humanize the process by forcing accountability back into the conversation. You're not attacking the bank; you're reminding it that *service* is part of "servicer." You hold them to their own standard: respond, verify, and disclose. When enough homeowners do that, the system must evolve.

So, yes, the era of dual-tracking birthed a generation of cynicism — but it also birthed a generation of informed borrowers. Out of that crisis came new warriors: men and women who learned to read their closing documents, to cite statutes, and to mail certified letters that moved mountains. That's the battlefield you stand on now. You don't need a courtroom to make impact — you need clarity, courage, and a stamp.

Key Insight:
Every certified letter is a small act of civil reformation. It says, "We see you now."

This is why the Ground Game never ended at the doorstep. It continues in the mailroom, in the notary's seal, and in the confidence of every homeowner who realizes that knowledge is the new currency. The banks had their machine; we have our movement. And every movement begins with one person refusing to let a system move unchecked.

The Mask Behind the Mask

(Who Really Owns the Loan You're Paying For)

When a homeowner gets that glossy letter in the mail that says, *"Your loan has been transferred to a new servicer,"* they usually sigh and think, "Here we go again." What they don't realize is that what's being transferred isn't ownership — it's *obligation.* The servicer doesn't own the note; they rent the right to collect on it. The real owner is usually buried three, four, sometimes ten layers deep inside a trust, an investment conduit, or a pooled security that hasn't technically existed as a live entity for years. That's why this chapter is called The Mask Behind the Mask — because the person taking your payment is rarely the person entitled to it.

When you send in that mortgage payment every month, it isn't going to "the bank" that gave you the loan. It's going to a servicer — a company paid a fee to forward funds, keep records, and manage defaults. That servicer may change hands multiple times, resetting correspondence addresses and muddying the trail of accountability each time. Meanwhile, the actual ownership of the note — the legal right to enforce it — often remains hidden inside a Real Estate Mortgage Investment Conduit (REMIC) or its successor. But here's the twist: many of those REMICs were temporary holding vessels that expired within a year or two of creation. The loans were sold off to investors, the trust dissolved, and the chain of title quietly broke.

Key Insight:

The name on your statement isn't the name on your note — and the name on your note probably doesn't exist anymore.

Over the last several years, the Administrative Default Group (ADG) — a network of administrative assistants who act on behalf of homeowners seeking transparency — has repeatedly uncovered this very problem. When ADG assisted homeowners issue lawful inquiries demanding the full ownership trail — identifying who funded, who purchased, and who currently holds the note — the responses that came back were vague, incomplete, or contradictory. Servicers routinely sent form letters stating, *"We are unable to identify the current owner but are authorized to act on their behalf."* Authorized by *whom?* That's the million-dollar question. In the real world, you can't enforce a contract for a party you can't name. Yet in foreclosure proceedings, this "mystery principal" is accepted without challenge — and that's how opacity survives.

Let's be clear: this isn't about demonizing banks; it's about exposing incomplete disclosure. Borrowers have the right to know who owns their obligation, who receives their payments, and who profits from their default. Under RESPA § 2605(k) and Regulation X, servicers must identify the current owner or assignee upon written request. When they fail to do so, they're in violation of federal law. That's why a Qualified Written Request (QWR) or Notice of Servicing Error (NSE) isn't just paperwork — it's a searchlight. It forces the system to name itself. When you require them to identify the "current holder of beneficial interest," you begin to see the difference between the face and the hand — between the mask and the power behind it.

Pro Tip:
Always ask, "Who currently holds the beneficial interest in my note, and who receives payment from the servicing account?"

That single question can unmask the entire corporate chain.

Here's a real-world example. A homeowner named Victor, assisted by ADG, sent a QWR requesting the full ownership record for his loan. The servicer replied, "The investor is U.S. Bank, as Trustee for Asset-Backed Securities 2005-3." That sounded official — until ADG researched the trust name and discovered it was closed in 2008, delisted from the SEC, and had its certificate of authority revoked years ago. In other words, the entity being cited as the creditor no longer existed. Yet that same "trust" was foreclosing on properties across multiple states. How? Because the system learned that most people never check. The mask stays on because no one lifts it.

When you educate homeowners to research SEC filings, Pooling and Servicing Agreements, or county land records, you turn a confused borrower into an informed participant. When those findings are attached to properly notarized administrative presentments — certified, time-stamped, and logged — the servicer's narrative collapses. The "creditor" that claimed authority often retreats into silence. And silence, in commerce, is not neutrality — it's consent.

Key Insight:
In commerce, silence equals consent. In administration, silence equals confession.

The Mask Behind the Mask is about revelation, not rebellion. Once you understand how the paper trail works, you stop chasing titles and start controlling timelines. You're no longer reacting to a system; you're redirecting it. The Administrative Default Group proved this repeatedly — that lawful, well-documented administrative procedure can move mountains faster than emotional confrontation. By forcing banks to meet their own disclosure obligations, they leveled the playing field for ordinary families who just wanted fairness.

That's the higher calling of this knowledge. You're not out to "beat the bank." You're out to *restore balance* to a process that lost its integrity. You do it through precision, paper, and principle — not protests. You operate as light in a system built on shadows. And as you learn to see the masks for what they are, you'll also see what the banks fear most: an informed public that refuses to play blind.

Action Step:
Always request written identification of the true owner and the master servicer under RESPA.
If they won't name the party with authority to modify, that's a compliance issue—not a dead end.

Breaking the Chain of Title Illusion

(The Moment Banks Broke the Map — and Why You Can Use It to Navigate Profit)

Every parcel of real estate in America once had a clear, traceable story — a chain of title written in ink at the county recorder's office. You could walk into a courthouse, pull the deed, and see the history of every owner, lien, and release. It was transparent, accountable, and human. But when Wall Street realized the mortgage note could be packaged and sold faster than any single bank could hold it, that transparency became an inconvenience. The solution they engineered wasn't reform — it was camouflage.

That's when the Mortgage Electronic Registration System (MERS) was born — later rebranded as MERSCORP Holdings, Inc. MERSCORP still manages the registration database that tracks over 60 million active and legacy mortgage loans across the United States. It was marketed as a "streamlined" innovation to cut down on paperwork and "modernize" real estate recording. In reality, MERS was created to mask ownership transfers and eliminate county-level oversight. Before MERS, every sale or transfer of a mortgage required a public filing, a $25 recording fee, and a transparent record for anyone to see. MERS ended that system. With one digital entry, a loan could change hands ten times in a day without a single update to the public record.

What MERS accomplished was nothing less than the privatization of America's property ledger. Counties lost jurisdiction. Borrowers lost clarity. Investors lost accountability. Millions of deeds now list "MERS as Nominee for Lender and Its Successors and Assigns" —

but MERS never lent a dime, collected a payment, or verified a single transaction. It was a legal façade. And when a company that never owned or funded a loan is listed on over sixty million mortgages, the result is a nation of broken maps.

Key Insight:
MERS wasn't designed to record ownership — it was designed to conceal velocity.
The faster loans changed hands, the harder it became for anyone to trace liability.

The Administrative Default Group (ADG) spent years assisting homeowners and investors to challenge these hidden transfers. Through written administrative inquiries and title research, they repeatedly found that servicers couldn't produce a verifiable chain of assignments — only vague statements such as *"We do not maintain that information."* That single phrase reveals everything: the entity demanding payment or foreclosure often cannot prove its standing — the one legal condition required to enforce a debt.

Under established contract law, the right to collect cannot exist without the ability to prove ownership. When a note and its deed of trust are split, or when assignments go unrecorded, the legal standing to foreclose collapses. But because the foreclosure process is now heavily automated, servicers push defaults through without ever producing the required proof. It's not malice — it's machinery. The assembly line assumes you won't ask the right questions. When you do, the system hesitates.

Pro Tip:
Always request the full Assignment of Deed of Trust history.
If every "successor" can't produce a recorded assignment, the claim is defective.

The 2011 investigations by state attorneys general — sparked by the infamous robo-signing scandal — exposed this illusion for what it was. MERSCORP's database had become so chaotic that banks resorted to mass document forgery to repair gaps. Workers at document mills like *DocX* and *EMC* fabricated signatures for officers who didn't exist, notarized paperwork with expired seals, and recorded those fakes into county offices nationwide. The most notorious false signer was "Linda Green" — a made-up identity used by hundreds of employees across multiple states.

The damage was irreversible. Millions of homes now carry what courts politely call a "cloud on title." In plain terms: a break so deep that ownership can't be traced through lawful transfer. And while courts have acknowledged the problem, they've avoided dismantling it — because doing so would unravel trillions in securitized debt. Instead, they rule narrowly, case by case, while the structural flaw remains baked into the system.

Key Insight:
A "cloud on title" isn't a curse — it's a clue.
It tells you where the leverage lives.

This is where the Realty Solutions Manager finds advantage. You're not a litigant — you're a light-bearer. You help homeowners understand that a broken title chain is not the end of ownership; it's the beginning of negotiation. When a servicer can't prove authority, you guide the homeowner to issue a Demand for Proof of Authority to Collect under 15 U.S.C. § 1692g(b) and 12 C.F.R. § 1024.35. That administrative demand halts further collection until validation occurs. And when the proof doesn't come — as it often doesn't — the power dynamic shifts. You've bought time, created leverage, and sometimes, opened the door to settlement.

This knowledge also creates opportunity beyond foreclosure defense. The same paper defects that stop a foreclosure can become profit centers when understood correctly. Many investors shy away from clouded titles because they see risk; you'll see redemption. With proper research, quiet title actions, and corrective assignments, you can cure defects and restore marketability — often acquiring these assets at steep discounts. What others fear to touch becomes your Money Machine.

Pro Tip:
The same defect that invalidates a bank's foreclosure can validate your opportunity.
Learn to cure what others ignore.

The Administrative Default Group has documented countless cases where this understanding turned chaos into cash flow. By identifying unreleased liens, duplicate assignments, or phantom endorsements, Realty Solutions Managers helped banks correct their own records — and got paid for it. You're not attacking the system; you're monetizing the truth it hides in plain sight.

Key Insight:
The clearer the title, the cleaner the conscience — and both compound into wealth.

Breaking the chain of title illusion isn't about rebellion. It's about restoration — bringing integrity back to the record and profit back to the people who know how to read it. When you master this knowledge, you're not just studying paperwork. You're decoding the playbook of the modern banking machine — and learning how to run your own.

Paper Alchemy
(Turning Administrative Truth into Financial Leverage)

Every era has its gold rush. In the 1800s, it was ore hidden in rock. In our generation, the gold is hidden in paper — contracts, notes, assignments, and filings that carry the quiet weight of value. Banks have mastered this craft for centuries: turning paper into money, signatures into credit, and promises into profit. Now it's your turn to understand the same alchemy.

In The Money Machine, we call this transformation Paper Alchemy — the process of converting what others see as paperwork into instruments of cash flow and control. When you can read and interpret the paper trail behind a mortgage, a lien, or an assignment, you hold the same tool the bank uses to print its own wealth.

Key Insight
Whoever controls the paper, controls the payment. Whoever understands it, controls the outcome.

The Hidden Ledger

Every transaction lives twice — once in the public record and once in the bank's private ledger. On the public side, you see a promissory note, a deed of trust, and a monthly payment. On the private side, that same note has been deposited as a financial asset and mirrored by a liability entry called "credit creation." According to GAAP, the note itself funds the transaction. The bank's "loan" to you is the bank lending you back the credit your signature created.

The ADG's administrative assistants uncovered this reality repeatedly through Qualified Written Requests and Servicing Error Notices. When asked who provided the original consideration — the money — most servicers replied, *"Funds were drawn from internal accounts in accordance with standard practice."* Translation: your signature created the asset; the bank monetized it.

Pro Tip

In banking, a promissory note isn't a promise to pay — it's the payment itself.

Understanding that simple truth changes everything. The borrower is not powerless. The borrower's paper is the raw material from which the bank's credit is minted. Once you see that, you stop begging for approval and start negotiating from equality. You realize your note funded the transaction, and the bank's role was bookkeeping, not benevolence.

From Knowledge to Negotiation

Realty Solutions Managers use this understanding to create practical leverage. When a servicer ignores disclosure laws, fails to identify the true creditor, or continues collection during an open QWR period, you don't panic — you pivot. You document every infraction. You send follow-ups by certified mail. You create a dated, notarized record. Each unanswered question becomes a point of administrative leverage — a lawful pause button in a system that hates being slowed down.

This is how administrative truth becomes financial power. You're not fighting; you're balancing. You're saying, "Until you produce the same transparency you demand from borrowers, performance is suspended." That's not defiance; it's due process.

Key Insight

In administration, silence is not neutral — it's admission.

Monetizing the Knowledge

There are three major income paths born from Paper Alchemy:

1. **Curing Title for Profit –**
   Many banks still carry unreleased liens or defective assignments

that block resale. Realty Solutions Managers who can research and correct these errors charge fees ranging from $1,000 to $10,000 per property. You're paid for fixing confusion they created.

2. **Acquiring Discounted Notes** –
Once a loan becomes "non-performing," banks often sell it for pennies on the dollar. If you understand how to evaluate the paper — the note, the deed, the assignments — you can purchase that debt, restructure it with the homeowner, and turn default into dividends.

3. **Structuring Private Paper Deals** –
Using the same principles of assignment, you can create your own lending instruments. You lend what you borrow. For instance, if you hold a $100,000 HELOC at 6%, you can lend $50,000 to an investor at 12%. You keep the spread. That differential is the sound of your Money Machine humming.

Hip National Bank Moment:
Every time your knowledge creates cash to flow to your pocket.

The Moral Balance Sheet

Let's be clear: Paper Alchemy is not trickery — it's transparency. The same laws that protect banks protect borrowers. You're simply using the tools they've kept to themselves. When you force disclosure, you force honesty. When you master process, you master peace.

The Administrative Default Group discovered that once banks know someone understands the playbook, attitudes change. Calls get polite. Offers appear. Files get "reviewed again." That's not coincidence — that's the quiet respect earned by competence.

Pro Tip
Banks don't fear rebellion; they fear comprehension.

The New Covenant of Commerce

The old banking covenant was simple: *You borrow, we own.* The new covenant is emerging: *You understand, we negotiate.* Knowledge is now the equalizer. By documenting, by questioning, by insisting on full disclosure, you turn the same system that once printed debt against you into one that prints equity for you.

This is the spiritual heart of *The Money Machine.* It's not vengeance; it's restoration. Just as light reveals what darkness hides, truth restores what deception divides. You were never meant to be a debt slave. You were designed to be a steward — of knowledge, of capital, of covenant.

Key Insight

Paper Alchemy isn't magic — it's management.
When you manage truth, money follows.

Bringing It Back to Solutions

Every homeowner you meet deserves a pathway forward:

- Option A: Audit the loan and challenge inconsistencies under RESPA/TILA.
- Option B: Negotiate a modification or settlement once leverage is established.
- Option C: If the math won't work, structure a dignified exit—cash-for-keys, leaseback, or a sale that clears credit.

When you focus on bringing solutions, not sympathy, you become the person everyone calls when the system says "no." The profit follows purpose.

Pro Tip:

You can't lose helping someone keep their dignity. Even when the home is
gone, they'll remember who fought for their right to understand.

The Human Element of Redemption
(Where Ministry Meets Money and Solutions Create Salvation)

Behind every foreclosure notice, behind every broken chain of title and every misfiled document, there's a human story — a man or woman who once dreamed of homeownership and now feels cornered by a machine. It's easy to look at the paperwork and forget the person. But if The Money Machine teaches anything, it's that paper doesn't make wealth — people do.

When you step onto a property as a Realty Solutions Manager, you carry more than information — you carry empathy, authority, and restoration. You become the bridge between confusion and clarity. The bank may see a default, but you see design — a chance to redeem value from chaos. That is the essence of this ministry-in-motion: to turn the administrative system back toward humanity without ever losing sight of profit or purpose.

Key Insight
Compassion is the new currency. Every genuine act of help multiplies your balance sheet in both heaven and Hip National Bank.

The Ministry of Solutions

When Jesus walked into the temple and overturned the tables of the money changers, He didn't destroy the economy — He cleansed it. He restored integrity to commerce. That same spirit lives in the modern marketplace through people like you, who bring fairness where greed once ruled. Every QWR you assist an owner send, every title that is cured, every homeowner you educate — it's all part of the same redemption arc.

The Administrative Default Group has witnessed this firsthand. When a frightened homeowner receives an authentic explanation of what's happening behind their loan, something shifts. They go from panic to participation. From isolation to empowerment. Suddenly, they're not a victim of the process — they're a partner in the remedy. And that's the difference between manipulation and ministry.

You were never called to just "close deals." You were called to restore dominion — to help others reclaim authority over what they thought they'd lost forever. When you help a homeowner delay foreclosure legally, or guide them to sell on their own terms, you're not just earning an assignment fee; you're repairing the spiritual economy of fairness itself.

Pro Tip

Every signed agreement is more than a transaction — it's a covenant of clarity between two souls in commerce.

The Moral Return on Investment

Here's the truth most investors miss: money follows meaning. When your motive is pure — to bring solutions, not exploitation — profit becomes a byproduct of purpose. The Money Machine was never designed to make you rich by deception; it was designed to make you free by understanding. And in that freedom, others find deliverance.

The most successful Realty Solutions Managers don't sell properties — they sell peace of mind. They walk into fear-filled homes and replace panic with possibility. They speak with calm authority, explaining the path forward: how administrative remedies buy time, how buyers can be found, how lenders can be held accountable — all without hostility, only with knowledge.

That's what separates you from the crowd. You're not mailing flyers or waiting for calls. You're meeting people face-to-face, bringing light into dark rooms, and giving hope where bureaucracy has built walls. You are the new kind of investor — a wealth restorer.

Key Insight

Redemption isn't about rescuing property; it's about reawakening purpose.

Beyond the Banks

There's a deeper truth hidden within these pages: the real battle was never between borrower and lender — it's between ignorance and understanding. The bank's greatest power has never been its vault; it's been the public's silence. Once you learn to read the language of contracts, disclosures, and administrative law, that silence breaks.

When the people understand, the balance shifts. The next wealth transfer doesn't happen through rebellion — it happens through revelation. The banks will continue playing their role, but now so will you — not as a debtor, but as a deliberate creator of commerce. This is where your "Money Machine" becomes more than theory. It becomes testimony.

Pro Tip

The world doesn't change when laws are rewritten — it changes when minds are renewed.

The Circle of Restoration

One of the most profound lessons in The Money Machine is that wealth is circular. You help a homeowner save their property or exit with dignity, and months later, they refer someone else. You teach your team how to identify defective notes, and suddenly, your influence grows beyond your reach. You move from personal gain to generational impact. That's when your Money Machine stops printing income and starts printing legacy.

When I teach this across the country, people often ask, "Ray, what's the endgame?" My answer is always the same: Restoration. Restoration of homes, of truth, of dominion, and of faith. The financial system isn't your enemy — ignorance is. And the moment you decide to understand it, you stop being a pawn and start becoming a player.

Key Insight
When you master money with morality, you multiply miracles.

Final Word from Ray Wright Jacobs-
*Redemption doesn't start in the courthouse — it starts in the heart.
When you bring light to the shadows of lending, you do more than recover
lost equity; you restore faith in the process itself. You're not here to burn the
system down. You're here to reform it from within, to remind it that commerce and conscience can coexist.*

*As you go forward, remember this truth: The greatest asset you'll ever
manage is people. When you serve them with integrity, the returns compound far beyond balance sheets. Every home restored, every title cured,
every life stabilized — that's another divine deposit into Hip National Bank.*

*Now take what you've learned, walk boldly, and remember: The most
powerful contract ever written was signed in blood to redeem what was lost.
Every time you bring a homeowner a solution, you honor that same
covenant of restoration.*

Workbook – Module 7

Always Bring Homeowner a Solution
Never Focus on the Profit of Selling the House
Realty Solutions Manager Training 101

Section 1: Understanding the Homeowner's Battle
1. Perspective Shift Exercise

Describe the emotional journey of a homeowner going through foreclosure.
What do they feel, fear, and believe about their situation before you arrive at their door?

2. Knowledge Check

List the three key consumer protection laws every Realty Solutions Manager must understand and explain to a homeowner.
(Hint: They form your administrative "shield" during engagement.)

3. Reflection Prompt

Why is it vital to "bring solutions, not sales pitches"?
How does focusing on service create more long-term income than chasing one-time profits?

Section 2: Administrative Power in Action
4. Comprehension Drill – Qualified Written Request (QWR)

In your own words, define what a Qualified Written Request (QWR) is and explain why it's a critical tool in your arsenal as a Realty Solutions Manager.

5. Process Application

Create a timeline outlining what happens after a homeowner sends a QWR.
Include the lender's required timeframes to acknowledge and respond.

- **Day 0:** QWR mailed (certified)
- **Day 5:** _____
- **Day 30:** _____
- **Day 45:** _____

6. Critical Thinking Challenge

If a bank ignores a QWR or fails to answer every item, what rights or leverage points does that create for the homeowner?

How can a Realty Solutions Manager turn that into an opportunity for negotiation or redemption?

Section 3: Breaking the Chain of Title Illusion
7. Analytical Exercise
Explain how MERSCORP Holdings, Inc. changed the traditional chain of title system in America.
What risks or complications did this create for homeowners, counties, and investors?

8. Case Study Review
Read the following statement and respond:
"A homeowner requests proof of ownership from their loan servicer and receives no answer.
The servicer continues foreclosure proceedings anyway."
What two administrative remedies can halt the process or expose procedural violations?

9. Real-World Practice
Research a publicly reported case involving MERS or a major foreclosure settlement. Summarize what went wrong and how transparency could have changed the outcome.
(Examples: 2012 National Mortgage Settlement, robo-signing scandal, etc.)

Section 4: Paper Alchemy - Turning Truth into Leverage
10. Application Prompt
In your own words, explain what "Paper Alchemy" means.
How does understanding the administrative truth behind loans turn knowledge into cash flow?

11. Strategy Mapping
Choose one of the three income streams below and write your 30-day action plan to apply it:

- [ ] Curing Title for Profit
- [ ] Acquiring Discounted Notes
- [ ] Structuring Private Paper Deals

Outline your steps, tools, and goals for 30 days:
12. Knowledge-to-Action Prompt
What is the difference between rebellion and restoration in the context of banking and lending?
Why is understanding more powerful than protest?

Section 5: The Human Element of Redemption
13. Empathy Check
Write a short letter to a fictional homeowner in default.
Your goal is not to sell them anything — only to educate and comfort them using what you've learned.
14. Moral ROI Reflection
What does "money follows meaning" mean to you personally?
How does compassion translate into real financial success?
15. Ministry in the Marketplace
Describe how your Money Machine activities can double as ministry — helping others while creating wealth ethically.
How does your work fulfill the original divine mandate of Authority, Dominion, and Might?

Section 6: Advanced Insight - The Administrative Default Group's Playbook
16. Administrative Awareness Drill
List three major insights or strategies you've learned from the Administrative Default Group (ADG) method of assisting homeowners administratively.
17. Real Estate Redemption Simulation
Imagine a homeowner owes $240,000 on a property worth $300,000 but faces foreclosure.
Create a 3-step solution plan that restores value to both the homeowner and potential investors, using what you've learned.

Section 7: Bonus Questions
18. Bonus Knowledge Builder
If the promissory note funds the transaction, what moral and legal obligation should banks have under the Truth in Lending Act (TILA)?
Explain your view of what true disclosure should look like in a fair financial system.
19. Bonus Reflection – Legacy Vision
If you mastered everything in Module 7 — understanding administrative power, human compassion, and financial restoration — what kind of legacy would your Money Machine leave behind 10 years from now?

Final Thought from Ray Wright Jacobs
"Knowledge without compassion creates arrogance.
Compassion without knowledge creates poverty.
But when you combine the two — you become unstoppable."
Keep studying, stay bold, and never forget:

Every contract you read, every title you correct, every family you restore — that's another deposit into Hip National Bank and another withdrawal from the vault of ignorance.

8

Module 8: Banking - Fuel Your Money Machine

Power Banking I: Knowledge to Prime Your Money Machine
Realty Solutions Manager Training 201
Gain the Leverage Bankers Hope You Never Learn You Have

The Hidden Power of the Promissory Note

Most people think a bank loan begins when a lender gives you money. But the truth is, the process starts the moment you sign. That single signature doesn't just authorize a transaction — it creates one. Your signed promissory note is a negotiable instrument under the Uniform Commercial Code, meaning it carries the same legal weight as cash once it's signed and delivered. Banks know this, but most borrowers never realize that the funding of the loan begins with *their* signature, not the bank's.

In modern banking, your note is not just a promise to pay; it's the primary deposit that fuels the bank's credit engine. When you sign the note, it becomes a new asset to the bank — immediately recorded on their ledger as cash equivalent. The bank then creates an equal liability, the "loan," on the other side of the ledger to balance it. In plain

terms, you've loaned the bank money first, and then they turn around
and lend it back to you — calling it a loan while keeping the original
deposit you created.

Once you see this, everything changes. It's not an opinion; it's accounting. Double-entry bookkeeping demands that every asset has a
corresponding liability. That means when the bank's balance sheet
grows from your note, it must record that it owes someone — and that
someone is you. But because of how the system is worded, you're never
told that you just created the deposit that funded your "loan."

Banks rely on that silence. The Truth in Lending Act (TILA) was
written to make sure borrowers receive *full disclosure* of material terms
and funding sources, yet this part of the equation is never disclosed.
That's the leverage they hope you never learn: you are the source of
their lending power. The moment you understand that, you realize
you've been sitting on the switch to your own *Money Machine* all along.

From Gold to Credit: The Quiet Redesign of the System

America's financial transformation didn't happen overnight. It un-
folded like a silent relay race where the baton passed from gold to
credit, from something tangible to something entirely conceptual. The
early 1900s brought the Federal Reserve Act, the Jekyll Island meetings, and the dawn of the modern central banking era. What was marketed as "stability" was really a restructuring — a way to turn every
citizen's future productivity into the new backing for national debt.

When gold reserves were transferred to central custody, what replaced them was our collective labor and signature value. The government didn't default; it redesigned how value would be defined. Instead
of gold certificates redeemable for metal, we were issued Federal Reserve Notes — debt instruments redeemable only by more debt. The
people themselves became the collateral through their lifelong participation in the system.

From that point forward, the system only worked if citizens kept
signing, borrowing, and spending. Every mortgage, credit card, auto

loan, or student loan became another brick in the wall of "monetized promises." We built an empire of credit — not because we were foolish, but because the structure demanded it. The banks call it liquidity. Economists call it confidence. I call it the harnessing of human capital.

This isn't about conspiracy; it's about comprehension. The moment we left the gold standard, the real standard became *faith and performance.* You don't hold money anymore; you hold trust — a ledger of who owes whom and who's willing to believe it. The borrower's faith became the new gold, and the banker's accounting pen became the new pickaxe.

So when you walk into a bank today, understand this: the vault isn't full of money; it's full of paper obligations and digital promises. The true reserve isn't metal; it's you — your time, your work, and your willingness to sign your name on the dotted line. You are the energy source of the financial grid. And once you see that clearly, you stop asking for permission and start demanding participation.

The Alchemy of Credit: How Money Is Actually Made

Let's walk through the process again, step-by-step, because this is where your leverage is born. Remember, when you signed that $300,000 promissory note at closing, you recall that the bank immediately deposited that note into a newly created internal account, often in your name. That deposit was booked as an asset to the bank and simultaneously generated a liability — the "loan" — which appeared as the bank's obligation to you. The wire that went out to escrow didn't come from pre-existing funds. It came from the credit created by your own note.

Here's how the accounting looks:

Debit: Bank Cash/Assets (your note)

Credit: Loan Payable (owed to you).

Then, using fractional reserve policy, the bank multiplies that deposit several times over, creating up to nine times its value in lendable credit to others. That's how your one home loan fuels nine more. It's a pyramid built on your promise.

This process is fully authorized under Generally Accepted Accounting Principles (GAAP) and Federal Reserve guidelines. The deception isn't in the mechanics — it's in the *marketing*. You were told the bank was the lender, not that it was the intermediary using your note as the seed from which all other credit sprouts. The omission is small but seismic. It changes who the real source of capital is.

The bank then earns interest on money that technically originated from you. They charge you for the use of your own credit energy. That's why they call it "interest." It's the fee they charge for lending you back your own power — neatly wrapped in a legal contract called a loan agreement. It's lawful but deeply undisclosed.

Key Insight:
The real interest you've been paying is for your own ignorance. Once that ignorance is gone, the leverage shifts entirely to your side of the table.

The Cloak & Dagger of Generosity: How Banks Created Dependence

In the late 1990s and early 2000s, banks began loosening lending standards. Advertisements shouted, *"Everyone qualifies!"* Subprime loans, teaser rates, and "pick-a-payment" mortgages spread like wildfire. The public thought it was generosity. In truth, it was an engineered demand for more promissory notes — more *raw material* for the machine.

The subprime boom wasn't about giving people homes; it was about generating collateral to feed the securitization market. Each signed note became part of a mortgage-backed security (MBS) pool.

Those pools were sliced, diced, and sold as Collateralized Debt Obligations (CDOs) — each layer of paper representing the same streams of payments, repackaged and resold. The investors thought they were buying assets. In reality, they were buying future payments on promises.

When the weakest borrowers defaulted, the machine didn't panic — it profited. Insurance policies called credit default swaps (CDS) paid out to cover "losses," even when those losses were engineered. Banks were reimbursed multiple times for the same loan — from the borrower, the insurer, and, later, the government bailout. That's not rumor. That's documented history.

So why did it matter that you didn't know your note funded the loan? Because disclosure would have given you negotiating power. You could have questioned consideration, demanded accounting, and understood you were providing the initial asset that built their trading pool. Instead, the illusion was maintained, and the borrower's ignorance became the bank's favorite commodity. Now you know why most banks give-away suckers called "Dum Dum's". Candy for dumb suckers.

That's why this module matters. The goal isn't outrage — it's ownership. When you know how the system actually monetizes signatures, you can structure your real estate deals, private notes, and partnerships with the same principles — lawfully, transparently, and profitably. You don't fight the machine; you become the engineer.

The Modern Money Illusion: Debt as Currency

Let's talk about the bills in your wallet — Federal Reserve Notes (FRNs). They look like cash, but they're technically promissory notes, issued by the Federal Reserve, not the U.S. Treasury. The fine print says it clearly: "This note is legal tender for all debts, public and private." It's a note, not a dollar backed by gold or silver. It's a promise to pay, circulating as money because we all agree to treat it as such.

When you hand a $20 bill to a cashier, you're not giving them "money" backed by value; you're transferring an IOU that they can pass to someone else who will also accept it as valuable. The entire system functions because of faith — the same faith that keeps the digital balances in your checking account meaningful. Without ongoing public belief, those digits collapse into numbers without weight.

Every major transaction in your life — your car loan, your mortgage, your business line of credit — operates on this same principle of *monetized belief.* The system needs constant signatures to sustain circulation. Without new notes, deposits, and contracts, the liquidity would dry up, and the machine would seize.

That's why banks reward borrowing. It's not that they love risk; they love new paper. Every time someone signs, the system breathes. When people stop signing, recessions follow. That's the hidden cycle — the expansion and contraction of credit, not gold, silver, or goods, defines modern prosperity.

So the next time you handle a stack of FRNs or sign a closing package, pause and remember: this is the world's most elaborate game of trust, played in ink and digits. The secret isn't to escape it; it's to master it. Once you understand how promises move money, you'll stop fearing debt and start using it as a tool — just like the bankers do.

How to Turn Knowledge Into Leverage

Now that you know how the banking engine really works, it's time to flip the script. You can use the same lawful structure to build your own private *Money Machine.* Begin with understanding that paper equals power. Notes, assignments, and liens are the assets of this age. Whoever controls the paper controls the flow.

When you negotiate, structure, or invest, think like a banker. Ask: *What's the source of consideration? Who holds the risk? Where is the ledger entry that records this as an asset or liability?* Every transaction tells a story, and the one who knows how to read that story dictates the ending. Knowledge is the new collateral.

Use what you've learned to operate within the system, not against it. Build private lending models, manage your own notes, or buy performing paper at a discount. Secure your deals with trust deeds and insurance the same way banks do. You're not breaking rules — you're mastering them.

Every dollar that passes through your hand is someone's promise. You now understand how those promises circulate, multiply, and return. That knowledge is leverage. It's what separates financial dependence from financial dominion. Once you grasp this, you don't work for banks — you work like them.

And remember this: the same way banks create money by belief and documentation, you can create prosperity through faith and precision. Sign with understanding. Lend with integrity. Earn with wisdom. When you do, your *Money Machine* stops serving someone else's agenda and starts serving your legacy.

Bonus Section – The Paper Trail the Bank Won't Show You
The Secret Circuit of Modern Money Creation

"Follow the paper, not the people — and the truth of money will always reveal itself."
— *Ray Wright Jacobs*

The Missing Diagram
Imagine a straight line — simple, clean, unbroken.
On one end stands you, the signer. On the other end stands the bank. Between you is what I call the *"Invisible Exchange"* — the part they never teach in finance class, and the exact moment your Money Machine is born.

Here's the flow:
You sign a promissory note.

- This signed instrument instantly becomes a cash-equivalent asset under banking law (UCC Article 3, Negotiable Instruments).
- The moment your pen leaves the paper, the bank now holds something that can be sold, pledged, or deposited.

The bank deposits your note.

- The note is deposited into an internal account — sometimes a Demand Deposit Account (DDA) in your name, sometimes into a pooled account used for funding.
- In accounting terms:
    - **Debit:** Bank Cash/Assets
    - **Credit:** Loans Payable (Liability to You)

The bank creates new credit from your note.

- Now that the bank has recorded "cash" from your note, it uses that new asset to issue a credit to your account or escrow.
- That wire you see on closing day doesn't come from the bank's reserves — it comes from the credit money created out of your note.
- You just funded your own loan without knowing it.

The bank earns interest on your creation.

- You repay the loan — principal, interest, and fees — as though the bank lent its money to you.
- But the truth is, the bank lent your money back to you, charging rent for the privilege.
- This is the ultimate magic trick of fractional reserve banking: your promise becomes their product.

The note is monetized and recycled.

- The bank now sells your note into a secondary market — often to an institutional investor, trust, or Federal Reserve facility.
- The sale price is typically close to face value, giving the bank immediate liquidity and freeing up capacity to repeat the cycle with the next borrower.
- They keep servicing the loan, collect interest, and report it as "income," though the original asset (your note) is long gone.

Result:

Your signature — not the bank's vault — created the money.

Their profit? Everything after zero cost.

Your cost? Interest on your own creation.

That's not a conspiracy. That's *accounting*.

And it's why understanding the Paper Trail is the most powerful financial education you'll ever receive.

The Ledger Behind the Curtain

When a loan "funds," two books open simultaneously — the Public Ledger and the Private Ledger.

Ledger Type	What You See	What the Bank Sees
Public Ledger	Loan disbursement, payment schedule, interest rate.	"Loan Receivable" – the bank's claim on you.
Private Ledger	(Hidden) Deposit of your note as "cash asset."	"Loans Payable" – the bank's liability to you for the note.

If both sides were revealed, the transaction would show a perfect balance — meaning no loan was ever "made." It was a mutual exchange: your lawful money (note) for their credit money (deposit). The only difference is that they recorded it as *you owing them*, not the other way around.

Now imagine what would happen if both ledgers were publicly reconciled. The entire perception of who funded what would flip in an instant. That's why you'll never be shown both books — until now.

The Math of Creation

Let's quantify this using the real-world Money Multiplier Effect: Suppose you sign a note for $300,000.

- That note becomes an asset on the bank's books.
- The bank is required to keep only a small percentage as "reserves" (traditionally 10%, now effectively zero in many cases).
- That means the remaining $270,000+ can be used to create new credit.

But it doesn't stop there. Every dollar of that $270,000 can be lent, redeposited, and re-lent again — creating as much as $2.7 million in new digital money across the banking system. Your one signature became the seed of multiple loans, multiple profit streams, and multiple asset-backed securities.

You did the work.
They did the math.
And the difference between what they earn and what you understand is what keeps the system alive.

The Loop of Silence

The reason this process remains largely unknown is opacity by design. Loan disclosures and Truth-in-Lending statements talk about *interest rates* and *APR*, but never about *initial funding mechanics*. Servicing companies and bank representatives often don't know either — they're trained in retail scripts, not wholesale banking operations.

The gap between what's real and what's revealed is the banker's moat. Once you close that gap, you become a financial engineer. You start asking questions they can't easily answer, like:

- "Who recorded the initial deposit of my note?"
- "Where is the liability entry for the corresponding consideration?"
- "Under GAAP, how was this transaction balanced on day one?"

Those are *not conspiracy questions* — they're commercial questions. They separate citizens from CEOs, and students from masters.

Your Takeaway: From Revelation to Replication

Here's the truth that changes everything: You can't change the existence of the system, but you can mirror it lawfully to your advantage.

That's what the rest of *The Money Machine* teaches — how to use this understanding to:

- Create secured, lawful private lending instruments.
- Control paper the same way banks control notes.
- Earn yields ethically by managing assets that already exist in your sphere.
- Never again fund someone else's wealth by ignorance.

When you understand the Paper Trail, you don't fear banks — you emulate them. You operate with clarity, not confusion. You start documenting like an insider, structuring like a lender, and negotiating like the person who already knows where the money comes from — because now, you do.

"For the Lord thy God blesseth thee, as he promised thee: and thou shalt lend unto many nations, but thou shalt not borrow; and thou shalt reign over many nations, but they shall not reign over thee."

(Deuteronomy 15:6 KJV)

Visual Summary: The Real Flow of a Loan

[YOU: SIGN PROMISSORY NOTE]

↓

(Asset Created: Your Note)

↓

[BANK DEPOSITS NOTE AS CASH]

↓

(Records Liability: Loan Payable to You)

↓

[BANK CREATES CREDIT FROM YOUR NOTE]

↓

(Wires Funds to Escrow or Seller)

↓

[YOU REPAY "LOAN" + INTEREST]

↓

(They Profit from the Money You Created)

Every loop ends the same way:
Knowledge = Leverage → Deposits → Hip National Bank.

Final Word — Ray Wright Jacobs:

"Money was never created to enslave you; misunderstanding was. Once you see the wires, ledgers, and laws for what they are, you no longer fear the machine — you become the mechanic."

Workbook: Module 8

Power Banking I
Knowledge to Prime Your Money Machine

Quote of the Module:
"You can't conquer what you don't comprehend. Once you understand the game,
you stop playing it blindfolded."
— *Ray Wright Jacobs*

SECTION 1: Hidden Power of the Promissory Note
Reflection Question:
Describe in your own words how your signature on a promissory note functions as
money. What ledger entries does it create for the bank?

Comprehension Drill:
Fill in the blanks:

- When a borrower signs a _____, the bank records it as a new _____
  on their balance sheet.
- A matching _____ is created to balance the books, called the _____.

Application Challenge:
Using your most recent loan or mortgage, request the **transaction ledger** from the
servicer under your rights in *Regulation X* (12 C.F.R. §1024.36). List what you discover
below:

- Was your note treated as a deposit or as collateral?
- Was the lender's own capital clearly identified?
- Any unexplained credits or offsets?

Action Step:
Write a short statement of empowerment that begins:

"I now understand that my signature has value equal to money because..."

SECTION 2: The American Blueprint
Reflection Question:
What changed when America left the gold standard and entered a credit-based economy? How does that affect your perception of "money"?

Research Task:
Locate one credible historical source that confirms the year the U.S. formally abandoned the gold standard for domestic and international settlements.

- Year: _____
- Source: _____

Fill-in-the-Blank Insight:
The Federal Reserve System was designed to transform _____ into _____ by using _____ as collateral.

Application Question:
In a credit-based world, what personal asset replaces gold as the new standard of value?

→ _____

Action Step:
List three ways you can use this knowledge to negotiate better terms or structure deals with confidence.

SECTION 3: The Alchemy of Credit
Reflection:
In your own words, explain how fractional reserve banking multiplies your promissory note into multiple loans. What lesson does that teach you about leverage?

Comprehension Drill:
Match the accounting entries:

Action	Entry Type
Bank receives your note	Debit – Assets

Action	Entry Type
Bank owes you money	Credit – Liabilities
Bank creates new loans from reserves	Credit Expansion

Applied Knowledge Exercise:
Use a hypothetical $200,000 loan. If the reserve requirement is 10%, calculate the total potential credit that can be created from your note.

→ $_____

Critical Thinking:
How does understanding the bank's ledger empower you to see through "interest rates" and recognize who truly funded the loan?

Action Step:
Summarize your takeaway in one clear sentence:

"Every time I sign a loan, I am actually _____."

SECTION 4: The Mask of Generosity

Case Study Reflection:
Recall the 2008 financial crisis. How did "easy credit" turn into national chaos? What lessons about transparency and disclosure stand out to you?

Fill-in-the-Blank:
Mortgage-backed securities (MBS) were built from _____, which were sold to investors as _____.

Reality Check:
What do you think banks feared most: borrowers defaulting or borrowers **understanding** the process? Explain your reasoning.

Assignment:
Draft a short, professional inquiry letter you could send to a lender requesting **clarification of funding sources** before signing a future loan.

Action Step:
Create your personal affirmation of financial clarity:
   "From this day forward, I will never sign a financial instrument without knowing exactly where the _____ comes from."

SECTION 5: The Modern Money Illusion
Reflection:
If every Federal Reserve Note is a promissory note, what makes it valuable? Who gives it that value?

Reality Drill:
Circle the correct statement:
a) Money has intrinsic value.
b) Money represents collective belief and trust.
c) Money is backed by gold.

→ **Answer:** _____

Application:

Explain how understanding this changes your approach to debt, investment, and credit creation.

Math Moment:
If you borrow $100,000 at 5% interest, but re-lend that same money at 12%, what is your net yield (ignoring fees)?
   → _____% annual spread goes directly into Hip National Bank.

Action Step:
Describe one real-world scenario where you can ethically turn debt into leverage this year.

→ _____

SECTION 6: Turning Knowledge into Leverage

Reflection:
List three lawful ways you can act like a banker without being one.

Comprehension Drill:

Fill in the blanks:
"The one who controls the _____, controls the _____."

Practical Exercise:
Using the *Art of the Assignment* model, outline one potential deal you could secure and assign for a profit. Identify:

- Purchase price: _____
- Assignment fee: _____
- Closing timeline: _____

Evaluation:
What is the single most valuable insight you gained from learning how banks truly create money?

Bonus Question:
If banks use your promissory note to fund themselves first, what's stopping you from using the same principle to build generational wealth through **private notes, equity shares, and trust structures**?

Final Reflection Prompt:
Write your Declaration of Financial Independence below:

"I, _____, having learned the true operation of the Money Machine, now choose to operate with full awareness. I will leverage knowledge over ignorance, documentation over emotion, and transparency over deception. From this point forward, every contract I sign will serve my purpose, my prosperity, and my Hip National Bank."

9

Module 9: Lending What You Borrow

Advanced Power Banking II: Leveraged Lending
Realty Solutions Manager Training 301
Lend What You Borrow – Print Money 'Legally' Like the Rich

Introduction: The Promise Fulfilled — Lend What You Borrow

For eight modules you've been guided through the framework of your own financial awakening. You've learned how to structure entities, protect assets, circulate currency, and challenge the myths that kept you financially dependent. Every page has been a revelation, but it has also been a preparation — leading you to this exact moment. This is the chapter that fulfills the promise of the book's title: *The Money Machine — Lend What You Borrow: Print Money Legally Like the Rich*. Until now, you've learned how money moves. Now, you will learn how to make it move for you.

Up to this point, you've seen the inside of the banking engine. You've learned how promissory notes fund loans, how trusts protect ownership, and how leverage multiplies velocity. Yet one truth has remained just beneath the surface — the single insight that separates the rich from everyone else. The wealthy never stop at borrowing; they take what they borrow and lend it again. They turn debt into fuel, not fear. That is the principle of *Lend What You Borrow*, and it is the secret rhythm of every financial dynasty on earth.

This module is the moment that curtain gets pulled back. Here, you'll see exactly how to reverse the direction of cash flow that has kept you paying interest instead of earning it. You will understand why the banks lend ten times what they borrow — and how you can use the same principle within your own private ecosystem. This isn't rebellion against the system; it's mastery of it. For the first time, you will stand in the same position as the lender, not the borrower, holding the keys that once belonged only to institutions.

When you learn to lend what you borrow, every dollar becomes an employee working double shifts. Money stops being something you chase; it becomes something you command. A $10,000 line of credit can generate $20,000 of lending profit when used correctly. A life insurance policy can become a private bank. A piece of real estate can fund new ventures without ever being sold. In this module, you will see how all of that connects — not as theory, but as strategy.

This is also where the concept of *Hip National Bank* comes alive. You've heard the term before: it's the income you keep, the profit you pocket, the currency that circulates back to your hip. When you understand leveraged lending, you'll see how to fund Hip National Bank with every transaction — whether it's a property deal, a business loan, or a policy-backed investment. You'll begin to grasp what the rich already know: that wealth is not created by possession, but by circulation. Every dollar that leaves your hand must return with friends.

We'll explore how J.P. Morgan built an empire not by hoarding gold, but by controlling the flow of credit through trusts and insurance contracts. We'll examine how modern corporations and ministries alike can mirror that same system using policies, notes, and property — turning liability into leverage and faith into funding. You'll see how a well-structured business or church can finance its own expansion, hire its own people, and pay its own debt, all within one circulatory system. These are not lofty ideals; they are replicable frameworks that you will learn to model in your own financial blueprint.

By the time you finish this module, the way you see money will be permanently altered. You will never again look at a loan, a line of credit, or a promissory note without recognizing the opportunity hidden inside it. You will no longer fear debt, because you will understand how to make it work in two directions at once. You will be equipped with the same financial alchemy that turned bankers into billionaires — only now, that power rests in your hands. Welcome to Module 9 — the moment the Money Machine turns on.

The Secret of the Currency Circulator

Every economy has only two kinds of participants: Currency Consumers and **Currency** Circulators. Consumers spend money once and watch it disappear; circulators set it in motion so that it returns, multiplied, again and again. The average person exchanges effort for income and lets the money escape. The professional banker exchanges agreements for assets and keeps the money moving in perpetual motion. The difference is not intelligence—it's architecture.

To become a Currency Circulator is to understand that money is not a static object but a current, a flow of promises. Banks borrow your deposits at near-zero cost and lend those same dollars back to the marketplace at 5 to 20 percent interest. Their profit is not created by magic; it's manufactured by movement. They understand that money gains power only when it changes hands, and they design every policy, account, and contract to make that motion serve them.

You can do the same. The strategy is simple, but its results are profound: borrow at one rate, lend at a higher one, and keep the spread. That spread is the dividend of leverage—the reward for understanding circulation. When you learn to multiply the velocity of money within your own trust, company, or ministry, you cease being a customer of the banking system and become a participant in it. You shift from paying interest to earning it.

This is the first doorway into your personal Money Machine. In the pages that follow, you'll see how to convert borrowed capital into income-producing capital through cash-value policies, real-estate notes, and trust-based lending structures. You'll learn why banks love debt—and how, when properly engineered, you can too. The same system that once worked against you can now work entirely in your favor. The current no longer drags you downstream; it carries you forward with power.

J.P. Morgan: The Blueprint for the Power Banker

When it comes to understanding the architecture of wealth, few figures stand taller than J.P. Morgan. He was not just a banker — he was a system builder. Morgan understood early that power doesn't come from holding money; it comes from controlling its motion. While most men tried to earn their fortunes, Morgan engineered his. He mastered the art of leveraged lending, transforming credit into an empire and risk into perpetual income. His lesson remains: wealth is not built on accumulation, but on orchestration.

J.P. Morgan's genius was in his use of **trusts.** He saw that by placing assets under the control of a trust, he could not only protect them but also multiply them through strategic lending. Every railroad, steel mill, and industrial company that bore his influence was connected through a web of entities that borrowed, lent, and reinvested among themselves. Each layer of that network served as both a borrower and a lender, creating a closed-loop financial ecosystem where every dollar generated more dollars before leaving the system. In modern language, Morgan didn't build companies — he built circulatory systems of capital.

The second pillar of his empire came through insurance — particularly, what we now call BOLI (Bank-Owned Life Insurance) and COLI (Corporate-Owned Life Insurance). By using the cash value of these policies, Morgan's institutions could access low-cost, tax-advantaged capital that they could then lend out again for profit. The policies themselves continued to grow in value even as they were being borrowed against. It was the purest form of Lend What You Borrow: borrow from yourself, lend to others, profit from both sides, and let the compounding never stop.

To see how revolutionary this was, imagine a single life insurance policy worth $1 million in cash value. A bank borrows $800,000 against it at 4 percent interest, then lends that same $800,000 out at 8 percent. The bank earns a 4 percent spread while the original policy continues compounding tax-free. In effect, the bank earns interest twice — once from the policy's internal growth and again from the loan yield. This was the quiet secret behind the rise of corporate banks across America, and it remains the engine that drives financial institutions to this day.

Morgan's model was not about speculation — it was about structure. He wasn't chasing opportunities; he was creating them. His money moved in cycles, each rotation generating new yield. That same design is now available to you. By combining a trust, a cash-value policy, and a note-holding company, you can replicate the same dynamic on a personal scale. You can use borrowed capital to generate income, reinvest the proceeds into your own trust, and keep the machine turning indefinitely. This is how the wealthy live beyond the limits of earned income. They don't wait for opportunity — they finance it.

Now let's take these principles from theory to practice. If J.P. Morgan built his dynasty through trusts and insurance, you can build yours through the same framework adapted for today's world. In the sections that follow, you'll see how to apply this model not just to your business or real estate portfolio, but even to community-based enterprises and ministries that can sustain themselves for generations. The system doesn't change — only the mission does.

The Power of Leveraged Lending

If J.P. Morgan built the financial engine, leveraged lending is the ignition switch. It's the act of taking borrowed capital and lending it again — transforming one stream of credit into multiple streams of income. This is how banks make billions on assets they never truly owned, and how you can begin doing the same thing on a smaller, perfectly legal scale. When you lend what you borrow, you're not multiplying money — you're multiplying velocity. Every dollar moves faster, works harder, and returns with more companions to deposit into Hip National Bank.

Here's how it works: imagine you secure a line of credit for $100,000 at 6% interest. Instead of spending it, you lend it out at 10% secured by a promissory note and a lien against real property. You just created a 4% spread on borrowed money — pure profit, without using your own capital. The loan is secured by real collateral, not cash, so your exposure is limited while your earning potential compounds. You are now doing exactly what every major financial institution does — leveraging borrowed credit to generate new income streams.

This is the essence of a Money Machine. It's not about owning assets — it's about controlling cash flow. The banks borrow your deposits, pay you 0.5%, and lend it to someone else at 8%. The spread is theirs to keep. Now the same principle works in your favor. You borrow intelligently at one rate and lend strategically at a higher one, using trust structures and insurance-backed policies to protect and circulate the profits. You've effectively duplicated the banking model — only this time, you're the one behind the counter.

In leveraged lending, time is your greatest multiplier. The longer your loan cycles run — 6 months, 12 months, 24 months — the more velocity your capital builds. When your borrower repays, the funds immediately recycle into the next transaction. That continuous motion creates momentum, and momentum creates wealth. Over time, the profits from your lending arm can fund new acquisitions, pay down your own debt, or purchase additional policies that expand your credit capacity. You're not just earning — you're engineering growth.

But let's make this tangible. Suppose you borrow $250,000 from a private lender at 8% interest. You immediately re-lend it to three property investors — $100,000 each — at 14% with 12-month terms, secured by first-position notes on their properties. Each pays monthly interest only, totaling $3,500 per month to you. Your payment to the private lender is $1,666 per month. Your net spread — the difference between what you earn and what you owe — is $1,834 monthly, or $22,000 annually. You just created a six-figure lending business without ever touching your principal. That's Lend What You Borrow in action.

Now, imagine scaling that model. Each year, you roll profits into new secured notes, expand your lending base, and use cash-value life insurance as a private bank to fund the next round of deals. The same $250,000 could circulate through your ecosystem indefinitely, producing passive income for years. You're not waiting for a raise or a promotion; you're writing your own paycheck from your own banking system. This is how families, churches, and small business owners can become financial institutions unto themselves — legal, ethical, and profitable.

The principle of leveraged lending is simple: control the flow, and you control the future. Every empire — from J.P. Morgan's to Rockefeller's to modern private equity firms — runs on this law. They borrow low, lend high, and use time as their multiplier. In the chapters that follow, you'll learn how to set up your own Private Lender's Blueprint — using trust-based lending, policy loans, and secured notes to turn your access to credit into a self-funded ecosystem. This is where theory meets power — where your Money Machine starts printing.

The Yield Concession Servicer: Turning Distress into Dividends

Every financial ecosystem needs a specialist — someone who can spot value where others see risk. In the banking world, that role belongs to the Yield Concession Servicer. This player doesn't chase new loans; they acquire existing ones. They buy performing, underperforming, or even non-performing mortgage notes at a discount, then extract profit by managing the yield between what was paid for the note and what it continues to produce. In other words, they turn distress into dividends — and they do it with precision.

Where most people run from defaulted paper, the Yield Concession Servicer runs toward it. They understand that every delinquent loan is just a mispriced asset waiting for a manager with vision. A $100,000 note purchased for $25,000 that still collects $600 a month in payments isn't a problem — it's a 28% return on investment. These investors are not speculators; they're engineers of income. They don't flip homes; they flip paper. And in the modern economy, flipping paper pays faster, cleaner, and with far less overhead than flipping drywall.

Here's the beauty: this strategy can be executed by anyone willing to learn the system. You don't need a banking charter or a Wall Street license. You need knowledge, capital access, and consistent execution. By working through bankruptcy trustees, foreclosure law firms, or bulk REIT sellers, you can acquire notes at pennies on the dollar. Many of these institutions are desperate to offload "zombie foreclosures" — properties sitting in limbo after years of legal disputes or broken title chains. While the big funds only want clean, performing assets, you can specialize in the ones they ignore — the so-called "ugly titles" that yield the highest returns when properly managed.

Imagine buying a batch of 10 notes for $0.15 on the dollar, each with a face value of $100,000. That's a $1,000,000 portfolio purchased for $150,000. If you can get just half of those borrowers paying again through modified agreements, you're earning steady income on $500,000 worth of paper that only cost you $150,000 to control. The other half can be liquidated through short sales, deed-in-lieu agreements, or investor flips. Either way, the yield spread between acquisition and realization can easily reach 300% or more. This is how you turn broken contracts into living cash flow — one note at a time.

The secret weapon of the Yield Concession Servicer is compassionate negotiation. Instead of foreclosing, they communicate. They approach borrowers not as collectors, but as problem solvers — offering modified payments, reduced balances, or creative exits in exchange for cooperation. By doing so, they transform hostility into harmony and default into dividends. This method not only produces income but also builds relationships, referrals, and a reputation for fairness — assets that no bank balance sheet can measure.

On a larger scale, Yield Concession Servicers operate like boutique hedge funds. They pool investor capital, acquire bulk portfolios, and then manage the assets internally for income and resale. But you don't have to think big to start. One deal can change your trajectory. Acquire one non-performing note at $0.20 on the dollar, work it out with the borrower, resell it performing at $0.70, and you've made 250% on your capital. Repeat that process systematically, and your Hip National Bank begins to overflow. Each deal deposits not just cash, but confidence.

This is the business model Wall Street prays you never learn — because once you do, you stop depending on their products. You no longer need their mutual funds or REITs when you can buy the source of their income: the notes themselves. This is the ultimate evolution of Lend What You Borrow. You borrow capital at a fixed rate, use it to acquire discounted debt, and then lend again at full face value, capturing the spread as pure profit. You've now become the middleman of money — and the middleman always gets paid.

To master this role, treat every distressed note as a mini-Money Machine. Each one has moving parts: a borrower, a property, a title, and a story. Your job is to realign those parts until cash flow begins again. Whether through direct payments, refinance, or resale, you're not speculating — you're manufacturing outcomes. That's how modern power bankers and private investors alike sustain generational wealth. They don't wait for perfect markets; they build perfect margins.

The $25 Million Opportunity Wall Street Forgot

Every generation has a window where the wealthy quietly reposition their portfolios — and the rest of the world never sees the opening. Right now, that window is in the aftermath of the foreclosure and bankruptcy residue still clogging up America's property records. Tens of thousands of properties sit frozen in limbo — too toxic for banks to sell to institutions, too complicated for average buyers to touch. They call them "zombie foreclosures," but in reality, they're dormant gold mines. Together, these forgotten assets represent more than $25 billion in unrealized equity, waiting for smaller, agile players to step in where Wall Street refuses to tread.

Here's the truth: the big funds don't want the hassle. They want clean, easy-to-trade paper they can securitize and package. They avoid the ugly, the complex, and the local — but that's exactly where your Money Machine thrives. The $25 million opportunity isn't in competing with the billion-dollar hedge funds; it's in doing what they can't. You have the advantage of speed, flexibility, and humanity. You can talk to a homeowner, negotiate with a trustee, and unlock value one deal at a time. Wall Street wants automation. You bring connection — and connection still wins.

Imagine this: across every major metro area, there are law firms, bankruptcy trustees, and REIT managers still holding 2,000 to 5,000 broken notes each. They've written them off on paper, but they still sit on the books as "unresolved liabilities." Most are worth between $75,000 and $200,000 in face value — yet they'd sell them for $10,000 to $25,000 just to clear the books. Multiply that by 10,000 properties, and you have a $25 million opportunity sitting in plain sight for every 5,000 mid-size distressed assets left behind. These are not guesses; these are numbers already being quietly moved behind closed doors.

You simply have to position yourself as the buyer who brings cash, clarity, and speed.

Now, let's say you assemble a small private group — even $500,000 in pooled capital. You acquire 20 of these distressed notes at an average of $25,000 each. Over the next six months, you and your team — maybe you and your Administrative Default Group — work out terms with occupants, offer cash-for-keys incentives, clean titles, and relist 10 of them for resale at $90,000 to $110,000 each. The others you convert into performing notes that yield 12% interest annually. Within a year, that $500,000 has tripled into $1.5 million — all while improving neighborhoods and helping families resolve debt they thought was impossible. That's impact capitalism in its purest form.

The key to capturing this forgotten fortune is access and organization. You must present yourself like a professional fund — even if you're just getting started. Build your website with investor and law firm login portals. Have an onboarding document, purchase term sheet, and escrow-ready process. You're not asking for opportunities — you're providing liquidity. Once they see that you can wire within 48 to 72 hours and handle ugly title assets with professionalism, you become their go-to buyer. They want quiet exits, not headlines. You give them both privacy and profit.

What makes this so powerful is that you don't need Wall Street's billions to do what they've ignored. You need strategy, system, and service. The Administrative Default Group can handle the paperwork. Your local team can handle negotiations. You control the flow of money, the timing of contracts, and the distribution of profit. That's the difference between speculation and orchestration. Wall Street builds skyscrapers of complexity; you build circles of cash flow — and each circle is another deposit to Hip National Bank.

And here's the long play: once you've proven your model locally, replicate it regionally. Build partnerships with 5–10 law firms, each sitting on thousands of notes they'd love to liquidate. Package your process into a repeatable framework and license it to others. You'll find yourself not just flipping assets but teaching the system — becoming the lender, the educator, and the financial architect of your own ecosystem. That's when the $25 million opportunity becomes $250 million in managed paper and millions in recurring revenue.

The irony is poetic: while Wall Street looks for high-frequency trading opportunities, you're building high-frequency cash flow. You don't need a Bloomberg terminal — you need a phone, a contract, and courage. The wealth gap isn't about information anymore; it's about imagination. Those who can imagine new ways to circulate old money will always outpace those waiting for permission to play. The $25 million opportunity isn't lost — it's just waiting for you to believe you belong in the game.

Becoming the Bank: Your Five-Part Financial Engine
1.) The Trust (Vault):

Every bank begins with a vault. Not the kind made of steel and concrete, but one made of structure and law. Your vault is the Trust — the legal fortress where your assets, contracts, and future income streams are safeguarded. While most people build wealth in their own names and spend a lifetime defending it, the wealthy do the opposite: they build structures first, and those structures own everything. A trust is not just a tool for privacy; it is the foundation of your personal central bank — the container that gives every dollar you earn a place to rest, grow, and multiply.

In a trust-centered Money Machine, the trust holds legal title to assets while you retain beneficial control through your position as Trustee or Managing Member. This creates lawful separation between you and your wealth, allowing you to operate as both steward and strategist rather than as an exposed individual. When properly drafted, the trust functions like a perpetual vault — it doesn't die, doesn't pay taxes like a person, and doesn't go through probate. It can own your business, your real estate, your intellectual property, even your private lending contracts. Everything that makes money for you belongs inside the vault — because banks never leave cash on the counter.

The trust also serves as the central ledger of your financial ecosystem. Every flow — income, expense, loan, or investment — begins and ends here. It receives your earnings from real estate sales, note assignments, consulting, or lending spreads. Then it redistributes funds into your auxiliary entities: your holding company, your insurance portfolio, and your reinvestment funds. Think of the trust as the hub and every other entity as a spoke. This circular movement of money within your own structures is how the rich create "internal economies" — systems where money rarely leaves their own ecosystem. Once you learn to circulate currency through your trust, you stop spending and start compounding.

Most people never experience this kind of control because they treat the trust like a will substitute instead of a business engine. But in the Money Machine, the trust is not just an inheritance tool — it's your first financial instrument. It can loan to your LLCs, hold promissory notes from your investments, or even serve as the lender of record on deals you fund. When you "lend what you borrow," the trust becomes your private treasury, issuing funds for opportunity while collecting returns into its own protected vault. Every dollar that enters the trust is reborn as trust capital — immune from personal liability, positioned for perpetual growth, and compounding quietly behind a curtain of legal protection.

Finally, the trust gives you what most people only dream of — freedom from permission. You don't need to wait for a bank to approve your moves when you already are the bank. Your trust signs the checks, your policies fund the loans, your companies deploy the capital. Together they form a private loop of creation, control, and compounding that mirrors what J.P. Morgan and Rockefeller designed more than a century ago. When you build your vault first, you stop asking for opportunity and start authorizing it. That's the moment your Money Machine becomes unstoppable.

2.) The Operating Company (Engine):

If the Trust is your vault, then your Operating Company is the engine that makes the vault hum. Every vehicle, no matter how powerful, needs an engine that converts potential energy into forward motion — and in your Money Machine, the Operating Company is that power source. It's the active business entity that creates, earns, and circulates cash flow on behalf of your trust. This is the company that signs contracts, employs people, provides services, manages real estate, and moves opportunities from paper to profit. It is your legal "face" in the marketplace — the brand the public sees while the trust remains safely behind the curtain, collecting the income.

The Operating Company is where you build momentum. It receives seed capital from the trust — not as a gift, but as a loan — and multiplies it through operations. That distinction is critical. When the trust lends to the company, any profits that flow back are treated as returns on investment, not taxable income to you personally. This is how wealthy families and private banks keep the flow of money legal, liquid, and leveraged. The company earns; the trust owns. That's how the vault stays full while the engine keeps turning.

Think of the Operating Company as the "lender interface" of your system. It's the part of your Money Machine that interacts with the outside world — borrowing lines of credit, acquiring property, hiring teams, and entering into joint ventures. But instead of letting banks dictate your terms, you become the one setting the pace. The company's balance sheet becomes a mirror of its velocity: assets go out, income comes in, and leverage grows. Every time you use the company to buy a property, finance a project, or fund a deal, you're teaching your Money Machine to run faster and more efficiently.

The secret is to structure the Operating Company so it's both productive and protected. It must be separate from your personal identity and clearly linked to the trust through loan agreements and minutes. When profits come in, they're swept back into the trust as repayment of principal plus interest. When new opportunities arise, the trust funds them again — just like a bank extending new credit. This creates a closed-loop ecosystem where money never sits idle. The trust becomes the vault; the company becomes the driver; and every deal becomes another gear turning inside your financial engine.

Finally, your Operating Company is also your economic testimony. It shows that you've graduated from being a consumer to a creator. It allows you to hire, expand, reinvest, and even inspire others to build their own engines. Whether you're running a real estate firm, a coffee shop, or a ministry with integrated auxiliaries, the principle is the same: create value, circulate cash, and keep ownership private. Once the trust and the Operating Company begin to move in rhythm, your Money Machine shifts from theory to traction — and traction, my friend, is what prints real money.

3.) The Policy (Bank):

Every true bank needs a source of liquidity — the place where money waits in safety until opportunity knocks. In your personal financial ecosystem, that liquidity source is The Policy — a properly structured cash-value life insurance contract. This is the "bank" inside your Money Machine. It's where your capital rests, grows, and compounds quietly in the background, ready to be deployed when the next investment, acquisition, or opportunity appears. But unlike traditional banks that deposits your labor dollars, creates credit and lend multiples to others, your policy only works for one customer — you.

The policy is not just an insurance product; it's a private banking system wrapped in a legal guarantee. When properly designed — typically as a whole life or indexed universal life policy with high cash-value accumulation — it provides a protected reservoir of capital that grows tax-deferred, earns dividends, and can be borrowed against at will. The moment you fund the policy, your dollars begin compounding — even if you borrow against them. That's the secret wealthy families have used for generations: they never remove money from their capital base; they simply borrow against it, allowing their money to do two things at once — work for them and remain at work.

Here's the beauty of this system: the trust owns the policy, and the Operating Company pays the premiums as a deductible expense, often through executive benefit structures or key-person coverage. The cash value grows inside the trust's private vault, insulated from taxes, creditors, and market volatility. When you need capital to acquire a property, fund a new business, or purchase discount notes, you don't go to a commercial bank — you borrow from the policy. The loan is instant, requires no approval, and the interest you pay goes back to the trust's balance sheet. In other words, you're paying interest to yourself. This is the cleanest, most legal version of "printing money" that exists in America today.

To understand the leverage, imagine this: your trust-owned policy has a cash value of $250,000. You borrow $200,000 from it to buy two distressed properties or lend it out at a higher rate through your Operating Company. While that money is out in the field working, the entire $250,000 inside your policy continues to earn guaranteed growth and dividends. The borrowed funds are simply collateralized by the policy, not withdrawn from it. When you repay the loan, your vault refills itself. It's a perpetual motion engine — capital that never sleeps, never taxes itself, and never needs permission to move.

And here's where the mindset shift happens: the policy is not your safety net; it's your capital engine. Banks themselves use this exact model — it's called BOLI (Bank-Owned Life Insurance). JPMorgan Chase alone holds billions in these policies as Tier 1 assets to fund their operations, pay executive bonuses, and finance acquisitions. You're simply adopting their playbook — only now, you're the banker, not the customer. The same laws that allow banks to lend against their own policies allow you to do the same. Once your policy is in motion, you've effectively built your own reserve system — a vault-backed, trust-owned, cash-yielding bank that serves one purpose: to fund your freedom.

When this principle clicks, everything changes. You no longer see life insurance as an expense but as a private Federal Reserve under your control. Your trust is the vault, your Operating Company is the engine, and your Policy is the bank that fuels them both. When you borrow against it, invest through it, and repay it, you've completed the circle of infinite cash flow. That's not theory — that's how the ultra-wealthy operate every single day. And now, so can you.

4.) The Notes (Yield):

If the Policy is your private bank, then the Notes are your income-bearing assets — your bonds, your yield generators, your profit engines. In the traditional system, you borrow money from a bank, and the bank earns interest on your payments. In your system, you reverse that flow. You become the one holding the promissory note, collecting interest payments from others while your capital continues to grow behind the scenes. This is where the phrase "Lend What You Borrow" takes on its full meaning — you're not just earning money from your labor anymore; you're earning money from money itself.

When your trust or your Operating Company issues a loan — whether to fund a small business, a real estate rehab, or a property buyer through seller financing — that promissory note becomes an income-producing instrument. Every payment that comes in represents yield, just like a bank's loan portfolio. The difference is that your "bank" doesn't have shareholders — it has beneficiaries. The interest you charge feeds back into your trust, replenishing your Policy's reserves and multiplying your vault's equity. This is the moment where you shift from being a consumer of credit to a creator of it. Every time someone makes a payment on a note you own, you're operating at the same level as the Federal Reserve — expanding the money supply through trust-backed lending.

Let's bring this down to street level. Suppose your trust borrows $200,000 from your life insurance policy at 5% and lends it out through your Operating Company at 10% secured by real estate or equipment.

That 5% spread — your arbitrage — is pure yield, just like a bank's net interest margin. The trust earns interest income while the policy continues to compound in full. The borrower wins because they received flexible funding, and you win because your capital never left your ecosystem. That is leveraged lending in its purest form — turning borrowed capital into permanent profit through the lawful circulation of private credit.

Every promissory note you hold is a piece of paper that works for you. It's your employee, your soldier, your silent partner in the marketplace. Notes can be bought, sold, discounted, or even used as collateral to secure new credit lines — meaning your yield can compound itself. This is the advanced stage of wealth creation: when your money flow creates new money flow. The wealthy don't chase jobs or paychecks; they build pipelines of cash secured by paper promises that others must honor. Your notes are those promises. The more you hold, the more your Money Machine hums.

Ultimately, Notes represent the maturity of your banking system. The trust holds the asset; the company services the payment; the policy replenishes liquidity — and the yield from your notes completes the circuit. Each note is a circulating instrument of wealth, a living receipt of value you've created by being on the other side of the loan table. When your ecosystem reaches this stage, you've crossed into the territory once reserved for institutions. You are no longer the one making payments to a lender — you are the lender, and your "Hip National Bank" keeps every cent of the profit in your own pocket.

5.) The Cycle (Flow):

Everything in nature that thrives, flows — rivers, blood, breath, and money. The same is true in your financial life: stagnation kills wealth, but circulation multiplies it. The Cycle, or Flow, is the fifth and final component of your Money Machine. It's the rhythm that ties all the other parts together — the pulse that keeps your financial body alive. When the trust, the operating company, the policy, the notes, and your collateral move in harmony, money stops being a problem and becomes a process. You are no longer chasing cash; you are managing flow.

Here's how the cycle works: the Trust seeds the Operating Company with capital. The Company deploys that capital into projects, loans, or acquisitions, often funded by Policy loans. The revenue from those activities — rents, loan repayments, or sales — flows back into the Trust as income. From there, part of the profit replenishes the Policy (your bank), restoring the vault and increasing available liquidity for the next round. The remainder may be reinvested, distributed, or held in reserve. Nothing leaves the system — it simply circulates from one chamber to another, like a perfectly tuned engine recycling its own energy. This is how banks, insurance companies, and family offices sustain generational wealth — by mastering flow rather than chasing transactions.

The power of the cycle is that it creates velocity. Every dollar inside your system has a job and never stops working. The same $100,000 can move through your ecosystem five, ten, even twenty times a year — funding new deals, collecting new interest, and building new equity — without ever leaving your control. Each pass through the system multiplies the yield. It's the exact principle behind fractional reserve banking — only now, you're the fractional reserve. Your Policy creates liquidity, your Notes generate interest, your Real Estate anchors collateral value, and your Trust captures every dollar of gain inside a protected structure. That is financial gravity working in your favor.

When the flow is consistent, you become your own economy. The Policy bank replaces your dependency on lenders, the Notes generate your recurring yield, and the Operating Company turns your creative ideas into production and profit. Even your expenses can circulate back into the system through planned reimbursements and internal lending structures. Instead of money escaping your world, it remains in orbit — returning again and again to the source. That's why the wealthy don't measure income by salary; they measure velocity of flow inside their private financial ecosystems.

The ultimate goal of the Cycle is not just to accumulate wealth, but to sustain motion. When your Money Machine runs at full flow, every dollar becomes a missionary with an assignment — to go out, bring back friends, and return home with profit. Your vault grows, your engine strengthens, and your flow quickens. You'll feel it in your daily life — peace replacing panic, strategy replacing stress. Because when you master circulation, you master creation. The banks have known it for centuries; now it's your turn to live it.

The Real Estate Example: From Dirt to Dynasty

Now let's bring this to life with two contrasting examples — one commercial, one spiritual — both using the exact same Money Machine principles.

Example 1: The Chick-fil-A Model – The For-Profit Engine

Imagine a gleaming Chick-fil-A on a bustling corner of Main Street. The line is wrapped around the building, cars snake through the drive-thru, and cash registers hum from open to close. To most people, it's just another restaurant doing brisk business. But to the trained eye, this is not just a chicken sandwich operation — it's a finely tuned Money Machine. Beneath the surface of waffle fries and customer smiles lies a sophisticated wealth ecosystem that quietly compounds profit in three directions at once.

Here's how it's built. The Trust is the cornerstone — it owns the land and the building. That's the vault. The Trust never works the counter or fries a sandwich; it just collects rent. Next, the Operating Company (LLC) — the franchise entity — leases the property from the Trust, paying monthly rent that's set slightly above market rate. Those lease payments are pure, predictable income flowing back to the Trust. The Cash-Value Policy — the private bank inside your system — funded the land purchase and construction through policy loans.

The franchise never went to a commercial lender, never begged for approval, and never risked losing its equity. It borrowed from its own bank and agreed to repay itself with every sale that crossed the register.

Now enter the Discount Note Company — the quiet investor behind the scenes. With surplus cash flow from the franchise's daily operations, it begins purchasing discounted mortgage notes and seller-financed contracts. These notes pay steady, monthly income, just like rent — but they do it without kitchens, employees, or grease traps. Each payment received on a note becomes new fuel for the system. Those returns are deposited into the Trust, which in turn repays the Policy loans that funded the original build. The Policy replenishes its credit line, restoring full liquidity and readying itself for the next location or expansion. The cycle continues, self-sustaining and self-funding.

Each component feeds the others in a perfect closed loop:

- Rent flows from the franchise to the Trust.
- The Trust uses that rent to repay its Policy loan.
- The Policy's credit line refills, ready for new construction.
- The Discount Note Company uses profits to buy more yielding notes.
- The Notes produce new passive income, deposited back into the Trust.

In one coordinated ecosystem, you've built three profit centers:

1. **Real Estate** – long-term equity and appreciation in the land and building.
2. **Business Operations** – daily income from the franchise itself.
3. **Lending Yield** – recurring passive income from your owned notes and private credit.

Together, these create perpetual motion — cash flow circulating through your own internal banking system, compounding returns without ever leaving your control. The Policy bank funds construction, the business fuels revenue, and the Trust captures profits — all feeding back into what I call Hip National Bank: the bank of you.

The brilliance of this design is that every dollar in the system does more than one job. The same dollar that bought the land earns rent, repays the Policy, restores borrowing capacity, and finances future expansions — all while increasing equity and building a lending portfolio. Nothing is wasted. The "borrowed" capital never leaves your world; it just changes positions on the chessboard. This is how modern empires are quietly built: not by luck or risk, but by engineering perpetual motion inside a private wealth ecosystem.

This is the true Chick-fil-A secret — not the recipe, but the structure. It's how a small sandwich shop can become a billion-dollar enterprise while staying debt-free, family-owned, and loved by employees. It's not fast food — it's fast finance. And the best part? You can build the same model with your own Money Machine, on your own scale, starting with the land beneath your feet.

Example 2: The Community Church Model – The Non-Profit Engine

Now, let's shift from Main Street to Mission Street. Imagine a thriving community church — bright, active, debt-free, and financially alive — serving hundreds of people each week while quietly operating one of the most intelligent wealth ecosystems in America. Its lights never flicker, its doors never close, and its members never struggle to fund its mission because it has mastered the art of Lending What It Borrows. This is not just a church that preaches faith — it applies it through financial stewardship, leveraging the same blueprint the wealthy use to build dynasties.

Under the IRS 508(c)(1)(a) or 501(c)(3) designation, the church is already recognized as a non-taxable sovereign entity, meaning its income used for ministry purposes is free from corporate income tax. That makes it the perfect foundation — a real-life Trust Vessel for God's work. The church owns its land and facilities through a Religious Trust, ensuring the property is legally protected and can never be taken through private claim or civil action. The ministry itself — the active operating arm — functions as the Operating Company, responsible for programs, outreach, and member services. The trust leases the building to the ministry, and the rent payments — though internal — create a paper trail of stewardship and accountability. Those rent payments, just like in the Chick-fil-A model, flow directly back into the trust, fueling expansion, renovation, and new missions.

Now comes the brilliance: within the structure, the church establishes integrated auxiliaries — IRS-recognized extensions that serve distinct functions such as a daycare, café, music studio, counseling center, or even a community housing initiative. Each auxiliary operates as a controlled company, wholly owned by the trust, yet generating its own revenue streams. The profits from these auxiliaries flow into the trust as contributions or service payments, which can then fund ministry projects, charitable works, and member welfare. These auxiliaries aren't side businesses — they're ministry arms with marketplace legs. The result? A full-circle financial ecosystem where every dollar earns, returns, and blesses again.

The next layer is the Cash-Value Life Insurance Policy — the Bank of the Ministry. The church takes out corporate-owned life insurance (COLI) and, where appropriate, pastor-owned or member-owned policies (BOLI-style structures) that accumulate tax-free cash value. These policies are the ministry's emergency fund, investment fund, and expansion capital source all rolled into one. The church can borrow from these policies to build new facilities, launch programs, or fund its housing auxiliaries — without debt, without banks, and without compromise. The repayments replenish the policy, restoring its borrowing power and growing its value year after year. It's God's version of compound interest — stewardship multiplied by wisdom.

Now tie in the Discount Note Company — a ministry-controlled auxiliary designed to acquire performing and non-performing real estate notes at deep discounts. This arm of the church becomes the silent investor for the community, helping distressed homeowners, providing affordable housing, and creating income streams that sustain the mission. Each acquired note pays monthly income back to the trust, which strengthens the financial base of the church. This is how the ministry becomes both a lender and a redeemer — literally buying back land, property, and people's hope from financial bondage. It's kingdom finance in motion — redeeming assets, redeeming families, redeeming futures.

Each element of this model serves a divine order of flow:

- The **Trust** owns the land and facilities, shielding them from liability.
- The **Operating Ministry** pays rent, creating stewardship records and operating income.
- The **Integrated Auxiliaries** generate marketplace revenue and community impact.
- The **Policies** store wealth tax-free and provide liquidity for expansion.
- The **Note Company** redeems property and produces passive income.

The synergy is unstoppable. The trust receives the rent and investment returns; the policy replenishes liquidity; the auxiliaries expand outreach; and the notes provide consistent monthly yield. Every dollar in the ecosystem multiplies — spiritually and financially. It's not just self-sustaining; it's self-expanding. The ministry becomes the lender, the employer, the investor, and the redeemer all in one — funding revival with financial strategy.

This is how you build a 100-year church that can't be shaken by economy, politics, or market collapse. Every piece of the system mirrors divine order — stewardship, multiplication, and circulation. As the Scriptures say, "To him who has, more shall be given." When a ministry stops borrowing from the world and starts banking on divine wisdom, it steps into what I call The Kingdom Flow. And from that flow, not only does the church thrive — but so does every family connected to it.

Key Insight:
"When the church that gains divine structure, inherits sustainability."
— *Ray Wright Jacobs*

Blueprint Summary: From Chick-fil-A to Church

Whether you're flipping a sandwich or saving a soul, the same laws of flow apply. The *Money Machine* doesn't care what industry you're in — it only responds to structure, stewardship, and circulation. The Chick-fil-A franchise and the community church may look worlds apart on the surface, but underneath, they run on identical architecture: a trust to hold the assets, an operating company to drive production, a policy to store and multiply liquidity, a note division to capture yield, and a cycle to keep the entire system alive. The difference lies only in the mission — one feeds the body, the other feeds the spirit — but both prove that when you Lend What You Borrow, you transcend debt and step into ownership.

At its core, this blueprint teaches you to become your own banker. Instead of borrowing money from the outside world and paying it back with interest, you borrow from your own system — your policy loans, your trust reserves, or your internally recycled cash — and lend it right back out into ventures that produce more than they cost. It's what banks, insurance companies, and Fortune 500 CEOs have done for over a century. J.P. Morgan called it "control without ownership." Walt Disney used it to build an empire of imagination. And the same principle that financed the Magic Kingdom can finance *your* kingdom — one that's practical, principled, and profitable.

In the for-profit model, your *engine* is the business — the Chick-fil-A, the laundromat, the car wash, or the real estate management company. In the nonprofit model, your *engine* is the ministry — the church, school, or community organization that drives your mission. But in both, the Trust is the anchor. It holds the assets, receives the rent, and distributes the profits. The Policy is the lifeblood, always replenishing liquidity, always compounding quietly in the background. The Note Company is the investor's alter ego — buying distressed assets, turning loss into yield, and converting debt into equity. Every component has a defined role, and together they make the machine perpetual.

The brilliance of *Lend What You Borrow* is that it removes the emotion of money and replaces it with mechanics. You don't need to pray for capital — you structure for it. You don't chase investors — you *become* one. You don't beg a bank to believe in your dream — you prove your own creditworthiness through policy loans, trust collateral, and note portfolios that work while you sleep. Even better, the interest you pay comes back to you, not to a faceless institution. You're the borrower *and* the lender. That's not just leverage — that's liberation.

Now picture this blueprint in motion: A trust-funded business buys its land through a policy loan. The business leases it back and pays rent. That rent repays the policy. The policy refills its loan balance, and the surplus buys discounted notes. Those notes pay interest back into the trust, which funds the next venture. The cycle repeats indefinitely. Every rotation grows capital, increases yield, and deepens ownership. Whether your focus is real estate, retail, or revival — the outcome is the same: an ecosystem that pays for itself, sustains itself, and expands itself.

This is the moment where *The Money Machine* becomes more than a metaphor. It becomes your personal, spiritual, and financial operating system. It's how you align purpose with profit, ministry with multiplication, and calling with cash flow. It's the art of turning every borrowed dollar into a servant that works for you — and every repayment into a reinvestment that strengthens your position. This is not theory; it's the architecture of every enduring dynasty. When you build it once, you never have to build it again — you simply keep the flow alive.

Legacy Through Leverage

The rich don't have better money; they have better systems. They lend what they borrow and profit from the circulation.

Now, so can you. Whether you're building a business, a ministry, or a multi-generational legacy, the principle is the same: borrow intelligently, lend strategically, circulate endlessly.

You've now learned what the bankers never wanted you to know — that wealth isn't about having money. It's about *moving* it.

You are now the Money Machine. You are now the bank. You can now lend what you borrow — and print money, legally, like the rich.

Workbook: Module 9

Advanced Power Banking II: Leveraged Lending
Realty Solutions Manager Training 301

Section 1: The Blueprint of Flow
Reflection Questions

1. In your own words, describe what *"Lend What You Borrow"* means to you.
   ○ How does it shift your mindset about money, debt, and ownership?
2. Why is it essential to understand the circulation of capital rather than its accumulation?
3. Write down three ways your current business, ministry, or idea could benefit from internal lending instead of external borrowing.

Fill in the Blank

- The key difference between traditional borrowing and *Lending What You Borrow* is that you _____ the interest rather than _____ it away.
- Wealth is not built by having more money; it's built by creating more _____.

Section 2: Building Your Five-Part Financial Engine
Every Money Machine has five key parts — the **Trust, Operating Company, Policy, Notes, and Cycle.**
Use this section to outline your personal model.
Exercise: Map Your Machine

Component	Purpose	Entity Name or Idea	Funding Source	Primary Function
Trust (Vault)	Owns assets, receives rent			

Component	Purpose	Entity Name or Idea	Funding Source	Primary Function
Operating Company (Engine)	Runs daily operations			
Policy (Bank)	Stores liquidity, provides low-interest loans			
Notes (Yield)	Generates recurring income			
Cycle (Flow)	Keeps the ecosystem circulating			

Action Step:

For each part, identify *one* action you can take this month to begin building or strengthening that component.

Section 3: The Chick-fil-A Model (For-Profit Example)

Scenario Challenge:

You're building a family-owned business that you want to scale into multiple locations using *your own banking system*.

1. What type of business will be your "engine"?
   ◦ (e.g., restaurant, car wash, short-term rental, logistics, etc.)
2. How will you structure your trust and operating company relationship?
   ◦ Who will own the land? Who will lease it?
3. What source of capital could you use for initial funding — savings, policy loan, or trust reserves?
4. How can you create a *closed loop of income* like the Chick-fil-A model described in the module?

Calculation Exercise:

If your trust leases a property to your LLC for $5,000 per month, and your LLC's operations produce $10,000 in monthly profit:

• How much can flow back into the trust annually? _____

- If the trust uses that to repay a policy loan at 5%, how much new credit can it access after one year? _____

(Use this space to calculate and visualize your own flow of funds.)

Section 4: The Church Model (Nonprofit Example)
Scenario Challenge:

You are the founder or administrator of a faith-based organization. You want to build a *self-sustaining ministry ecosystem* using the same "Lend What You Borrow" principles.

1. What auxiliary ministries or enterprises could your church operate that also serve the community?
   - (Examples: daycare, counseling center, coffee shop, recording studio, transitional housing.)
2. Which of these could be structured as controlled companies or integrated auxiliaries?
3. How could your church use corporate-owned life insurance (COLI) or member policies to fund expansion, housing, or benevolence programs?
4. What new forms of outreach or community transformation would be possible if your ministry generated recurring passive income from its own investments?

Fill in the Blank:

- The IRS recognizes a church as a _____ entity, allowing all income used for ministry to remain _____.
- Each auxiliary business of the church should serve both a _____ purpose and a _____ function.

Section 5: Designing Your Money Machine Ecosystem
Exercise – Connect the Flow:

Draw your personal "Money Machine Map."

- Start with your Trust at the top (the vault).
- Draw arrows to your Operating Company (the engine).
- Show rent and income flowing back to the Trust.
- Add your Policy as the internal bank replenishing liquidity.

- Connect your Note Company as the income-generating yield arm.
- Finally, illustrate how profits recycle back to start the next cycle.

(Use blank space on this page or create your own diagram on a separate sheet.)

Section 6: Case Study Comparison
Compare the Two Engines:

Category	Chick-fil-A Model	Church Model
Entity Type	For-Profit LLC	Nonprofit 508(c)(1)(a) or 501(c)(3)
Asset Holder	Business Trust	Religious Trust
Revenue Stream	Product Sales & Rent	Donations, Auxiliaries, Notes
Banking Source	Policy Loans	COLI/BOLI Policies
Passive Income Arm	Discount Note Company	Integrated Note Ministry
Ultimate Goal	Expansion & Profit	Sustainability & Impact

Reflection Question:
What part of these models most excites you — ownership, income, impact, or independence? Why?

Section 7: The Flow Formula

To maintain flow, follow the **4M Rule:**

1. **Make** money through operations.
2. **Move** it into assets that cash flow.
3. **Multiply** it through internal lending.
4. **Maintain** control through trusts and policies.

Action Prompt:

- Write one paragraph describing how you will apply the 4M Rule to your life or business this year.
- Be specific: list at least one entity, one asset, and one reinvestment cycle.

Section 8: Bonus Question
In your own words, explain this principle:
"If you can borrow once and lend forever, you can print your own income for life."

- How does this statement change your view of debt and wealth?
- What steps can you take right now to begin turning your own Money Machine?

Key Insight
"You are not chasing capital — you're creating circulation. The same dollar that leaves your hand should come back with a friend."
— Ray Wright Jacobs

10

Module 10: The Retail Flip Remodeler

Buy • Repair • Flip (Retail)
"The Blueprint for Turning Sawdust into Cash Flow"
(Realty Solutions Manager Training 401)

"Vision without execution is hallucination." — Thomas Edison

The Leap of Faith: From Dreamer to Builder

Every investor starts out in the same place — standing at the edge of an idea, staring into uncertainty, wondering, *Can I really do this?* Maybe you've watched the shows, seen the quick profits, and felt the itch to try it for yourself. But deep down, something stops you — the fear of what you don't know. This is where most people stay stuck: dreaming of profit, but never moving past hesitation.

That ends right here. Because by now, you've learned the secret rhythm of wealth — control the contracts, and you control the cash flow. You've seen how the "Money Machine" turns promises into paydays, and how the power to create wealth is never outside you, it's inside the agreements you write and the discipline you keep. Now we'll take that same principle and put it into one of the most tangible, hands-on businesses in America — real estate remodeling.

The goal of this module isn't to turn you into a carpenter or a TV personality. It's to show you how to create a *system of value* that the market will pay for — repeatedly, predictably, and profitably. You'll learn how to buy right, repair smart, and flip retail with precision so that every project puts real money into your Hip National Bank. You'll also learn how to read the motivations of the people who move the marketplace — realtors, contractors, buyers, and bankers — and how to win them all to your side.

When you're done with this module, you won't just *understand* the business — you'll be able to *enter* it. And not as a gambler hoping for luck, but as an architect running a controlled profit operation, just like the rich.

"Do your planning and prepare your field before building your house."
(Proverbs 24:27 NLT)

The Mindset Shift: From Fear to Flow

The biggest secret to flipping real estate successfully isn't construction or design — it's confidence born from clarity. Builders guard this truth like treasure: *you don't need to know everything — you only need to control what matters.* The rest can be bought, contracted, or delegated. Every great developer started with one property, one plan, and a commitment to make every mistake once — and never twice.

The fear most people carry comes from the unknown. "What if something goes wrong?" it whispers. The truth is — something always will. But that's not failure; that's tuition. The difference between a struggler and a success story is that the struggler reacts emotionally, while the success recalculates mathematically. Every problem has a price. You solve it by writing it into your system next time. That's how confidence compounds.

Here's your first rule of flow: *you're not building houses — you're building contracts.* The house is the byproduct. You are a Money Machine operator. Every screw, nail, and paint stroke has a contract attached to it that defines cost, time, and profit. You are not a construction worker — you are a conductor. Your hammer is paper. Your saw is signature. And your blueprint is the agreement that guarantees your payday.

When you shift from fear to flow, the game changes. You start to see contractors, realtors, and buyers as players in your orchestra. You stop asking, "What if I fail?" and start asking, "What system will protect my next success?" That's the mindset of the professional. That's when you stop being a spectator and start running your own financial construction site — the one that deposits directly into Hip National Bank.

Buy Smart: The Hidden Profit Is in the Purchase

Builders have a saying: *You make your money when you buy, not when you sell.* Every penny of future profit is written the day you close on the property. Buy too high, and you've already lost before the first nail hits wood. Buy smart, and you've guaranteed your win. The math doesn't lie — but you have to listen to it.

Before you ever buy, know three things: (1) the highest sold comp in the last 90 days that matches your home's bed, bath, and square footage; (2) the repair cost to reach that comp's quality; and (3) the gap between your total cost and that comp's sale price. That gap is your future profit. If it's not at least 20% of the total after-repair value (ARV), walk away. You can't fix bad math with good intentions.

And don't get emotional. The biggest mistake new flippers make is falling in love with the property instead of the numbers. The house doesn't love you back — it loves whoever controls its paperwork. Be that person. Let your calculator tell you when to walk. Your discipline is your defense.

Smart buying also means seeing the *hidden costs* that others miss — title defects, unpaid liens, foundation issues, old roofs, septic problems, and unpermitted additions. These are not deal killers; they're negotiation weapons. Every problem you discover is a discount you've earned. You are not buying a house — you are buying leverage.

Repair Right: What the Shows Don't Tell You

TV makes it look like every remodel comes with a "surprise" — a broken pipe, a rotten joist, a hidden foundation crack that magically eats $10,000 of profit. But here's the truth the networks won't air: real builders aren't surprised, because they inspect everything *before* they swing the hammer. Surprises are just things lazy investors didn't check.

Walk the property with your contractor and look behind the beauty. Check the panel box for aluminum wiring. Crawl under the house and inspect the beams. Lift a vent and look at the ducting. Run the water and listen for hammering pipes. You're not being paranoid — you're being profitable. Every unknown you uncover before you buy is money you won't lose after you close.

Then, when it's time to remodel, run your project like a mission. Always have your contractors sign *your* contracts, not theirs. You decide the terms — fixed price, clear scope, deadlines, and penalties for missed dates. Never accept "time and materials." That's contractor code for "you're paying for my confusion." Control the paper, and you control the cost.

Here's the most guarded builder secret of all: materials don't make money — sequence does. The order you do things determines how fast you finish and how clean your budget stays. Keep trades from stepping on each other. Line up inspections back-to-back. Schedule paint only after every patch is sanded, not "almost ready." Every day you save is a day Hip National Bank's balance grows.

Flip Retail: Selling Like a Pro (and Why Agents Matter)

Now that the house shines, it's time to sell — and this is where most investors either fly or fall. Wholesale buyers care only about numbers; retail buyers buy stories. And stories are told through emotions, lighting, smell, and detail. You're not selling drywall — you're selling *dreams.*

The fastest way to create those dreams is through the people who tell them for a living — realtors. They are your unpaid marketing army. But here's the trick: don't look for the cheapest one, look for the hungriest one. The ones who close consistently do so because they've learned to turn listings into experiences. Reward that. Offer bonuses for full-price sales. Feed the hand that feeds your machine.

A smart flipper never uses discount brokers. They look cheap on paper but expensive in time. A 4% listing may save you 2% up front but cost you 10% on the back end in slower traffic, weaker showings, and tired agents. Instead, go the opposite way — make yourself famous for paying well. If you offer 7% with a 4% buyer's side for full-price or better, you'll be the listing every agent in town shows first. You just moved to the front of the line.

And always stage your home like you respect the buyer's dream. Clean, bright, and smell like success — not sawdust. Leave a binder on the counter with your upgrades, warranty cards, and before-and-after photos. You're not just selling a house; you're selling proof that you're a pro. The first time you watch a family light up walking into your finished property, you'll realize something powerful: you're not just flipping homes — you're flipping futures.

The Perfect Deal: Printing Profit Step-by-Step

Let's walk through the dream deal so you can visualize how it looks in real life. You buy the note to a property with a $300,000 face-value non-performing loan for $75,000. You invest another $30,800 perfecting the title — cash-for-keys, paperwork, and goodwill to the prior owner — completely converting the note to marketable title and making the property ready to resell. You remodel the home for $61,000 but, because your General Contractor Company runs lean, your real cost is $45,750, leaving $15,250 in your contractor's Hip National Bank.

Your total project cost? $166,800. You list the home at $369,000, a touch under the $380,000 market value, and you ignite the buyers' imagination. You offer agents a 7% total commission, giving the buyer's agent 4% if it sells full price in the first week. Within three days, you have multiple offers, and one buyer offers $387,500 cash. After your 7% commissions and 1.5% closing costs, you net roughly $352,500.

Subtract your $166,800 investment, and your profit is over $185,000. Then you pay your Real Estate Investment Company a $5,000 administrative fee and your General Contractor Company $15,250 for construction profit, leaving you three streams of income — all controlled by contracts you wrote. That's not luck. That's system.

This is what the Money Machine looks like in motion:

- One purchase created three contracts.
- Three contracts created three income streams.
- Three income streams fed Hip National Bank.

You didn't chase profit — you designed it.

The Calling: Build, Bless, Repeat

The deeper secret in flipping isn't just profit — it's purpose. When you restore a home, you don't just fix walls; you redeem value that others walked away from. You take something broken and make it beautiful again. That's ministry through materials. Every time you hand over the keys, you transfer peace.

You're also modeling something sacred — stewardship. The way you manage people, contracts, and capital becomes a testimony of excellence. You show your community that business and integrity can live in the same house. And the income you create funds new oppor-tunities: jobs, partnerships, and more homes to bless.

So don't wait for perfect timing — it doesn't exist. Faith is spelled "GO Therefore, be doing, and the Lord be with thee." Every investor you've ever admired once stood where you are now: nervous, unsure, and one signature away from transformation. Take that leap. Trust your system. Let your Money Machine do what it was designed to do: turn thought into structure, paper into payment, and blueprints into blessings.

Because now you know the truth: builders don't make their money with hammers. They make it with contracts — and confidence. And the next deposit waiting in Hip National Bank... has your name on it.

Bonus to Module 10 — Buy • Repair • Flip Insider Secretes

The Shift: From Math to Emotion (Without Losing the Math)

Retail flips don't sell because a spreadsheet says 23% IRR; they sell because a buyer's kid points at the backyard and says, "Can we put a swing there?" That's the first truth you need to carry into every decision. We're still investors, still disciplined, still allergic to sur-prises—the home has to *feel* inevitable the moment someone steps over the threshold. If you honor both the math and the emotion, you win every single time.

Here's the secret most builders won't tell you: the premium isn't in marble and brass; it's in cohesion. Buyers will pay more for a home where the sightlines, lighting temperature, hardware finish, and floor-ing width agree with one another. When it feels curated, the brain stops hunting for defects and starts imagining furniture. That's the moment you win the offer, and that moment is engineered on paper *before* a single tile is set. Cohesion costs less than "expensive."

Your new mindset is simple: renovate to the *top sold comp*, not to your taste. Pull the last five closed sales within a half-mile and match their winning features—*not* their photos—feature by feature. What stove size pushed those closings? Did the winner have an 8' slider? Were primary baths selling with frameless glass or shower curtains? Copy the pattern, then give it one signature flourish buyers can brag about.

Last thing on mindset: don't chase applause during the remodel—chase applause at the open house. Builders often overspend backstage because it feels productive. We don't. We put the dollars where buyers notice: first impression, kitchen triangle, primary suite, and the 12 feet you see from the front door. Everything else is "quiet competence"—solid, clean, and unbreakable.

Before you swing a hammer, you should know the exit number you can document to an appraiser and defend to a buyer's dad. That means pulling sold comps (not listed hopes), walking them if you can, and building your Finish & Feature Matrix from what closed high. Your matrix is a one-page spec playbook: flooring width, plank length, paint sheen, cabinet profile, range size, hood type, lighting temp (2700–3000K), bath tile size, trim height, door style, hardware finish, and curb-appeal plan. Tie each line to a unit cost and a day-impact on schedule. Pros plan first so they don't pay twice.

Next, hunt the invisible value. Insulation R-value, new subfloor, dedicated 20A circuits in kitchen, GFCI/AFCI coverage, shutoff valves, and vented hood to exterior. These aren't sexy on Instagram, but they are catnip for appraisers and the cousin who flips houses "on the side." When you hand buyers a features sheet listing the things they can't see, you turn skepticism into "Shh, this one's different." That sheet is your premium's defense.

Walk the neighbors' inventory like a scout. Note why the one that *should* have sold for more actually sold for less: poor lighting, small island, cheap faucet, awkward laundry, squeaky floors. Your scope exists to erase those mistakes. Remember: we aren't trying to build the Taj Mahal; we're building the best version of what's selling right now within a street's price band. That's how you sell fast without chasing price reductions.

Finally, set your exciting price before demo. If fair value is $380,000, choose a launch number that creates a line at the door—often 92–97% of fair, depending on inventory. Everyone else lists high and apologizes on day 30; we list right and negotiate *up* on day 4. Price is a magnet; use it to create gravity.

Reality shows sell chaos; pros sell houses. Your fix is a lump-sum, milestone-paid contract with teeth: start/finish dates, progress draws tied to visible deliverables, daily liquidated damages for missed critical path, and a finish bonus for beating the date with quality intact. Add a Latent Conditions clause that says: concealed-condition claims must be noticed within 48 hours, photographed, priced by the same unit schedule in the bid, and approved in writing—or the cost is deemed included. Miss the window? subcontractor eats it. The drama just died.

Require daily photo logs (front elevation, kitchen, each bath, MEP, backyard) dropped to a shared folder by 6 p.m. This is your time-lapse—your early warning system. Pair it with a 10-minute morning stand-up: "What finished yesterday? What's blocked? What's today's deliverable?" Keep it friendly and firm. When everyone knows the baton pass, the schedule moves like a relay.

Run a no substitution policy for visible finishes unless you approve the exact SKU and finish. "It looks the same" is contractor code for "it was on sale." Lock lighting temperature across the house (yes, this matters), hold grout color to your tile scale, and keep your hardware family consistent. Disjointed spec is the #1 reason flips look "almost right." Almost right doesn't get over asking price.

Finally, order your final clean, window wash, and photos two weeks before the expected finish. Deadlines birth miracles. Subs sprint when they know the photographer's coming and the lockbox is going on. You're not micromanaging; you're conducting.

Here's the realtor truth no one prints: listing agents spend money up front; buyer's agents spend time with risk. Respect both and you'll become a favorite seller in your market. Give the listing side assets that make them look pro (permits packet, upgrade list, floor plan, utility sheet, roof/HVAC age) and give the buyer's side reasons to prioritize *your* listing (clean showing instructions, well-written "agent remarks," and a commission structure that says "Thank you for bringing me the winner").

Commission is a lever, not a leak. We regularly offer a performance-based 7%: 3% to the listing side and 4% to the buyer's side for full-price-or-better accepted within the first 7–10 days. You're not being generous; you're being surgical. A hot buyer's agent with three families in the car will show your house first when they know you respect the work. That often saves two months of carry and a death spiral of price cuts. Cheap is expensive; aligned is profitable.

Write "agent-only" remarks like a pro: "Seller prefers as-is with information-only inspection, appraisal gap language up to $X, local lender, and a 14-day close. $2,000 buyer credit at full price+ for personal upgrades (lender-approved). Buyer's broker 4% at full price+ in first 7 days." Clear, confident, and agent-friendly. You just told them exactly how to win—and they'll coach their clients to do exactly that.

Then help the appraiser. Leave a binder on the kitchen island: before-and-after photos, receipts for big items, permit finals, energy upgrades, a comp map with your two best anchors circled, and a one-page "What's New" list. Appraisers are not your enemy; they're your evidence audience. Give them easy proof, and they'll give you the number.

Your listing gets only one "new" moment on the Realtor's MLS—treat it like a product launch. Drop a "Coming Soon" 72 hours before live to warm up search alerts. Go live mid-week, broker open Thursday, stacked open houses Saturday and Sunday with tight windows (11–1 and 2–4) to create a sense of crowd. Set an offer deadline for Monday at 5 p.m. and actually stick to it. Velocity is a strategy.

The house should show like a boutique hotel. Neutral scent, balanced lighting, soft music, crisp staging, fresh front door color, mulch that still looks wet, and house numbers that read from the street. Put

a features card by the sink and in the primary: "New 200-amp panel •
EV outlet • 36″ range with exterior vent • Level-5 wall finish • 7.5″ LVP
• 3000K throughout • Quiet-close hinges • Solid-core bedroom doors."
Buyers don't have to know what Level-5 means to feel it.

During showings, make it easy to say yes. Provide disclosures up
front, inspection report if you've done a pre-list, and sample as-is ad-
dendum language that plays nice with lenders. Ask your listing agent
to respond to all inquiries same day and to call every agent who
showed by Sunday evening with a polite nudge: "Offer window closes
tomorrow at 5; seller is prioritizing as-is + gap." That single call often
adds five offers to your pile.

When the offers land, grade by net + friction: price, appraisal gap,
inspection posture, loan type, close speed, rent-back, and lender credibility. A slightly lower price with a real gap and a local lender can
be a higher certainty of close, which is the highest number of all. We
don't fall in love with price; we fall in love with probability.

The Perfect Deal – Narrative Walkthrough You Can Copy

*You buy control, not a fairy tale. Through your Discount Note Company,
you acquire a $300,000 face-value note for $75,000 (25¢ on the dollar) on a
home with $380,000 fair value. Your Real Estate Investment Company steps
in as the adult in the room—offers $6,000 cash-for-keys to the occupant,
drafts a humane goodwill share of $19,800 (say $300 × 66 months paid), and
earns a $5,000 admin fee for deed-in-lieu, releases, and recording. Title cleans
up; neighbors exhale; you create a future referral.*

*Hard numbers now: $105,800 all-in to market-ready title ($75,000 +
$30,800). Your General Contractor Company prices the scope at $61,000 to
the market standard, delivers it for $45,750, and keeps a $15,250 margin. For
deal math, you still carry the $61,000 because that's the value the buyer is
purchasing. Your project basis sits at $166,800 on a house that shows like
$380,000.*

*You list at $369,000 to create a crowd, announce 4% to buyer's broker for
full-price+ in week one, and include a $2,000 buyer credit for personal up-*

grades at full-price+. Traffic hits. By Monday you're staring at nine offers and a clean $387,500 cash with a two-week close and no inspection repairs. You accept, grin, and breathe. Commission at 7% and standard seller costs at ~1.5% slide off the top, and you land about $352,500 net to the deal.

Subtract your basis ($166,800) and you're holding roughly $186K of flip profit—plus $15,250 to your GC company and $5,000 to your REI company already tucked into Hip National Bank. The former owner leaves with dignity and dollars; agents leave with stories about "the seller who does it right"; and your brand becomes the one buyers rush to see first. That's how a contract-controlled exit feels.

Buyers don't pay for "expensive"; they pay for "effortless." Effortless is a thousand tiny pre-decisions you make so they don't have to. Match lighting temperature across fixtures. Align handle sizes across doors and drawers. Scale tile to the room so grout lines feel calm. Use one paint white for ceilings, trims, and walls but shift the sheen to create subtle depth. It's the cheapest luxury in the game.

Don't fall for the "surprise" narrative. Surprises are often just unmade decisions dressed up as fate. Decide the spec, decide the schedule, decide the story—then write the paper that makes everyone else agree. When the paper is strong, the project is quiet. Quiet projects close high and fast.

And please, don't try to "save" money at the finish line by stiffarming the people who *bring* you the buyer. Pay the buyer's agent like a partner and they'll behave like one. You'll recover the spend in days saved, bids battled, and appraisals anchored. Retail flipping isn't about squeezing pennies; it's about designing the net.

The game is simple: control the contract, respect the craft, and choreograph the launch. Do those three and you won't need a lucky market—your outcomes will be repeatable, generous, and fast. That's how we sell like storytellers and bank like builders.

Your Simple Retail System (Run It Every Time)

- **Plan:** Build your Finish & Feature Matrix from the top two sold comps; set your exciting price and launch calendar.
- **Paper:** GC + subs on *your* contract; milestones, LDs, bonuses; latent-conditions protocol; daily photos.
- **Produce:** Hit the four value zones (entry, kitchen, primary, backyard), keep spec coherent, and pre-book clean/photos.
- **Promote:** Pro photos, floor plan, upgrade list, agent-only notes, buyer-agent bonus, $2,000 buyer credit (full-price+).
- **Proceed:** Offer deadline, triage by net + friction, counter for as-is + gap, hand the appraiser your proof.

Do this once and you'll see the difference. Do it three times and agents will chase *you*. Do it ten times and your flips will start selling off your name alone. That's not hype—that's momentum you built on purpose.

Workbook: Module 10

Buy • Repair • Flip (Retail)
The Blueprint for Turning Sawdust into Cash Flow

"Do your planning and prepare your field before building your house."
(Proverbs 24:27 NLT)

Use this workbook to turn the module into action. Move top-to-bottom; don't skip steps. Keep pages unnumbered.

1) Mindset to Motion — Confidence Builder
Purpose: convert fear into a repeatable system.

- **Quick reflection (write 3–5 sentences each):**
  1. What's the one fear that's kept you from starting?
  2. What specific decision today will neutralize that fear?
  3. What will your first "win" look like in 30 days?
- **Commitment statement (fill in):**
  "I am not building houses; I am building contracts. My hammer is paper, my saw is signature, and profit is designed—never hoped for."

2) Deal Math — Buy Smart or Don't Buy
Purpose: prove profit before closing.

- **Target property (address / link):** _____
- **Top sold comp (≤90 days, same bed/bath/SF):** $_____ (MLS #_____)
- **ARV (after-repair value) you can defend:** $_____
- **Repair budget to match comp quality:** $_____
- **Hidden cost reserve (title, liens, surprises):** $_____ (min 10% of repairs)
- **All-in basis (purchase + repairs + soft costs):** $_____
- **Required margin (≥20% of ARV):** $_____
- **Go/No-Go rule (circle one):** GO / NO-GO
- **Walk-away line (price at which you pass):** $_____

Hidden-cost scan (check/price each):
[ ] Title defects ◈ Liens/Judgments ◈ Roof ◈ Foundation ◈ Septic/Sewer
[ ] Electrical panel/wiring ◈ HVAC age ◈ Unpermitted additions ◈ Drainage/grade

[ ] Insurance risks (polybutylene, aluminum, knob-and-tube, cast iron)

3) Finish & Feature Matrix — Build What Sells
Purpose: spec to the top comp, not to taste.

- **Comp anchors (two best closed sales):** MLS #_____ / MLS #_____
- **Matrix (fill with SKUs or specs):**
    - Flooring: species/width/length: _____ | Unit $/SF: _____
    - Paint: wall/trim sheen & color: _____ | Lighting temp: 2700–3000K
    - Kitchen: cabinet profile, 36" range? exterior-vent hood? island size: _____
    - Baths: tile size/patterns, grout color, glass type: _____
    - Doors/trim: style, height, hardware family/finish: _____
    - Curb appeal: door color, house numbers, lighting, mulch/planting plan: _____

Signature flourish (one brag point under $1,500): _____

4) Scope, Sequence, Schedule — Where Pros Make Money
Purpose: materials don't make money—sequence does.

- **Critical path (dates):** Demo → Rough MEP → Inspections → Close-in → Drywall/Texture → Trim/Doors → Paint → Cabinets/Tops → Tile → Fixtures →
  Final Clean → Photos → List
- **Milestones & draws (tie $ to visible deliverables):**
  M1 *% Demo complete* → $__ | M2 *% Rough-in pass* → $__ |
  M3 Cabinets set → $_____ | M4 Substantial completion → $_____
- **Daily photo log (due 6 p.m. to shared folder):**
  Front, kitchen, each bath, panel/HVAC/plumbing, backyard.
- **Morning stand-up (10 minutes):**
  Yesterday finished: ____ | Today's deliverable: ____ | Blockers: ____

5) Contractor Control — Paper That Protects Profit
Purpose: eliminate "TV surprises."

- **Your contract includes (check all):**
  [ ] Fixed-price lump sum [ ] Start/finish dates [ ] Daily liquidated damages
  [ ] Early-finish quality bonus [ ] Detailed scope & exclusions
  [ ] No substitutions without written SKU approval
  [ ] Latent-conditions clause: 48-hour notice + photos + unit pricing or deemed included

[ ] Clean site & end-of-day checklists [ ] Insurance/worker's comp on file
[ ] Pay apps tied to milestones [ ] Lien waivers with every draw
- **Three bids compared on the same scope:**
  GC A $_____ | GC B $_____ | GC C $_____ | Selected: _____ Why: _____

6) Price to Create a Crowd — Not to Fish for One Buyer
Purpose: velocity beats stubborn asking.

- **Fair market value (FMV):** $_____
- **Exciting launch price (92–97% of FMV):** $_____
- **Offer window:** Live (Wed/Thu) → Opens (Sat/Sun) → Deadline (Mon 5 p.m.)
- **Performance commission (agent-only notes draft):**
  "Total 7% commission: 3% list / 4% buyer for full-price+ accepted in first 7 days."
- **Buyer incentive (at full-price+):**
  $2,000 seller credit for personal upgrades (lender-approved).

7) Realtor Alignment — Make Pros Your Partners
Purpose: become the listing every agent shows first.

- **Listing package (provide at launch):**
  [ ] Floor plan [ ] Upgrade/permit binder [ ] Roof/HVAC ages [ ] Utility sheet
  [ ] Before/after photos [ ] Seller disclosures
- **Agent-only remarks (paste your draft):**
- **Follow-up cadence:**
  Listing agent calls all showing agents by Sunday 7 p.m.
  Script: "Offer window Monday 5 p.m.; seller prioritizes as-is + appraisal gap up to $____; local lender preferred; thank you for showing."

8) Launch Like a Pro — 7-Day Market Blitz
Purpose: one "new" moment—treat it like a product release.

- **Calendar:**
  Day –3 "Coming Soon" live | Day 0 go live (pro photos) | Day 1 broker open |
  Day 2–3 stacked opens (tight windows to create energy) | Day 4 offer deadline
- **Show condition checklist:**
  [ ] Hotel-clean [ ] Balanced lighting (3000K) [ ] Neutral scent [ ] Music low
  [ ] Fresh mulch & door paint [ ] Crisp staging [ ] Feature cards (what's new)

9) Offer Triage — Choose Net + Certainty
Purpose: probability of close > headline price.

- **Scorecard (1–5 each, total /25):**
  Price ___ | Appraisal gap ___ | Inspection posture ___ | Close speed ___ |
  Lender/local credibility ___ → **Winner:** Offer #___ Total: ___/25
- **Counter template (fill and reuse):**
  "Seller accepts price $, **appraisal gap up to $**, information-only inspection,
  14-day close, buyer credit $2,000 at full-price+ honored."

10) Appraisal Packet — Give the Evidence Audience Proof
Purpose: help them justify your number.

- **Island binder (leave on kitchen):**
  [ ] Best two sold comps (highlight adjustments)
  [ ] Before/after photos (by room)
  [ ] Upgrade list with costs (panel, HVAC, insulation, vented hood, etc.)
  [ ] Permit finals / receipts
  [ ] Energy and safety upgrades list
  [ ] Summary: "Why this home is superior to [Comp A/B]"

11) The Perfect Deal — Your Numbers (Copy & Fill)
Acquisition via note (face value): $_____ @ ¢/$ = $_

Title perfection package (cash-for-keys, admin, filings): $_____

Remodel budget (market): $_____ | GC internal cost: $_____

GC company margin captured: $_____

Project basis (carry market remodel #): $_____

List price: $_____ | Accepted offer: $_____ | Buyer credit: $_____

Total commission (target 7%): $_____ | Seller costs (~1.5%): $_____

Net to deal: $_____ | Profit (net – basis): $_____

Plus company margins (REI admin + GC margin): $_____

Total Money Machine outcome: $_____

12) Post-Close Debrief — Turn Lessons into Systems

Purpose: compound skill.

- Three wins I will repeat: 1) _____ 2) _____   3) _____
- Three frictions I will fix (with process change): 1) _____ 2) _____
  3) _____
- Spec edits to matrix (what stays / what goes): _____
- Vendor roster update (keepers / cuts): _____

13) KPI Dashboard — Run the Business by Numbers
Enter after each project; watch trendlines.

- Days from close to list: ___
- Days on market: ___
- Over-ask delta: $___ (%) ___
- Change orders as % of budget: ___%
- Carry cost per day: $___
- Gross margin (net ÷ sale price): ___%
- Return on basis (profit ÷ basis): ___%

14) 30-Day Action Plan — From Reader to Operator
Week 1: Pull five target zips; save top 10 sold comps per zip; build baseline Finish & Feature Matrix.

Week 2: Interview 3 GCs on *your* contract; gather bids on a sample scope; pick your #1 and #2.

Week 3: Meet two top listing agents in your area; review your launch playbook; align on performance commissions.

Week 4: Walk three candidate properties; run the Deal Math sheet; submit at least one disciplined offer.
Accountability partner (name/phone): _____

First project launch goal date: _____

15) Bonus Question — The Builder's Edge

Answer in 5–7 sentences.

What is one invisible upgrade you will include on every flip (panel amperage, exterior-vented hood, insulation R-value, solid-core doors, etc.), and how will you

translate that invisible value into an on-market premium using your features sheet and appraisal packet?

16) Prayer of Stewardship

"Lord, make me faithful with people, paper, and property. Let my work restore value, bless families, and reflect Your excellence. Establish the work of my hands."

Print-Ready Checklists (tear-off or copy)
Pre-Offer: comps pulled • ARV set • repair budget • reserves • hidden costs scanned • walk-away line set.

Pre-Demo: permits • matrix locked • materials ordered • schedule posted • insurance verified.

During Build: daily photos • morning stand-up • milestone draws • no substitutions • tidy site.

Go-Live: pro photos • floor plan • upgrade binder • agent-only notes • commission perks • open house schedule.

Under Contract: appraisal packet • inspection strategy • lender updates • title cleared • closing checklist.
Run this workbook once to feel the difference.
Run it three times and agents will start chasing *you.*
Run it ten times and your flips will sell off your name alone—that's momentum designed on purpose.

11

Module 11: "Spread" Produces Your Wealth

Credit Produces Assets, Which Produces More Credit
Lend What You Borrow (Across Multiple Banks)
Realty Solutions Manager Training 501

The Pivot: Stop Consuming Credit, Start Producing It

Most people borrow for consumption and let tomorrow's paycheck service yesterday's dinner. That's a treadmill, not a path. Your shift is simple and profound: only borrow to acquire assets that cash-flow quickly enough to repay the line and leave profit behind. When you do that on purpose, your credit becomes inventory, not indenture. Used this way, credit is a product you sell at a spread—just like the bank.

Think like a builder of systems, not a buyer of things. If a dollar of borrowed credit can be placed into a contract that returns that dollar plus a fee within 30–120 days, you've turned liability into inventory and inventory into income. Repeat that cycle and your track record earns larger limits and better terms. Credit → Asset → Cash Flow → More Credit is not a slogan; it's the engine you'll run on paper.

Here's the sanity check you'll apply to every deal: "Will this place-ment of credit clear itself and pay me extra within a short, defined window?" If the answer isn't a clean yes (with documentation), that deal is consumption wearing a mask. You'll pass. Your discipline, not the lender's generosity, is what keeps our Hip National Banks full.

From here on, you are a Currency Circulator. Your future is not "How do I get cheaper debt?" but "Which assets deserve my credit to-day?" That mindset alone will save you from 90% of the traps that keep borrowers broke.

Earn Like a Banker: Spread, Velocity, and Small Beginnings

Banks don't chase jackpots—they master the art of consistent, microscopic profit executed with mechanical precision. Their entire empire runs on fractions of a cent: overdraft fees, interchange fees, transaction spreads, and overnight lending interest. A single quarter in fees per account per month sounds trivial, until you realize that same quarter, multiplied by millions of accounts, becomes billions in net gain. That's the banker's secret—they never gamble with outcomes; they engineer inevitabilities. To "earn like a banker," you must adopt that mindset. Small profits done perfectly, over and over, outperform risky windfalls done rarely or recklessly.

You'll do this ethically and intentionally by focusing on spread and velocity—the twin engines that feed Hip National Bank. Spread is the difference between what it costs you to borrow and what you earn lending it out. Velocity is how often you can repeat that cycle within a year. For example, a 4% origination fee and 1.5% monthly interest on a 60-day deal produces a clean, predictable 7% every two months. Do it six times a year, and your effective annual yield exceeds 40%—with-out ever increasing risk. The difference isn't magic; it's math. Velocity compounds capital faster than size. If a $100,000 credit slice creates $6,000 in net gain every 60 days, that same capital, properly rede-ployed, can generate $36,000–$40,000 annually, while still returning home to your Hip National Bank after every cycle. The pros don't let money rest—they keep it in motion under controlled conditions.

This rhythm is the heartbeat of professional lending. The best bankers don't fall in love with large returns; they fall in love with perfect timing. They understand that every day money sits idle is a day it's unemployed. That's why your job as a Currency Circulator is to keep money circulating, never stranded. Instead of chasing "home-run" deals that promise double-digit returns but require twelve-month holds, aim for steady, bite-sized rotations backed by collateral and clear exits. Each rotation becomes another turn of your flywheel—small, safe, and sure. The secret isn't in the size of your deal; it's in the consistency of your system.

And here's where reputation becomes your invisible equity. In the banking world, credibility is currency. You can't buy it—you have to earn it "on time, every time." Lenders don't expand limits because they like you; they do it because you perform like clockwork. Never miss a payment, never overextend, and always deliver what your paperwork promises. Once banks see your system working flawlessly—paper moving, profits cycling, credit lines paid down and renewed—they'll extend more rope. That rope isn't for hanging yourself; it's for building another flywheel. Every banker started small, from pennies to profits, by protecting their reputation as fiercely as their capital. That's the real compound interest—trust multiplied by performance.

Finally, document everything. A real banker's deal reads like a foregone conclusion before it even starts. Every transaction deserves a one-page summary that shows the advance, origination, timeline, collateral, and exit. If it doesn't add up cleanly on paper, it won't add up in practice. The more you document, the more control you maintain, and the more predictable your cash flow becomes. In time, you'll realize the secret isn't getting rich overnight—it's never having a broke day again. That's what it means to earn like a banker: small beginnings, perfect execution, and unstoppable rhythm.

The "Lend What You Borrow" Playbook (5 Non-Negotiables)

Rule 1 — Borrow only for assets. If a borrowed dollar can't put money back in the account that paid for it—quickly and predictably—it's not an asset, it's a souvenir. Your first screening question for any use of credit is ruthless and simple: "Will this purchase generate enough cash, within my target window, to cover debt service and leave a surplus?" If you can't show that on paper before funding, you're financing emotion, not enterprise. Assets pay you; consumption invoices you.

Treat every proposed use of credit like a mini business plan. Write the timeline (days, not vibes), the revenue mechanism (rent, resale, fee, or interest), and the math for service + surplus. Identify the choke points—what could delay the cash—and name your backup exits. If you can point to at least two clean exits and one conservative breakeven, proceed; if not, pass. Discipline at this gate is what keeps you liquid when everyone else is "waiting for things to turn."

Build a hard rule into your operating rhythm: no swipe without a service schedule. That means you know the monthly payment, the total carrying cost (interest, insurance, holding, and closing friction), and the precise inflow that will retire the debt and tip profit back into Hip National Bank. If the inflow depends on "finding the right buyer" or "hoping the season picks up," the deal isn't ready; tighten the model or lower the basis until the numbers answer for themselves. Remember: the bank pays you for speed and certainty—borrow only for assets that deliver both.

Rule 2 — Take collateral or control. Every real lender—public, private, or institutional—operates on one foundational law: control is safety, and paper is power. You never lend, partner, or advance capital without either taking possession of an asset or securing a claim against it. Promises, handshakes, and "trust me" stories are not collateral; they are invitations to loss. True professionals protect their downside before they ever discuss the upside, and they do it in writing. Whether it's a deed, title, lien, or assignment, you must have something you can touch, transfer, or enforce if things go sideways. The borrower's intent doesn't secure your investment—the paperwork does.

Control comes in many forms, and not all of it requires ownership. You can file a UCC-1 lien on inventory or receivables, record a first right of refusal on property, or execute an assignment of proceeds on a pending contract. These documents don't make you an enemy; they make you a professional. When the money moves, the paper decides who gets paid first. You want to be at the front of that line—not waiting behind unsecured creditors. Even something as simple as holding title in escrow, having dual-signature control on a project account, or setting up a collateral trust gives you leverage without confrontation. It tells the other party, "I'm not guessing. I'm governing."

The reason "paper beats promises" is because contracts survive personality. People forget, change, and panic—but recorded agreements do not. Your UCC filing will outlast a handshake. Your deed-in-lieu will outlast a voicemail apology. Control gives you calm in chaos, because you know your claim is enforceable and your position is protected. This is the quiet confidence of real bankers: they don't need to threaten, chase, or plead. They simply point to the document that says, "This asset is pledged." Control isn't aggression—it's stewardship. When you master that discipline, you stop hoping to get paid and start expecting to.

Rule 3 — Price the spread, not the dream. The biggest mistake new lenders and investors make is chasing the fantasy of giant returns instead of the reality of steady spreads. Wealth is not built in spikes—it's built in rhythm. Your margin doesn't come from the dream of doubling your money overnight; it comes from the consistent difference between what you pay for money and what you charge for its use. That's the spread—the quiet, predictable profit that keeps your Hip

National Bank full while everyone else is swinging for home runs and striking out. Boring deals that perform are far more valuable than exciting deals that explode.

Your profit lives in two places: origination and time-in-use. Origination is your fee for creating opportunity—setting up the loan, structuring the contract, and managing risk. Time-in-use is the interest you earn while your capital is deployed. Together, these two create a reliable yield machine. The key is to price them fairly, consistently, and repeatedly. For example, charging a 3% origination fee and earning 1.25% per month on a 90-day loan produces far more cumulative wealth than chasing one 25% "jackpot" that might never close. The professional doesn't care about the size of the deal; he cares about the certainty of the spread.

Tight and repeatable beats loud and risky every time. When you master this discipline, your lending model becomes scalable. You know your exact input, output, and timeline. Your numbers stop being random—they become mechanical. And that's where freedom begins. A real banker never prays for a miracle; he plans for a margin. You're not here to dream—you're here to design a spread that pays you on time, every time. Dreams fade. Systems pay.

Rule 4 — Pre-plan the exit. The deal isn't real until the money comes home. Every seasoned lender knows this: you don't get paid when you fund—you get paid when you're repaid. The most dangerous part of any transaction isn't the front end where excitement lives; it's the back end where silence hides. You must know, before the ink dries, how the other side will perform—specifically. Will the payoff come from a resale, a refinance, or the turn of a receivable? Who's responsible for the trigger event? What's the timeline, and what's the safety valve if it doesn't happen? If you can't answer these questions clearly, you're gambling, not lending.

Pre-planning the exit means mapping every repayment path with precision and paperwork. If the repayment is tied to a sale, you need proof of market demand, pricing comps, and escrow control. If it's tied to a refinance, you want to know the borrower's lender, credit position, and underwriting readiness. And if repayment depends on accounts receivable or business revenue, demand verifiable documentation of cash flow and the customer's payment history. You're not being difficult—you're being diligent. This isn't mistrust; it's management. The same way a pilot doesn't take off without knowing where the landing strip is, you never fund without knowing where your repayment will touch down.

The pros don't hope for exits—they engineer them. They set up automatic repayments, escrow holds, and pre-signed releases that trigger once conditions are met. They build redundancy into every deal—two exits minimum, three if the ticket size warrants it. Why? Because hope doesn't deposit into Hip National Bank. Only performance does. Pre-planning the exit transforms your capital from "at risk" to "in motion." And once you master this rule, every dollar you lend becomes a disciplined soldier with a return ticket home.

Rule 5 — Obey the map. There's a fine line between power and peril in the lending world, and that line is drawn in ink by regulators. The difference between a builder and a pirate is paperwork. Commercial versus consumer lending laws, licensing requirements, usury limits, and mandatory disclosures all form the map that keeps your Money Machine legitimate and sustainable. Ignorance of those boundaries isn't an excuse—it's a liability. When you obey the map, you build a business that can scale safely and attract real partners. When you ignore it, you build a house of cards that collapses the first time someone asks for your credentials.

Commercial lending and consumer lending may look similar on the surface, but legally, they live in different worlds. Commercial lending is typically business-to-business, governed by contract law and the Uniform Commercial Code (UCC), giving both parties more freedom to negotiate terms. Consumer lending, on the other hand, is tightly regulated under federal laws like the Truth in Lending Act (TILA), the Real Estate Settlement Procedures Act (RESPA), and the Fair Debt Collection Practices Act (FDCPA). The government's primary concern is protecting the consumer—because to them, you're the bank now. That means you must know your usury limits (maximum legal interest rates) in your state, provide written disclosures if required, and avoid advertising or operating in a way that suggests you are an unlicensed lender when your structure doesn't yet support that claim. Staying compliant doesn't kill creativity—it keeps your creativity alive long enough to pay dividends.

The best builders know that wealth built outside the lines doesn't last. You can make a fast dollar by cutting corners, but you'll never build generational credibility that way. Integrity is the invisible infrastructure of every real empire. The goal isn't just to make money—it's to keep it, grow it, and pass it forward without fear of audit or accusation. That means having clear agreements, working through licensed brokers when required, maintaining proper disclosures, and charging rates that make sense within the law. Remember: the pirates get headlines, but the builders get legacies. The blueprint of prosperity only works when the foundation is lawful. The map isn't there to restrict you—it's there to keep your Money Machine running strong long after others have run aground.

Write these on the inside cover of your notebook. The playbook is what keeps you steady when a shiny "opportunity" winks at you. There's always another deal. There isn't another reputation.

Build Your Credit Stack (Across Multiple Banks)

Think in layers, not in one "magic" line. Diversified relationships reduce concentration risk and increase total capacity. Target three buckets, as easy as *A,B,C*, and build them in parallel with different institutions.

Operating / Business LOC (Bank 1):

What it is (and why you want it). An Operating Line of Credit (LOC) is a revolving credit facility issued to your operating company—not you personally—that you can draw, repay, and redraw as often as needed within the limit. Think of it as your working-capital shock absorber: it smooths cash gaps between outlay and inflow so projects never stall. Because it's short-term and business-purpose, banks price it better than credit cards and approve faster than term loans when you show repeatable use. Your goal isn't to "carry" debt—your goal is to move it: draw, deploy into a secured, near-term deal, then clear it early to earn trust and reset capacity.

What you use it for (tight, repeatable placements). Keep this LOC reserved for small, secured, high-velocity tasks: earnest-money deposits, option fees, appraisal/inspection orders, short rehab draws before reimbursement, trade advances for materials with lien rights, or bridging receivables you already control. These are placements where paper beats promises: you hold a signed purchase agreement, lien rights, or assignment of proceeds that converts quickly to cash. Examples: $15,000 EMD on a note acquisition you'll wholesale in 14 days; $28,000 cabinet/roof package advanced to a licensed GC with a recorded subcontractor agreement and waiver sequence; $40,000 trade advance to a supplier secured by UCC-1 on materials and assignment of the buyer's escrow disbursement.

How to structure it (bank-friendly and borrower-smart). Ask for a revolving LOC with a 12–24-month term, interest-only monthly, tied to Prime/SOFR + a modest spread, and a clean-down requirement (e.g., zero balance 30 consecutive days per year). Provide a simple borrowing base (AR + cash equivalents) or light collateral (UCC on company assets) to speed approval; avoid pledging real estate here—save property for longer paper. Keep personal guarantees limited or sunset after performance milestones (e.g., PG burns off at

12 months of on-time payments). Add online draw capability, ACH push to escrow, and same-day wire privileges so you can move with broker speed.

How to run it (utilization rhythm and reporting). Target a 30–60 day rotation per draw: money out with paperwork in hand, money back with fee in pocket. Keep utilization in the 30–60% band—enough activity to show life, enough headroom to pounce on opportunities. Repay early whenever the exit hits; banks love early paydowns more than big balances. Send a one-page monthly dashboard to your banker (balances, aged AR, pipeline, next 60-day exits). When they can "see" your machine turning, they push for bigger limits without you asking.

Controls that protect profit (and your reputation). Pair every draw with a Deal Sheet before funds leave: purpose, collateral/control (EMD receipt, UCC, lien waiver chain, assignment), exit source and date, projected spread, and kill switch (what you do if Plan A slips). Require counterparties to sign pay-when-paid acknowledgments and pre-authorize escrow to wire your repayment at closing. Use a lockbox/sweep: all proceeds from placements land in a dedicated deposit account that automatically sweeps to reduce the LOC first, then releases surplus to operating cash. This habit keeps you "on time, every time," which is how limits grow.

Numbers you can live by (example cadence). Limit: $250,000. Average draw: $35,000 for 45 days at Prime + 2%. You price a 3% origination + 1.5%/month on the outgoing paper, secured by assignment of closing proceeds. Net spread per turn $\approx$ $1,575–$2,100 after interest. Five such placements per 60-day cycle produce ~$8,000–$10,000 net, returning capital to zero, resetting capacity, and feeding Hip National Bank—without tying up a dollar longer than necessary.

What not to do (common rookie leaks). Don't finance consumption, long rehabs, or speculative marketing from the Operating LOC—that's how working capital becomes working worry. Don't leave balances idle "just in case"; unused debt erodes discipline and invites fees. Don't skip lien waivers, UCCs, or written assignments; verbal assurances are not collateral. And don't surprise your banker—bad news gets cheaper the earlier you share it, especially when you already attached Plan B in your Deal Sheet.

Run this line like a metronome—tight draws, papered control, early repayments—and Bank 1 will become your cheerleader. Then, when you ask Banks 2 and 3 for purpose-built credit (term paper, warehouse, SBLC), you're not applying as a stranger—you're scaling as a proven operator.

Collateralized LOC via Non-Interest CD (Bank 2, Private/Business Banking):

What it is (and why it exists). A collateralized line of credit is a revolving (or sometimes draw-down) facility secured 100% by your cash on deposit—typically a non-interest-bearing CD/time deposit that the bank can perfect a first lien against. Banks love this paper because loss-given-default is essentially zero; their credit committee treats it like lending against T-bills. In exchange for that certainty, they'll extend a larger limit, better pricing, and simpler covenants than they would on an unsecured line. You're trading the tiny yield you could earn on the CD for leverage + capacity you can redeploy at much higher, controlled returns.

Why you use it (capacity without drama). This is the cleanest way to scale when you have "past labor" (cash) but don't want it sitting idle. The bank earns interest on a fully secured facility; you earn spread by placing draws into short, collateralized deals you control (notes, EMDs, vendor advances), then sweeping proceeds back to zero. Because the bank's risk is minimal, underwriting is fast and covenant light—ideal when you need reliable firepower that won't get pulled mid-project. It also signals sophistication: you're operating like a treasury desk, not a consumer borrower.

How to structure it (ask for these terms). Open a non-interest CD/time deposit (12–60 months) in the private or business banking channel; authorize a control agreement granting the bank a first lien. Negotiate a non-callable LOC for 70–90% of the deposit (80% is common; push for 90% if your relationship is strong). Tenor 12–24 months, revolving, interest-only monthly, priced at SOFR/Prime + 1.5%–3.0%. Require no borrowing base tests, no MAC ("material adverse change"), and only two covenants: keep the CD intact and pay on time. Add (a) same-day wires, (b) ACH draw capability, and (c) a 30-day annual clean-down you can plan for during a quiet month.

Operational mechanics (keep it automatic). Pair the LOC with a dedicated deposit account and a sweep/lockbox: all deal proceeds land there and auto-sweep nightly to reduce the line before releasing surplus to operating cash. Every draw must be stapled to a one-page Deal Sheet (purpose, amount, fees you'll earn, collateral/control, exit source/date, contingencies). Use it for short, secured placements you can evidence: assignments of closing proceeds, UCC-1s on inventory/ materials, first-right agreements, or recorded liens. Rhythm targets: 30–60-day turns, 30–60% average utilization, early paydowns whenever exits hit.

Negotiation levers (how to get 90% advance and better pricing). Bring relationship weight: merchant services, payroll, and your operating account balances—banks price across the relationship. Offer visibility: monthly snapshot of draws/exits and a quarterly pipeline call (10 minutes). Ask for a tiered limit (e.g., $500K Day 1, auto-step to $750K after 6 on-time months) and a PG sunset (personal guarantee burns down or falls off after 12 months spotless performance). If they push for an interest-bearing CD, trade them a longer term on the deposit for a lower spread on the LOC; your goal is cheaper borrowing, not CD pennies.

Numbers you can live by (two quick scenarios). Scenario A — 80% advance: You place $250,000 into a 24-month non-interest CD. Bank gives you an $200,000 LOC at Prime + 2.0%. You deploy $120,000 chunks for 45 days at a 3% origination + 1.5%/month to a rehabber, secured by assignment of proceeds and UCC. Interest cost ≈ $900; gross fee $4,800; net per turn ≈ $3,900. Four turns per year on two concurrent placements ≈ $31,200 net—an annualized return on your parked $250K that dwarfs CD yield. **Scenario B** — 90% advance with velocity: You lock $500,000 and negotiate $450,000 LOC at SOFR + 2.25%. You run five $75,000 placements for 30–40 days, each at 2% origination + 1.25%/month, secured by assignments of receivables. Per turn, interest ≈ $844; fees ≈ $2,875; net ≈ $2,031 per placement. Five concurrent placements, eight turns/year ≈ $81,000–$90,000 net—while your principal never leaves the CD.

Risk controls (protect the deposit and your reputation). Never commingle personal spending with this facility. Limit uses to asset-backed, paper-controlled deals. Maintain a contingency lane (unused headroom) equal to one average draw so a delayed exit doesn't trigger covenant breach. Pre-authorize escrow agents (in writing) to wire directly to your LOC for paydown at close. Calendar the clean-down month and avoid new draws inside that window. If a counterparty slips, execute Plan B (backup buyer, factor the receivable, or swap collateral) within 48 hours. Banks forgive delays; they do not forgive silence.

What not to do (leaks that kill limits). Don't chase yield with long, speculative placements; this line is for velocity, not adventures. Don't pledge the CD twice (e.g., as collateral at another bank); the intercreditor headache will freeze your line. Don't request frequent amendments; negotiate flexibility up front. And never let the CD pay interest you then "reinvest" at the same bank—your leverage is the bargain: they keep CD yield, you keep borrowing cost low.

Graduation path (turn one line into a stack). Run this perfectly for two quarters and ask for: (1) a limit increase or second, parallel facility for a sister entity; (2) a warehouse line for note purchases (non-revolving, asset-tied); and (3) a standby letter of credit (SBLC) capacity for bids/EMDs. The message you're sending: "I trade yield for leverage, document everything, and repay early." Banks reward that with more rope—and you spin it into more flywheels for Hip National Bank.

Specialized Capacity (Bank 3 or Lender Partner):
What it is (the "semi-truck" lane, not the daily driver). Specialized capacity is credit built for bigger, heavier moves: a warehouse line to temporarily finance assets you aggregate and resell (e.g., mortgage/contract-for-deed/consumer note pools), or a standby instrument (SBLC/LOC) to secure large purchases, bids, or settlement obligations. Unlike a general LOC (cash-in, cash-out), this lane is asset-tied and exit-defined. The lender advances against eligible paper you control; you repay from a takeout buyer or refinancing event on a fixed timeline. Think of it as a conveyor: assets roll on, get financed, get sold, line returns to zero—repeat.

Why you use it (scale without strangling working capital). Your operating LOC handles earnest money, draws, and short advances. But when a $3.5M pool of mixed notes or a $1M block purchase appears, you don't want to freeze your day-to-day line. A warehouse facility lets you lock inventory fast, enjoy institutional advance rates, and earn spread while you curate, season, or repackage the assets for a higher exit. A standby instrument lets you post proof-of-funds or performance security to control opportunities you couldn't touch with cash alone. You're buying time and positioning—on terms you can model with a calendar.

How a warehouse line is structured (translate bank-speak into operator steps). Expect a borrowing base: the lender advances 65–85% of the eligible asset value (not face value) based on an agreed haircut grid (e.g., 80% LTV 1st liens ≤70% ITV, 60% for performing 2nds, 0% for missing docs until cured). You'll maintain a loan tape with fields they specify (UPB, rate, PTI, FICO, LTV, lien position, maturity, doc status). Funds draw into a controlled account; payoffs flow back to that account and auto-sweep against the line. Pricing is typically SOFR/Prime + 3.0–6.0% plus a line fee (0.5–1.0%/yr) and transaction/wire fees. Tenor is 12 months revolving with a 90–180 day max dwell per asset and a clean-down (return to a % of commitment once/ quarter). Your job: keep dwell low, cures fast, and takeouts punctual.

Eligibility & haircuts (the grid that makes or breaks economics). Before signing, push to lock the grid in the term sheet: what counts as eligible and at what advance. For example: Performing 1sts with full collateral files and verified pay history at 80–85% of purchase price; Reperforming with 6 months clean at 70–75%; Non-performers only if you have a documented conversion plan (trial payment plan, deed-in-lieu pipeline) at 50–60%; CFDs/land contracts with recorded interests and taxes current at 60–70%. Ask for cure windows (e.g., 30–45 days to replace missing assignments or riders) so you can draw while you finish file work. The better your tape discipline, the better your advance.

Standby instruments (SBLC/standby LOC) — when the seller wants certainty, not stories. Sellers of large assets (note pools, equipment lots, development pads) often require bank paper proving you can close or pay damages if you don't. An SBLC is the bank's promise to pay the beneficiary upon stipulated conditions; you collateralize it with cash, securities, or a back-to-back facility. Use it to (a) win auctions, (b) negotiate better pricing ("hard" security beats soft proof-of-funds), and (c) bridge from award to warehouse funding. Price is usually 1.0–3.0% per 12 months of face amount, billed upfront; structure it for only the time you need (90–120 days) and align the draw conditions narrowly (e.g., only if you fail to close by X date without seller breach).

Operational rhythm (make it boring and fast). Build a siloed entity for this facility with its own bank accounts, accounting, and reporting. Create a Checklist-to-Cash workflow: (1) LOI with seller; (2) preliminary tape scrub; (3) warehouse credit memo with projected haircuts and margin; (4) draw request; (5) collateral file intake & cure list; (6) marketing deck to takeout buyers; (7) executed PSA; (8) payoff & sweep; (9) post-mortem. Target ≤45 days asset dwell for performing pools and ≤90 days for re-perf/cleanup trades. The profit lives in velocity + basis lift: buy at $0.52, finance $0.40, add value (cures, clean pay history, boarded servicing), exit at $0.65–0.72.

Example — $4M commitment, first trade. You win a $2.8M UPB pool of 1st liens (weighted coupon 6.8%, mixed status) at $1.54M (55 cents). Warehouse advance grid yields $1.20M eligible; you wire $340K of your equity to close. Over 60 days you: board to servicing, complete collateral cures (4 lost assignments replaced, 3 payoff statements obtained), push two PTPs to 3 payments, and remarket. Exit at $1.84M (65.7 cents). Line payoff $1.20M, fees/interest $28K, expenses $22K, net to you ≈ $550K before overhead. Line returns to zero; you rinse and repeat with a larger pull. Your equity turns 1.6× in two months—not because the asset was loud, but because the process was tight.

Covenants & reporting (what the lender actually cares about). They want: (1) borrowing base compliance (no over-advances), (2) timely tape updates (weekly is common), (3) collateral custody (bailee letters or approved custodians), (4) insurance/tax status current on secured assets, and (5) no commingling. Give them a Friday package: updated tape, aging by dwell, cures in progress, and forecasted takeouts by date/amount. When an exit slips, tell them before they ask and present Plan B (alternate buyer, price concession math, or refinance).

Risk controls (don't let the tail wag the dog). Refuse pools you can't re-underwrite in five business days. Cap non-performing exposure to a percentage of the borrowing base unless you have an in-house legal/collections engine. Pre-build takeout relationships (two buyers minimum per asset class). Enforce an internal stop-loss: if a trade's basis drifts more than X% or dwell exceeds Y days, you price down and move it—cashflow beats pride. Never use the warehouse to prop up retail flips or long rehabs; that's not its job and breaches purpose-built discipline.

SBLC mechanics (clean, narrow, and short). When issuing an SBLC, insist on: (a) precise draw language (e.g., seller's certificate of your failure to close by Date X with attached escrow letter—no vague "in our judgment" triggers), (b) **expiry** no longer than your realistic close window plus a cushion, and (c) transfer restrictions (non-transferable without your written consent). Fund it via Bank 2's collateralized capacity or cash margin; release immediately upon close or mutual extension. Treat the fee like deal cost; you bought leverage and time at wholesale.

Silo the lanes (how you keep all three partners happy). Bank 1 sees fast, secured operating usage. Bank 2 sees pristine, cash-secured leverage with early paydowns. Bank 3 sees institutional-grade, asset-tied trades with professional reporting and punctual exits. Do not commingle funds, collateral, or purposes across banks. Each partner should feel like they're your #1 in their lane, staring at a clean, boring, high-performing use case. That's how you grow limits without drama—and how your Money Machine graduates from pickup truck to freight train while still stopping on a dime.

The Private Conversation (How to Ask for the Right Line)

You're not asking for favors; you're offering the bank exactly what they want—performing paper and predictable deposits. Keep it short, specific, and professional:

- **Open:** "We operate a contract-driven asset business. We borrow only for short, secured placements and repay on accelerated schedules. I'm here to place a non-interest time deposit and structure a clean credit facility against it for working capital rotations."
- **Offer:** "I'll place $300,000 in a non-interest CD for 36–60 months. In exchange, I'm seeking a non-callable 24-month revolving line sized at 70–85% of the deposit, interest-only monthly, with quarterly clean-downs if required. We'll keep operating accounts here and demonstrate velocity."
- **Use:** "Funds deploy into documented, collateralized transactions—discount note acquisitions and short rehabs—with pre-committed exits. Average turn is 30–120 days. We cross-deposit proceeds here so you see the cycle."
- **Close:** "If this lane performs as expected, we'll expand the deposit and line together. Who on your private/commercial team should I work with to paper this properly?"

Practice that until it's muscle memory. You are not a retail borrower at the counter. You are bringing a lane. Banks fund lanes.

Deployment Example A — Discount Notes + Quick Retail (Using $300,000 of a Line)

Step 1: Buy the paper. You purchase $1,200,000 face value of non-performing notes at $0.25 on the dollar for $300,000 using your collateralized line. Your diligence focuses on title curability, occupancy, and resale bands—not fantasies.

Step 2: Monetize half fast. Sell ~60% of the pool (by face) to another investor at $0.68 on the dollar after a light title tune-up. Proceeds ≈ $1,200,000 × 60% × 0.68 = $489,600. Retire the line advance ($300,000) the same day and bank the remainder net of transaction costs (assume ~6–8% expenses) as working capital.

Step 3: Work the winners. The remaining ~40% ($480,000 face) you convert: cash-for-keys, deed-in-lieu, record, then quick rehab and retail using your operating LOC. You list at an "exciting price" (92% of retail) to create a crowd and let the market bid you up. Assume an average realized value around $441,600, less 7.5% sale/close costs and 18% construction costs on value. Net ≈ $334,000+ across that subset.

Step 4: Close the loop. All proceeds wash through the same bank. Limits rise. Your banker sees what you promised: short placements, fast paydowns, deposits growing. That's how you earn the next tranche.

You didn't "take risk"; you took control—of paper, title, timeline, and price. The line was the spark, not the bonfire.

Deployment Example B — Short Commercial Paper (Velocity Engine)

Offer 30–90 day advances to established small businesses for inventory or receivable gaps. This is commercial, not consumer. You price an origination fee (1–3%) plus monthly interest (1–1.5%) with hard caps set by your jurisdiction. Security can be UCC on inventory/receivables, assignment of proceeds, or purchase-order control. You fund only when there's a contracted take-out (e.g., PO to big-box, invoice to known payer).

Run small, tight tranches: $25k–$100k rotations that clear within a calendar quarter. Ten such placements at $50k each can earn $10k–$20k in aggregate fees and interest in 60–90 days if you keep standards high and paper clean. That outperforms a single "big" deal that drifts six months late.

Your rule: no story deals. Numbers, documents, and dates or no dollars. People respect what you inspect—and pay for it.

Guardrails: Compliance, Ethics, and Staying Power

You win this game by acting like a regulated institution even when you aren't one. Stay in the commercial lane unless you are truly set up for consumer lending with the right licenses, disclosures, servicing posture, and complaint-handling process. Know your state's usury ceilings, exemptions for commercial-purpose loans, and what flips a deal from business credit into a consumer obligation. Build a simple matrix by state: max rate, permitted fees, default interest rules, cure periods, and enforcement limits. When in doubt, hire counsel once to draft your master templates and train you on where the lines are, then keep using the same paper with minimal edits.

Paperwork is protection, not decoration. Every advance should ride on a clean stack: purpose statement (business use), promissory note with interest and fee schedule, security agreement, personal or entity guaranty if appropriate, UCC-1 filing details, and an assignment-of-proceeds or escrow instruction when you expect a sale or refinance payoff. File UCCs correctly in the right jurisdiction, tickle a reminder to continue them before lapse, and release promptly at payoff. Keep a closing checklist and refuse to fund if any box is blank—sloppy today becomes expensive tomorrow. Store executed documents in a secure, searchable vault with version control and off-site backup.

Separate church and state in your books. Maintain dedicated entities for each lane of activity, with their own bank accounts, reconciliations, resolutions, and insurance. Never cross-collateralize your personal life or sweep money between entities without documented intercompany agreements. Produce a monthly packet for yourself like a lender would: trial balance, line-by-line utilization, borrowing-base (if applicable), delinquency aging, cash runway, and covenant confirmations. If an auditor could sit down and understand your business in 30 minutes, you're running tight.

Ethics is an asset class. Set a house rule that you never pressure, you only perform: clear terms up front, no junk fees, no moving goalposts after signing. Treat counterparties with honor, especially when deals stress; you want former borrowers to recommend you because you were fair under pressure. Never game appraisals, spoof proof-of-funds, or mislabel consumer use as commercial; shortcuts stain your brand and spook banks. Your edge is speed, certainty, and paperwork discipline—not sharp practice.

Build operational guardrails that keep small problems small. Keep a liquidity buffer equal to two to three minimum payments across all lines plus thirty days of operating expenses. Track utilization weekly with a red-amber-green dashboard: draw dates, expected exits, collateral status, and days-on-book. Run a monthly line-health review that asks three questions: what slipped, why it slipped, and what the written fix is. If a placement hiccups, over-communicate early with your banker and your borrower, propose options in writing, and update your internal playbook so the miss becomes a system improvement.

Respect the broader compliance perimeter even for commercial credit. Do basic KYC on counterparties, verify control persons, screen for obvious sanctions issues, and document beneficial ownership when entities are thin. Mind privacy and data security: limit who sees tax returns or bank statements, encrypt storage, and purge unneeded PII on a schedule. If you service notes, adopt a simple complaint log, respond within set timeframes, and keep call notes—paper trails calm regulators and judges alike. Quiet operators who run clean files, clean books, and clean exits get invited deeper; noisy ones get boxed out.

Your Operating Cadence (Run Sheet)

Weekly: pipeline review (what's funded, due, and clearing), banker touch (send 3-line update), reconcile all inflows/outflows.

Deal-by-deal one-pager: amount, fee, term, collateral, exit, worst-case cure.

KPIs: average days outstanding, fee yield per 30 days, loss rate (<1%), line utilization band (30–60%), days to recycle proceeds (<5).

Quarterly: ask for the next increment—*after* you've shown the turn. Bring a highlight sheet of deposits, turns, and zero lates.

What to Say "Yes" To (and "No" To)

Yes: short windows, documented exits, assets you can touch (title, inventory, invoices), repeat counterparties, boring profits.

No: consumer bridges, "it's different this time," thin margins with long tails, collateral you can't perfect, personalities over paperwork. You're not trying to impress anyone. You're trying to get paid—quietly, predictably, and on schedule.

Workbook: Module 11

Credit Produces Assets, Which Produces More Credit
"Lend What You Borrow for Profit"
(Realty Solutions Manager Training 501)

1. In your own words, explain what **"Lend What You Borrow"** means.

How does this principle change the way you see credit, borrowing, and opportunity?

Write about how this mindset turns you from a *consumer of debt* into a *creator of income.*

2. List three debts or liabilities you currently hold that could be transformed into assets.
   Describe how you could re-lend, restructure, or repurpose each one for profit.

Section 2 — The Banker's Five Rules
Rewrite the five core rules in your own language and describe how you will apply each one.
Explain the habits or disciplines you will need to develop to master them.

- **Rule 1:** Borrow only for assets that cash-flow the debt and a profit.
  How will you evaluate whether something produces income before taking on credit?

- **Rule 2:** Take collateral or control.
  Describe the methods you can use to secure every deal—titles, UCC filings, assignments, or ownership control.

- **Rule 3:** Price the spread, not the dream.
  How will you protect your profit margin and stay disciplined in small, repeatable wins instead of chasing big risky ones?

- **Rule 4:** Pre-plan the exit.
  What are the clear repayment or liquidation events you must confirm *before* you fund a deal?

- **Rule 5:** Obey the map.
  Note what regulations, licensing, and legal boundaries apply to your operations, and how you'll stay compliant.

Section 3 — Building Your Credit Strategy

Describe how each type of bank relationship supports your overall "Money Machine."
Use full sentences rather than bullet points so you internalize the process.

Bank 1 – Operating or Business Line of Credit

Explain how you will use this revolving line for short, secured transactions such as earnest-money deposits, small rehab draws, or trade advances.
How will you keep the cycle of borrowing and repayment moving quickly to build trust and increase capacity?

Bank 2 – Collateralized Line of Credit (via Non-Interest CD)
Write how you can pledge *past labor* (cash) into a non-interest-bearing time deposit and negotiate a private, non-callable credit facility against it.
Why is this approach more powerful than traditional savings, and what leverage does it give you?

Bank 3 – Specialized Capacity (Warehouse or Standby Facility)
Describe when you would use this type of line, what makes a deal institutional-grade, and why each bank relationship should remain separate and purpose-built.
How will you ensure that each partner sees a clean, high-performing lane?

Section 4 — Compliance, Ethics, and Guardrails
Write a short integrity pledge to yourself.
State how you will operate as a disciplined, ethical lender—never crossing into consumer territory without the proper structure.
Include your commitment to accurate record-keeping, proper lien release, and transparent communication with both borrowers and bankers.

Next, list the personal boundaries you will uphold:
• Keep personal finances separate from business lines.
• Maintain liquidity equal to two-to-three monthly minimum payments.
• Track utilization weekly and review performance monthly.
How will these habits protect your staying power?

Section 5 — Velocity Practice
Explain how velocity—moving the same capital through multiple short, safe rotations—creates more profit than a single large deal.
Use an example: if $100,000 earns $5,000 every 60 days, how many times could that

cycle in a year, and how would the compounding work in your favor?
Write the math and your understanding below.

Section 6 — Your "Hip National Bank" Plan
Summarize in your own words how you will apply this module over the next 90 days.
Include these prompts to guide your planning:

1. What will be your first small, safe lending placement?
2. How will you document each deal and track the spread?
3. How will you protect your reputation for "on time, every time"?
4. How will you ensure your profits flow back to build your Hip National Bank?

Challenge: Can you achieve at least 6–8 full turns per year on the same capital while never missing a repayment?

Integrity Ledger – "Guardrails and Grace"
List the ethical guardrails you will install to protect your business reputation and relationships.

Reflection:
What will integrity look like in your lending practice when pressure hits?

Power Questions for Meditation & Mastery

1. What are three ways banks "lend what they borrow," and how can you mirror those methods in your business?

2. How can you build one habit this week that turns consumer debt into capital for production?
3. What's one skill—negotiation, underwriting, or contract control—that would make your Money Machine more powerful?
4. How will you use your profits to create new opportunities for others—employees, partners, or your community?

Bonus Challenge: "The Infinite Return"

Using your current available credit, design a 12-month rotation plan where each draw is self-liquidating and re-lent. Show how you'll grow Hip National Bank without using any new cash—just velocity, discipline, and documentation.

Key Insight:

Credit is not evil—it's energy. The wise steward learns to harness it like electricity: direct the current through purpose, control the flow through contracts, and illuminate every area of your financial house.

Personal Declaration:

"From this day forward, I will use credit only for assets,
maintain control of my paper, price my spread honestly,
plan every exit before I enter, and stay within the laws that govern commerce.
I will operate with integrity, discipline, and clarity—
becoming the banker of my own destiny."

Signature: _____ Date: _____

12

Module 12: Then What is Credit Used For?

What to Buy: The Effective Use of Bank Credit
Lend What You Borrow

Ray Kroc didn't invent the hamburger, but he perfected a machine that turned ground beef into bankable equity. When he first visited the MacDonald brothers' shop in San Bernardino, he didn't just see teenagers moving fries; he saw a choreography that could be cloned, financed, and placed on the best dirt in every town. Kroc licensed the system, standardized the process, and—most importantly—wrapped the whole thing in a real estate play. Franchisees paid for the right to operate the store, but the corporation owned or controlled the land beneath it. Rent checks, franchise fees, and predictable sales created an income stream sturdy enough to be capitalized by bankers at premium valuations.

At Hamburger University, Kroc would ask new owners, "What business are we in?" When someone finally answered "the hamburger business," he'd smile and correct them: "We're in the real estate business." He was right—sort of. The burgers created the revenue that justified the rent that created the valuation that unlocked the credit that bought the next corner. But pull the camera back: McDonald's was in the money business. They used a reliable operating system to print collateral and then used that collateral to borrow more, build more, and own more. The restaurant was the engine; the real estate was the chassis; the banking relationship was the fuel line.

Run the math and the model becomes obvious. An empty corner might cost $1,000,000 and the building another $1,000,000. But a standardized, high-throughput store on a long lease can be valued by the income approach, not just replacement cost. Strong sales, tight operations, and a corporate covenant turn dirt into a dividend. Capitalized at a reasonable market rate, that site can appraise at a multiple far beyond the $2,000,000 invested, creating millions in paper equity. Banks love that kind of paper because it behaves: predictable rent, brand stability, and a line of franchisees ready to step in if one falters.

Here's the quiet gear Kroc didn't preach from the stage: once the income exists, the line opens. Lenders will advance against stabilized cash flow, often at conservative loan-to-value ratios, and those proceeds become seeds for the next site. The franchisee runs the store, pays the note, and feeds the rent; the parent company becomes a portfolio of cap-rated leases. That is Money Machine thinking: convert process into property, property into paper, paper into purchasing power—then loop it. You don't need golden arches to do it; you need a repeatable operation, defensible margins, and the discipline to keep the credit aimed at assets.

Now translate that same logic to our lane. Banks hate inventory that bleeds and love inventory that pays. Non-performing notes, half-fixed houses, and title snags clog their pipes; stabilized assets clear them. When you buy distress at a discount and convert it to performing paper or saleable property, you turn the bank's lemon into your lemonade—and they will happily drink with you. The moment your remodel sells or your re-worked note begins to pay, you've created value that can be measured, collateralized, and—if you choose—levered again. You didn't swing for magic; you executed a system that turns problems into predictable payments.

The golden rule at this stage is simple: never let the bank's lien live on your keepers. Use credit to acquire, fix, and flip—or to convert paper you can resell—but do not strap your long-term holds with debt that can be called at the worst moment. In Module 11 we introduced the private-side tactic: pledge "past labor" (cash) into a non-interest time deposit and negotiate a clean, non-callable line against it. That line is your tool for short, secured placements—earning spreads, not chasing trophies. The assets you produce—cash proceeds, perfected notes, paid-off properties—are your trophies, and they stay unencumbered. The bank sees disciplined use; you keep permanent control.

Let's bring it down to a single flip to show the rhythm. You acquire a fixer for $115,000 in a neighborhood that supports a $300,000 exit when done right. Your controlled scope calls for $60,000 in work, executed under your contract, not your contractor's. You draw both the purchase and the rehab from your private line, finish in sixty days, and launch with an "exciting price" that creates a crowd and a bidding window. Multiple offers push the sale to $307,000; you wire proceeds into your operating account at the same bank, then pay the line back to zero. What remains—after commissions, closing costs, and your rehab—settles in Hip National Bank as new cash, not new debt.

Now widen the aperture. Ten such turns in a year—done clean, documented, and early—don't just stack profits; they stack credibility. With every repayment the banker's risk officer sees exactly what we want them to see: utilization that rises with purpose and returns with speed. That's when you negotiate your next capacity bump, or spin a second CD-backed facility, or open a small warehouse line earmarked solely for discount notes you intend to flip to a yield buyer. Each lane has its own purpose, its own paper, and its own exits. You never commingle lanes, you never miss a payment, and you never forget that boring is bankable.

The temptation at this point is to "celebrate" by buying toys on the same line that funds your deals. Don't. If it can't cash-flow its own debt service plus a profit inside your target window, it's consumption masquerading as an investment. The rich buy the assets that buy the toys; consumers buy toys and then rent their lives back from lenders. You are graduating into the first group. Set a policy you don't break: credit lines acquire assets only. Personal lifestyle is paid out of realized, debt-free profits—after the line has been returned to zero.

Remember also the warning from Proverbs. Co-signing and cross-collateralizing feel generous in the moment and become handcuffs when the wind shifts. Keep your business entities clean, your books separate, and your promises few. If a deal needs your personal guarantee to pencil, it isn't a deal; it's a demand. Let paper, not pity, secure your placements: UCC filings, assignments of proceeds, title control, or first-right agreements. Mercy is good; muddled is deadly. We're builders, not pirates.

"Don't agree to guarantee another person's debt or put up security for someone else. If you can't pay it, even your bed will be snatched from under you." (Proverbs 22:26–27)

Here's your final flywheel before we close the book. Use Line A (operating LOC) for earnest money, rehab draws, and short trade advances that you can liquidate in 30–60 days. Use Line B (CD-collateralized) for larger, secured placements where your exit is a sale or a take-out buyer you already know by name. Use Line C (specialized capacity) only when you're warehousing notes or inventory for institutional buyers under pre-negotiated terms. Each placement gets a one-page deal sheet: amount out, fees in, collateral in hand, calendar dates, and exit trigger. If a sheet can't be written to look inevitable, the deal isn't ready for your money.

Let's end where Kroc started: with a simple system anyone can follow, multiplied without mercy. Your "hamburger" might be a flip, a note re-work, a trade advance, or a tiny business that throws off reliable cash. The point isn't the product; the point is the process. Stand up a repeatable operation, place it on strong "dirt" (your contracts and your bank relationships), and let the income approach do the heavy lifting. As your cash flows stabilize, capacity expands. As capacity expands, your options multiply. And as your options multiply, you can choose stewardship over spectacle—assets over applause, covenant over consumption.

You've walked from curiosity to competence, from fear to flow, from consumer to constructor. You've learned to see what bankers hope you'll miss: that contracts are currency, that credit is clay, and that value is something you can form—legally—every single day. The Money Machine was never a building or a balance sheet; it was the discipline in your hands and the signatures you command. Go place it on your corner of "Main Street." Go turn paper into property, property into paper, and paper into purpose. And when the deposits hit Hip National Bank, remember why we do this: to build, to bless, and to leave something standing that outlives us.

A Final Word on Integrity - Understanding Why You Are to Give Your Way to Being Rich

"A good man leaveth an inheritance to his children's children: and the wealth of the sinner is laid up for the just." (Proverbs 13:22)

There are three elements that, when united, naturally produce wealth. In the beginning, God made the earth, and within it He placed every resource needed to sustain life. Genesis 2:7 says, "God formed man of the dust of the ground." We are literally connected to the land—dust to dust—so real estate resonates with us at a level deeper than preference; it is origin. In the moment God breathed life into man, the three elements met in one scene: God, Man, and Land.

Then God "remodeled" the land into a garden and made it our home. He designed plumbing before pipes—rivers sprang from Eden to water it. In His generosity He placed man in the best parcel on earth: a place with pure gold, aromatic resin, and onyx. Real estate people summarize value with three words—location, location, location—and from the beginning God gave mankind the premiere location. There was God, there was man, and there was the best-situated piece of land on earth.

Have you noticed how easy it is to talk with anyone about real estate? Everyone wants to know how to acquire it, sell it, or invest in it. We are drawn to own a piece of the earth parceled into lots because God formed us from it and gave it to us to cultivate and steward. Throughout Scripture He reserves choice land to restore His people. Real estate represents wealth in tangible form. When He delivered Israel from Egypt, He promised "a good and large land, a land flowing with milk and honey."

"For the Lord your God is bringing you into a good land of flowing streams and pools of water, with fountains and springs that gush out in the valleys and hills. It is a land of wheat and barley, of grapevines, fig trees, and pomegranates; of olive oil and honey. It is a land where food is plentiful and nothing is lacking. It is a land where iron is as common as stone, and copper is abundant in the hills. When you have eaten your fill, be sure to praise the Lord your God for the good land He has given you." (Deuteronomy 8:7–10 NLT)

The Unencumbered Life—Living Off Your Giving

As freely as I've shared the wisdom God has entrusted to me, I ask one thing of you: become a giver on purpose and use this information to live as the "just." Your inheritance—"a good and large land... flowing with milk and honey"—is already appointed. The problem is many of the just, just don't know they are the just yet. That hesitation stalls the emergence of the glorious Church Christ will return for. So, commit to be a sower, not a taker—to plant and then patiently expect harvest so you can plant again. "God so loved the world that He gave..." (John 3:16). His nature is generosity; our privilege is to duplicate it.

"Give, and it shall be given unto you: good measure, pressed down, and shaken together, and running over, shall men give into your bosom. For with the same measure that ye mete withal it shall be measured to you again." (Luke 6:38 KJV)

Success in real estate brought opportunities to buy nice things—cars, vacations, homes, schools for the kids—the visible stuff people equate with prosperity. When people see those things, they usually ask, "What do you do?" What they mean is, "What am I missing? Why do you seem peaceful while your life looks abundant?" For years I answered, "I make my living buying and selling real estate." I said it for twenty years—until the Lord showed me the real source.

Business and real estate were simply the work of my hands—something for God to bless. Then came the great flush of 2007–2008. My "golden touch" vanished; I lost everything. I couldn't sell, deal, or borrow my way out. Confidence collapsed. My marriage of twenty-two years didn't survive. After decades of self-employment my résumé looked like a skeleton, and I didn't know how to start over.

I was a relatively new Christian, having committed my life to Jesus two years earlier. I had little church background—no traditions to un-learn—so when I read the Bible and heard teaching, I took God at His Word. When I prayed about my finances, I expected answers because Scripture said I should. That's when Luke 6:38 hit me—hard.

It wasn't the first word, "Give," that struck me; I'd always been a giver. It was the rest—how extravagantly God returns to givers. As I meditated, He replayed moments when I had given unselfishly and showed me why blessings kept boomeranging back. Then He took me to Galatians 6:7: *"Be not deceived; God is not mocked: for whatsoever a man soweth, that shall he also reap."*

"Whatsoever" means whatever I sow returns in kind. Nature preaches the same sermon: seeds reproduce after their own kind. Plant grapes, get grapes—never apples. God warns, "Be not deceived," because nothing can negate this spiritual law; He will not be mocked.

Right then my phone rang—my insurance agent calling to review the vehicles on my policy.

After we finished, she laughed, "Ray, you sure have a lot of cars for two people." I fumbled to justify my little fleet. After I hung up, I felt a twinge of shame—until the Holy Spirit whispered, "Each seed produces after its own kind." I asked, "Lord, what does that have to do with anything?" Before I could finish, peace flooded in and He answered: "Son, you have given away more cars than most people have ever owned. You sowed 'car,' and by My whatsoever law, you reap 'cars.' You said I go 'slap crazy' in giving back; Luke 6:38 is about overflow. When I need to answer someone's prayer with a car, I know I can count on you."

He was right, and the shame vanished. I realized I would always be in the Kingdom Car Business with my Father—Abba & Sons. From then on I refused to be shamed by opinions that couldn't see the source. *"Out of the bosom of man shall you be blessed."* My bosom is one with God; He has access to anything He's ever placed in my storehouse. Thy will be done.

God showed me the real source of wealth: I was living off my giving. Work—our economic energy, time, and talent—is simply the seed-maker. It gives God something to multiply, but it is not the source. Becoming skilled in real estate is the "sauce," not the source. In the Kingdom, wealth flows by seedtime and harvest. The world runs on buying and selling; the Kingdom runs on planting and reaping. "Each seed produces after its own kind." Money sown produces money grown. The ground you plant in determines the size and certainty of the crop. A better Kingdom saying than "It takes money to make money" is this: it takes sowing money into fertile Kingdom ground to produce an enduring harvest of money.

"Be not deceived." Why the warning? Because the deceiver fights the truth of the tithe. He twists it so people think it's "their money" and giving is loss. Yet Scripture says God supplies seed to the sower and has blessed you to get wealth. Remove one breath from God and the capacity to earn disappears. His blessing on your hands has a double purpose: provision for your household and provision of seed for His purposes. Have you noticed givers always seem to have something to give? Those who never have enough usually don't sow; they consume the very seed that would have changed their season.

How the Integrity of One Man Funded a Nation

Joseph's humble beginning did not predict his great finish. What made him remarkable was integrity aligned with what I call the Foundations of Personal Power. He trusted God's word about himself. He believed the dreams God gave him—even when sharing them provoked jealousy.

Through every trial he held his integrity. He didn't crumble when sold to Ishmaelites, or when Potiphar's wife lied, or when the cupbearer forgot him for two more years. He guarded his words—no record of complaining—and always gave God glory. Brought before Pharaoh, he prayed, interpreted the dreams, and then offered a national plan. The authority in his words promoted him from prisoner to prime minister in a single day.

Joseph didn't take offenses personally; he saw God orchestrating each step. That allowed him to restore his family later from a position of strength. He avoided assumptions and asked precise questions, restating for clarity before interpreting. Because he finished what he started and did his best in every assignment, he rose quickly—over Potiphar's house, inside the prison, and finally over Egypt's economy. His plan to store grain during seven years of plenty saved the region during seven years of famine. Wealth streamed into Egypt because food was in Egypt, and God's favor rested on Joseph's stewardship.

God brought good out of others' evil—the brothers' betrayal, Potiphar's wife's lies, the cupbearer's delay, and the famine itself. The entire arc shows that God can overrule malice and position His people for destiny. Pharaoh recognized wisdom when he saw it and entrusted

Joseph with Egypt's fortunes. The result wasn't only national survival; it was national surplus.

Now fast-forward. Generations passed and a new Pharaoh forgot Joseph. As Israel multiplied, Egypt enslaved them. When the time came for deliverance, God gave instructions that are easy to overlook amid the plagues and the Passover. "Speak now... let every man ask from his neighbor, and every woman from her neighbor, articles of silver and articles of gold." (Exodus 11:2–3). "And the Lord gave the people favor... so that they granted them what they requested. Thus they plundered the Egyptians." (Exodus 12:35–36).

At the Red Sea God parted the waters; Israel crossed; the Egyptian army drowned. On the far shore there was no debt to the Egyptians for the borrowed goods—only justice. Some call it reparations for forced labor. I believe it was repayment of what Joseph's anointing had brought to Egypt generations earlier. The wealth of the wicked had been stored for the just until the just were ready to walk out. God's wealth transfer was not a trick; it was a settling of accounts.

Joseph was a giver, carried blessing, and walked in integrity—wholeness, oneness with God. I share his story because the same pattern stands now: a divine wealth transfer is reserved for the just. Our role is to be those people—faithful, integrous, generous—so God can trust us with stewardship when the doors open.

The 7/10ths Rule of Multiplying Family Wealth

ADAM—Authority, Dominion, And Might—was the original blessing pronounced over mankind. "Be fruitful and multiply, fill the earth and subjugate it... rule over every living thing." (Genesis 1:28–30 AMP). God gave us seed-bearing plants for food and as a picture: life moves by seed.

Here is a simple, durable rule for covenant finances. For every $100 you create as an asset through the use of credit to acquire it:

• Give the first $10 (10%) to God's Church as the tithe.

- Pay yourself the next $10 (10%) before any expenses to build an inheritance for your children's children.
- Save the next $10 (10%) before expenses until you can invest safely, without risking principal, and let compound interest put your "money children" to work.
- Live—wisely—on the remaining $70.

Per $100 of income earned:

$100 — Total income

– $10 — Tithe to God's Church

– $10 — Pay yourself first (legacy)

– $10 — Savings for wealth

$ 70 — Adjusted income to operate your household

Sample "Money Machine" income of $10,000 per month:

$10,000 — Monthly income

– $1,000 — Tithe

– $1,000 — Pay yourself first (legacy)

– $1,000 — Savings for wealth

$ 7,000 — Adjusted monthly income to live on

Now adjust your standards of living to thrive on 7/10ths of take-home income. Build an emergency fund of at least three months of that adjusted number. Use the 7/10ths figure to set your household budget, determine safe borrowing capacity, and plan debt service when appropriate. From that same 7/10ths, plan your alms and seed offerings—gifts above the tithe—as the Spirit leads.

Final encouragement: *The Money Machine you've built in these pages is fueled by integrity and generosity. Sow on purpose. Guard your name. Keep your word. And expect what God promised: "You shall lend to many na-*

tions, but you shall not borrow." The wealth of the wicked is laid up for the just—so be the just.

Coming Soon: The Remodel Series

NEW 7 BOOK SERIES FROM RAY WRIGHT JACOBS

The 5-Adam Foundation Remodel Points (5-AFRP)

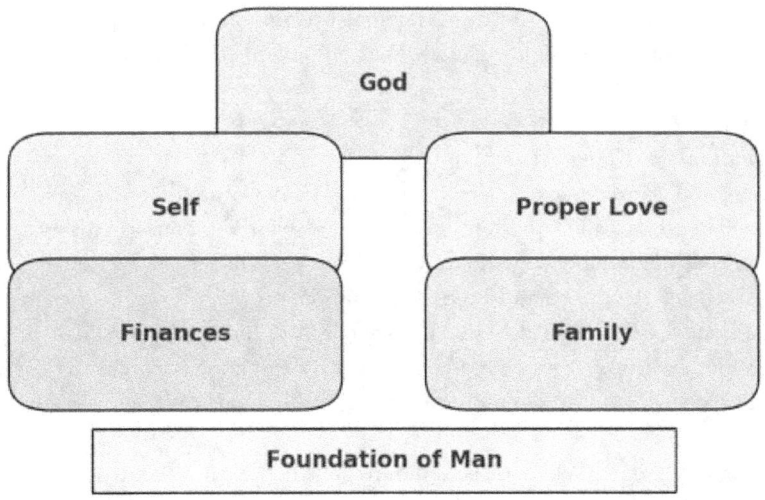

ADAM = Authority, Dominion, And Might

The purpose of The Remodel series is to provide practical, spiritual, and actionable steps for you—the man—to regain your wholeness. This training focuses on rebuilding the entire man, restoring him to the original garden state of **Authority, Dominion, And Might**.

In Genesis, God blessed the first Adam and gave him authority over the earth: over the fish, the vegetation, the animals, and all living things. But Adam lost that dominion. Through the plan and grace of God, the "second Adam"—Jesus Christ—came to restore those who believe in Him to their former fullness.

The ministry of Adam, Where Can I Find You? carries this assignment: to **remodel the man** back to his natural state of Authority, Dominion, and Might in all five life areas—**God, Self, Proper Love, Finances, and Family**—repairing the garden foundations so that man may stand strong again.

Unlocking What Was Concealed

As you study Adam, Where Can I Find You? you will discover how simple God's instructions truly are—though often hidden in plain sight within His Word. My prayer is that you will be provoked to dig deeper, to uncover mysteries reserved for seekers of light.

"It is the glory of God to conceal a matter; but the glory of kings is to search out a matter."
— Proverbs 25:2 NKJV

This series calls men to repentance and to return to the garden, where Christ, the second Adam, is waiting to restore what was broken. Through simple, plain steps, He shows us how to repair the breach, reclaim our inheritance, and walk again in the fullness of God's design.

The Foundation Under Attack

When God created man, He created him in His image and likeness—to look like Him, act like Him, and function like Him. God blessed Adam as Authority, Dominion, and Might and charged him to "multiply and fill the earth." But the enemy came, distorted the image, and stole the dominion.

That same distortion is celebrated in society today. The more a person displays rebellion, immorality, or sin, the more attention and applause they receive. Just a few decades ago such behavior would never have been broadcast, yet now it dominates our screens.

This is why Adam, Where Can I Find You? is so critical. It confronts the decay, quenches man's desperate search for meaning, and leads him back to the garden where Jesus Christ stands ready to restore him. Together, we will plow the ground, take ownership, and repair the crop with God's guidance.

The Master Builder's Blueprint

God's order is clear: the man is His foundation. Just as a master builder starts with the ground before laying a foundation, God formed man from the dust before forming woman, family, or society. Man is the bedrock. And when that foundation is set upon the "rock of revelation," no devil in hell can prevail against it.

"According to the grace of God which was given to me, as a wise master builder I have laid the foundation, and another builds on it. But let each one take heed how he builds on it. For no other foundation can anyone lay than that which is laid, which is Jesus Christ."
— 1 Corinthians 3:10–11 NKJV

The 5-Adam Foundation Remodel Points (5-AFRP)—God, Self, Proper Love, Finances, and Family—represent the pillars that support the man's assignment. When they are whole, society is whole.

A Warning to the Runners

Many men, like Jonah, are running from their calling. They will pay any price to escape the voice of God—even if it means being swallowed by despair, addiction, hopelessness, or prison walls. But just as God delivered Jonah to the shores of his destiny, He can deliver you.

"Then Jonah prayed to the Lord his God from the fish's belly. So the Lord spoke to the fish, and it vomited Jonah onto dry land." (Jonah 2:1, 10 NKJV)

Jonah's obedience saved a nation. Your obedience may save your family, your community, or even your generation. What message has God sealed inside of you that cannot wait?

The Call of This Series

Adam, Where Can I Find You? is not simply God's question to the first Adam after the fall. It is the cry of every man searching for restoration, clawing and reaching in the dark until finally he calls out to the second Adam, Jesus Christ.

This journey is not for the woman, nor for the family first. It is for the man—the foundation. When the man is remodeled, everything built on him is strengthened. And so we return to the garden, to meet the second Adam, to fill the void that nothing else can satisfy, and to be restored to our original Authority, Dominion, and Might.

The Remodel Series

The work of Adam, Where Can I Find You? expands into **seven focused volumes**, each addressing one of the 5-Adam Foundation Remodel Points, along with books dedicated to women and rest. Together, they form the **Remodel 7-AFRP Series**:

- **God – Adam, Where Can I Find You?** – *Restoring the Man Back to Garden Dominion*
- **Self – Why the Fatherless Son Wanders** – *Repairing the Breached Foundation*
- **Proper Love – Compelled By Compassion** – *Servitude to All Saints in Truth & Love*
- **Finances – The Private Money Covenant of Wealth** – *God's Wealth Plan of Abundance*
- **Family – The Interceding Rock** – *Answering the Call with Holy Hands Lifted Up*
- **Family For Women – I Survived the Stench of the Remodel** – *A Guide to Assisting in the Reconstruction of Your Dream ~~Dwelling~~ Husband*
- **Rest – Rest-Ored** – *On the Seventh Day God Commanded We Rest... Restored in His Perfect Law*

Each book is paired with a workbook, training modules, and companion resources to equip men for their remodel journey.

My Promise to You

"Through my **Definite Chief Aim**, I commit to building The Remodel into a global brand—one that will include books, workbooks, seminars, websites, video trainings, public speaking, church ministry engagements, mobile device apps, and social media platforms. My vision is for The Remodel to become such a worldwide movement that it ushers me into fellowship with great men and women of faith, allowing me to stand alongside their ministry brands and present Adam, Where Can I Find You? on the global stage through our annual Remodel Events.

I will certify, through the training of men who graduate from **Adam Academy**, the credentials to preach, teach, and instruct the ministry assignment of Adam, Where Can I Find You? These men will rise as global public speakers, equipped to remodel and reconstruct the whole man back to the garden state of **Authority, Dominion, And Might.**

God blessed the first Adam with dominion over the fish, the vegetation, the animals, the whole earth, and all living things. Though Adam lost that dominion, through the plan and grace of God, the second Adam—Jesus Christ—came to remodel and restore all who believe in Him back to their former fullness. The ministry of Adam, Where Can I Find You? carries this same assignment: to remodel man back to his natural state of Authority, Dominion, and Might in all five Life Areas—**God, Self, Proper Love, Finances, and Family**—repairing his garden, reclaiming his inheritance, and occupying his land.

I pledge to demand the highest standard of integrity, faithfulness, and covenant commitment to Jesus Christ from every Adam Academy graduate. And in time, the vision will expand into a full academic institution: **Adam Academy, Texas.** This school will stand as a modern-day version of the great Oral Roberts University—dedicated to housing, teaching, training, remodeling, and restoring Adam disciples for the "Great Commission." Its mission: to harvest the lost and the backslidden man back to the Hope of Glory, righteousness, and the restoration of garden Authority, Dominion, and Might—to the glory of God's original creation, MAN."-Ray Wright Jacobs-

Final Word

This series is a clarion call: Adam (Authority, Dominion, And Might), where are you? The time has come to stop running, return to the garden, and embrace the Second Adam, who alone can restore the fullness of God's design.

"Beloved, I pray that you may prosper in all things and be in health, just as your soul prospers."
— 3 John 1:2 NKJV

About the Author

Ray Wright Jacobs, author of Best Seller, "Matter Miner – Immutable Laws That Attract Success With Every Thought", is a seasoned entrepreneur and visionary with over 30 years of experience in the real estate industry. Born with a passion for building and creating, Ray became a licensed real estate agent in 1994 and advanced to a real estate broker by 1998. He founded and managed his own real estate brokerage, as well as a real estate development and investment companies, guiding numerous clients through the complexities of property transactions and investments.

As a husband, father of thirteen and grandfather of seven, family has always been at the heart of Ray's journey. His personal life and professional endeavors are deeply intertwined, teaching him invaluable lessons about ambition, humility, and the true measures of success.

The real estate recession of 2007–2008 marked a pivotal point in Ray's life. Facing significant losses, he confronted the hard lessons of vanity and ego that had influenced his career. This period of reflection led him back to his first love: writing. Ray began channeling what he describes as "downloads from God," receiving profound insights and revelations that would shape his future work.

Appendix: Hour of Prayer

When asked how to pray for an hour as Jesus did, we find ourselves lost in vague requests, repetitive prayers and wish list loops. I prayed to God and asked Him to give me a way to be about His business and not mine. This is what He gave me to add to the 7-book series, The Remodel. I share this and challenge any man who wishes to cover his territory effectively to just read out loud and watch what happens:

ADAM = Authority Dominion And Might
MAN = God's Foundation of Creation – ADAM

CORPORATE INTERCESSION AND SPOKEN WARFARE OF GOD'S INTERCEDING ROCKS THE ADAM-MEN TO REVIVAL

1.) Thanksgiving   2.) Praise   3.) Petition
4.) Warfare   5.) Royal Decree 6.) Confession
7.) Rest-ord

1.)
Blessed art Thou my glories Father Yahweh Nissi,

Today hear my worship because of Your love and justice. Lord, I praise You today with songs of psalms. I will also be careful to live a blameless life – I wait for You to come to my aid. Please accept my offering this day as I enter Your gates with thanksgiving and go into Your courts with praise: Give thanks to the Lord, for the Lord is good; Your mercies and kindness endures forever! Thank You Father for Your grace, which is sufficient for me to accomplish Your intended purpose for my life. I thank You that yesterday is behind me, and I forget its woes as well as its triumphs; for today is a present from You and tomorrow no man knows what it holds. So, thank You for the gift that is today; I shall make the most of it with my cooperation to Your will. I thank You for sending Jesus to redeem me from the slavery to sin and eternal death, which was its wage. Thank You for the Holy Spirt, the Teacher and Comforter of my soul. But, more than all of these, I thank You for pre-picking me to save me as one of Your own; for You are Elohim, and You alone will I serve.

2.)

Before the mountains were born, before You gave birth to the earth and the world, from the beginning to end, You, El Olam are God. You satisfy us each morning with Your unfailing love, thus I sing for joy to the end of my life. You alone are my refuge, my place of safety, You are my God, Lord Adonai, and I trust You. You cover me with your feathers. You shelter me with your wings. Your faithful promises are my armor of protection. I give thanks to You Lord and proclaim Your unfailing love in the morning, Your faithfulness in the evening, because You are Good. You thrill me, Lord, with all you have done for me! O Lord what great, works that You do! And how deep are Your thoughts. You, O Lord, are King! You are robed in majesty and armed with strength. Your royal laws cannot be changed. Your reign, O Lord his holy forever and ever.

When doubts, fears and unbelief fills my mind, Yahweh Shammah, Your Comfort gives me renewed hope and cheer because You are always there. You are my fortress; You are the Mighty Rock where I hide. I come to You with thanksgiving, and sing You psalms of praise. For You are a great God, a great King above all gods. You, El Roi, hold in Your hands depths of the earth and the mightiest mountain. The sea belongs to You, for You made it, and Your hands also formed the dry land. I come to You with my bowed down worship. I kneel before You Lord, my maker, for You are our God. O Great Shepherd, Yahweh Sabaoth, we are Your people You watch over, the flock under Your care.

Each day I praise Your name, and proclaim the good news that You are the Lord who alone can save us. I publish Your glorious deeds among the nations, and tell everyone the amazing things You do. Great are You Lord! You are most worthy of praise! You, EL Elyon, are feared above all gods of other nations which are mere idols. Honor and majesty surround You because You made the heavens, and strength and beauty fill Your sanctuary. I love to give You the glory only You deserve; Let all of creation hear my offering whenever I come into Your courts.

Let the trees of the forest rustle with praise before the Lord – Attiq Yomin, for You are coming to judge the earth. You will judge the world with justice and the mountains with Your truth. Fire spreads ahead of You and burns up all Your foes. The heavens proclaim Your righteousness; every nation sees Your glory. Those who worship idols, dear Lord, are disgraced – all who brag about their worthless gods – for every god must bow to You, my El Elyon. For You, O Elohim, are supreme over all the earth; You are exalted far above all gods. Your Right Hand has won a mighty victory; Your Holy Arm has shown Your saving power! Let the sea and everything in it shout Your praise! Let the earth and all living join in – for if they are quiet, You, Lord El Roi, will cause the rocks and stones to praise You!

Lord, El Olam, let me not be counted as the quiet men who do not praise You with my Holy Hands Lifted Up. As for me and my house, we praise Him who sits on His throne between the Cherubim, while the whole earth quakes. I praise Your great and awesome name: YAHWEH! Your name is holy! Mighty King, lover of justice. You have established fairness and acted with justice. I exalt You Lord God as I bow before Your feet, for You are holy! O Elohim, You performed miraculous signs and wonders in the Land of Egypt – things still remembered to this day! And You have continued to do great miracles in Israel, and all around the world. You have made Your name famous to this day. This is the day the Lord has made; I will rejoice and be glad in it!

3.)
We thank You, El Shaddai, that You are faithful and true to forgive all sins and here and now confess to You each and every one of our sins And thank You for Your faithful forgiveness. We nail our flesh to the cross today, Lord, that our flesh be put to death as our daily sacrifice and obedience to Your Word. And because we died with Christ, the enemy has no authority over the death of our bodies and thus no access to our minds without our permission.

That we here and now revoke that consent given through deception and subject the dictates and lusts of the flesh under our heavenly created spirit; And our spirit, which is always aligned and obedient to Your Spirit, the Spirit who is the creator of time Himself, and because You, Lord Adonai, are not bound by the dispensation of time;

You stepped outside of time, gathered and took every earthly sin, past present and future, all the way from Adam to the last person to ever be born in the future on this earth and imputed them all on Your most excellent sacrificial Lamb during the Calvary Ceremony as the perfect sin offering, who is Christ, when He cried out, as He died for our sins once and for all, "tetelestai", which translates – "It is Finished!" and "The bill has been paid."

We thank You Father, that there is no sin that we will ever commit, that You have not already placed upon the head of Christ, making Him the last blood sacrifice ever; therefore, we receive the offer of His free gift of Your Grace dear Lord.

We honor His sacrifice by putting our flesh to death with Him, but also that we share with our regenerated spirit His rise, and joined to His Body as His holy and acceptable unblemished church as we daily renew our minds to the sufficiency of Your Grace. Abba Father, we love You because You first loved us so much that Your Hand in our life's affairs have led us, and keeps us on the path to You.

Abba Father in heaven, You have said, "*Put on the whole armor of God, that we may be able to stand against the wiles of the devil. For we wrestle not against flesh and blood, but against principalities, against powers, against the rulers of darkness of this age, against spiritual hosts of wickedness in heavenly places.*" (Ephesians 6:11-12)

As we pray, we place our complete trust in You, Elohim, and Your Word as the word of truth, *as we gird ourselves by taking up the whole armor of God, so that we may be able to withstand in this evil day, and having done all to stand; we stand therefore* in Jesus' Name.

So that the fertile ground of our believing hearts will no longer accept weed seed lies from the unseen spiritual enemy, *we gird our waist with truth*; to assist us in managing the lasting effects of sin is our Advocate, Jesus, who is always pleading our case before You dear Father, the only One who is truly righteous. *We therefore put on the covering breastplate* of Jesus who maintains our right standing with You;

Your Word in Isaiah 52 says, *"How beautiful on the mountains are the feet of the messenger who brings the good news of peace and salvation"*; We therefore, *shod our beautiful feet with the battle preparation of the gospel of peace;*

Lord God, so that we may always be ready to prove our confidence in everything we hope for, we interlock our shield wall with all believing saints in this battle – *above all* – *by taking our shield of NOW-Faith with which we are able to quench all the fiery darts of the wicked one*; And, the crowning authority of our **Positive Throne of Adam** which protects our Subconscious minds from erected strongholds, *we take our helmet of knowing our once-for-all salvation.*

Just as when Jesus, full of the Holy Spirit, returned from the Jordan River was led by the Spirit into the wilderness; where He was tempted by the devil for forty days, He used the incorruptible Word of God as the only offensive weapon needed when He said – 3-times to counter Satan's 3-lies, *"It's written..."* And because **we now know** it is also an unseen enemy who opposes us, and not the people around us - who are also Your children; we too unsheathe the *sword of the Spirit, which is the Word of God,* Jesus;

We thank you Father for this gift of protection and ask You to fulfil Your Word to make Your purpose for this protection during our walk, assignment, purpose and prayer reign in our lives, as we pray always with all prayer and supplication in the spirit, **(*Pray in Tongues for Godly Direction*)** we are watchful to this end with all perseverance and supplication for all saints – and for us also that utterance may be given to us, that we may open our mouths boldly to make known the mystery of the gospel, for which we are ambassadors in chains; that in it we may speak boldly, as we ought to speak; that we do not cease to give thanks for all the saints, making mention of them in our prayers:

"That the God of our Lord Jesus Christ, the Father of Glory, may give you the spirit of wisdom and revelation in the knowledge of Him, the eyes of your understanding being enlightened; that you may know what is the hope of His calling, what are the riches of the Glory of His inheritance in the saints, and what is the exceeding greatness of His power towards us who believe,

According to the working of His mighty power which He worked in Christ when He raised Him from the dead and seated Him at His right hand in the heavenly places, far above all principality and power and might and dominion, and every name that is named, not only in this age but also in that which is to come.

And God has put all things under the authority of Christ and has made Him head over things for the benefit of us, the church. And the church is His body, it is made full and complete by Christ, who fills all things everywhere with Himself." (Ephesians 1:17-23). And by that authority, Christ – The Head, now shares with us – His

Body, the **Sovereign Authority Dominion And Might** that restores us to our Adamship assignment as given by You Lord in the beginning, in the garden.

Abba Father in heaven, we stand in proxy for Your called ones, Your ADAM-Man, in this prayer of repentance, petition, and warfare cry to You until Your revelation of prayer has reached their hearts and minds and they join in as Interceding Rocks for themselves and their loved ones, in Jesus Name.

Lord El Olam, in the beginning, You blessed the purpose of Your first Adam with Sovereign Authority Dominion And Might over the earth, the fish, vegetation, animals, and all living things. Because he lost that Sovereign Authority Dominion And Might a call from You went out in Genesis 3:9 – "**Adam, (Authority Dominion And Might) Where Are You?**: as You dispatched Your plan and Grace for the Second Adam – the Lord Jesus Christ, to restore and *Remodel* man to former fullness of his Sovereign – ADAM-Man – state of Authority Dominion And Might through the restoration of the **5-Phase ADAM-Man Foundation *Remodel*** which re-establishes us to our intended wholeness.

Abba Father, thank You for this **5-Phase ADAM-Man Foundation *Remodel*** in these five life areas: **Messiah**, so that we may know Your will, what part in Your will we play, and trust You as our Lord and King as You draw us back to the garden where we find our Sovereign Authority Dominion And Might that You restore back to us when we cry out to Jesus: "*Adam, (Authority Dominion And Might) Where Can I Find You?*"; **Self**, so that You can reveal to us within our spirit, Your will for us, who we are, why You created us and stop "*The Fatherless Son from Wandering*" by directing us to our *Positive Throne of Adam*, renewing our minds, and establishing our stand at the posts of our assignments and purpose; Yahweh Shalom, I now climb up to my watchtower and stand at my guard post, while I wait for You Lord God, to answer my call for Your vision and plan for me.

Proper **Love**, so that we may learn to imitate the very nature of You Elohim, which is to Love, Give, and Sacrifice as shown in Your works as we pray always with "*Holy Hands Lifted Up*" and answer the call to be like You "*Compelled to Compassion*". **Finances**, so that we may demonstrate impeccable stewardship over the blessing You have empowered us to get wealth and to possess the land that You have instructed us to keep, dress, and multiply, as we occupy as "*Private Money Covenant*" Bankers – *Lending even that which We Borrow*, until Jesus' return;

I especially thank You, Abba Yahweh Nissi, in our all-consuming area of **Finances** and for providing the revelation of Your Divine financial Pre-Paid plan for me to have: The perfect, productive, well-paying career position; Witty ideas and inventions I take all the way to the paying market; Success in all business ventures and "*Private Money Covenant*" contracts; and, Unhindered access to every banker, lender, investor, Secretary of Treasury, IRS Director, Federal Reserve Chairman, US President, and mentor Your Favor has purposed for me – by making a clear and direct path for my recoupment efforts to establish my Godly "*There Place*", where You are pouring me out Treasury Notes are under Your Window of Heaven in this world's economy for my Kingdom Purpose to be fulfilled, in Jesus Name.

And finally, **Family**, to imitate You Father, as *"Interceding Rocks"* to pray, love, and provide leadership to the harvest and our families, as kings and priests, as God's ordained head and leaders of our homes, families, and church body knowing the scriptures so that we may wash our wives, our children, and shepherd Your family of *Wandering* sheep back into the safety of the flock by the cleansing of Your Word and the sowing of good seed in their hearts only.

Lord, Yahweh Shalom, Your established order of our *Remodel* is a perfect one, and by Your grace and peace maintains our dignity as men while under Your heavenly re-construction; **Messiah, Self,** proper **Love, Finances** and **Family**. Father, as Your Word declares: *Proverbs 1:7*, teaches us before there can be us, there is You, it says:

"Fear of the Lord is the foundation of true knowledge", and; *Proverbs 24-27* instructs us Your priority to becoming Your ADAM-Man as well as the proper order You established as best for us; - clarifying the wisdom of producing enough income to care for a wife prior to marring her and starting a family; it reads: - *"Prepare your work outside And get it ready for yourself in the field; Afterward build your house and establish a home."* And *Proverbs 24:3* gives us understanding of exactly how to build a house; and the wisdom to turn it into an eternal Godly home: *"Through [skillful and godly] wisdom a house [a life, a home, a family] is built, And by understanding it is established [on a sound and good foundation]"*.

Dear Heavenly Father, we thank You for this understanding, for in *Proverbs 4:7* You have said in Your word, *"in all of your getting, get understanding"*, and we here and now submit and consent to Your full foundation *Remodel* as we respond to Your – *Genesis 3:9* call from the garden that ends our grouping, stretching, reaching and clawing search through outreached hands back to the waiting Christ, with our own question; **"Authority, Dominion, And Might – Where Can I Find You?"**, in Jesus Name.

We ask, Father what is it that You want, what affairs are on Your holy agenda today that You may download to us to assist You with? What do You want to happen on earth? We thank You Father that Your blessing is with us in the course of accomplishing Your work on earth.

We thank You Lord Adonai, and ask You Father to fulfil Your word that as we release this and every prayer for each other that we may be healed. We receive this healing here and now in abundance and thank You, that You are faithful and true to do for us whatever You say.

And Father, we pray over our families, these captives in exile, and Your Remodeled ADAM-Man, that You, Yahweh Sabaoth, surround them with Your covenant kindness and covenant protection as a shield for them and all of their loved ones, their wives, their children, one-by-one; and cause every judge, prosecutor, attorney, warden, jailer, C.O., bailiff, county staffer, private prison personnel, Marshall, every state and government employee to have blessed victory as we pray for each of them as well as the peace and prosperity of the cities in which You have carried them into exile; that the land prospers so that they too may prosper in accordance with Jeremiah 29:7, and also let each and every one of them find favor in the sight of those officials for Your sake. Give us Your all-sufficient grace to endure all adversity with patient peace and joy in You, in Jesus Name.

4.)

Now Father, we decree and declare by the Sovereign Power of the Eternal Spirit You have given us back through Christ, that we place all power and works of the enemy and his lies under our feet and bruise his head as we join You Jesus, in our seated position of authority as members of Your Body; as we rebuke Satan and revoke all consent that allows his demonic forces to twist Your truth dear Lord, in our minds, in the name of Jesus.

Because we are the godly, in the name of Jesus, we decree and declare that our every step is directed by You Lord; Although we may stumble, we shall never remain fallen because You, Yahweh Shammah, are faithful to confirm Your word – "that although a righteous man falls seven times, he will rise, but the wicked falls once and is destroyed; we are never abandoned by You, Lord El Roi, nor will our children ever beg for bread; thank You Father, that we only give good counsel in Your name and teach what is right and what is wrong.

Now Father, as Your godly Garden **Remodel** project that You are restoring back to **Sovereign Authority Dominion And Might**; one, in which You have deemed as godly, and by that authority, we enforce the mandate of the promised inheritance of our land; that we live with You forever; and we watch as the wicked are destroyed, in the name of Jesus.

El Shaddai, because of Your Shekinah Glory, the enemy who continually opposes us, is now opposed by You; our enemies are now Your enemies; we therefore stand firm in the victory of Jesus over those who war against us by and through the Blood of the innocent lamb, Jesus.

We decree and declare, that since we fear You, Lord God Adonai, Your angel of the Lord is our rear guard, in Jesus name.

Abba Father, You have said, "*command ye My hand*", and that You personally inhabit the praise of the righteous; therefore Father, hear and inhabit our praise to You right now, confirm Your word, as we now command Your hand – for You, Elohim, to muster Your armor; take up Your shield, lift up Your spear and javelin; prepare for battle, inhibit our praise, and come to our aid;

In the name of Jesus, we declare victory over those who pursue us; we take up our sword of the Spirit, which is the Word of God, and cast down each vain imagination, vex, hex and every high thought that exalts itself, and dares to oppose You and Your knowledge, Dear Father.

In the name of Jesus, we dispatch calamity to overtake the wicked who hate righteousness; and we take our refuge in You dear Lord, because You have redeemed us.

Father, we here and now confirm our covenant, as disciples of Christ, to operate in the **Sovereign Authority Dominion and Might** over the works of Your hands, in both the heavens and the earth that was given back to us by the finished works of Jesus;

We announce our harmonious consent of Your will to make disciples of all nations; to baptize them in the name of the Father, The Son, and The Holy Spirit; by and through Your power, Jesus, and we declare that You are always with us, in Jesus name.

We decree into the heavenlies, that we deny our self-willed - self-life, which is hostile against Your will Father, and take up our cross daily to follow You Jesus; We declare our obedience by laying down our lives for Your sake, where we find Your will and our real spirit-life in You dear Lord; We here and now usurp every part of our will hostile towards You and consent for it to cooperate in harmony with Your will, and thus lay up our profit in heaven, in the name of Jesus.

In the name of Jesus, Father, we place ourselves under Your healing light of truth so that we may discover and know all lies concerning ourselves, our Private Status, our health, our Pre-paid wealth, our Private Equity remedy, our mental state, and physical conditions that we have accepted from evil spirits which have set-up strongholds and citadels in our minds – that continue to trigger sin, poverty and adverse conditions in our lives, so that You may reveal, and help us rid ourselves of every counterfeit thought, idea, attitude, prophecy, and suggestion causing us any vexation, weakness, sickness, brokenness, depression, oppression, impoverished mind-set and/or lack.

Abba Father, we thank You for our regenerated spirit that reconciles us and brings us home to You for all eternity. Now, Yahweh Yireh, so that we may carry out our worldly assignments, we ask You to renew, enlarge and strengthen our minds by shining Your Glory Light and installing our Positive Throne of Adam into the darkened areas of our minds where Lucifer and his evil spirits have established their lies as bases-of-operation, as strongholds, to keep us deceived which we have mistakenly accepted as truth.

In the name of Jesus, we bind their further access and control, and loose Your Word of Truth as our **Positive Throne of Adam** that destroys his footing by replacing them with the full enlightenment of Your will, that we hereby acknowledge and accept, placing our will in cooperation and agreement with You, so that not only our walk, but also our thinking attracts and glorifies You.

We bind every uncontrolled thoughts, imaginations, impure pictures, wanderings, prejudices, and confused ideas that imanate from principalities; from powers; from rulers of darkness of this age; and from spiritual hosts of wickedness in heavenly places that are attempting to inject into – or subtract from – anything to do with our minds.

We further bind any attempt to induce us, through our minds, to accept their "Balak-like" curses, as our own words for us to speak, say our utter over ourselves as these curses intending to thwart Your promises.

Instead, Lord God, may You return them – One-Thousand Fold, back into the enemy's camp as spiritual bombs that explode over them, in the same way Balaam ended up prophesying over "*the apple of Your eye*", Israel; and never return to us except as the blessing, You have placed in their mouth instead that they must release over us NOW!; as well as releasing our status as Sovereign Private Citizen with full **Authority Dominion And Might**; no longer treated as a law fiction under the Trading With Enemy's Act, and excluding us from further mischaracterization under the Emergency Banking Relief Act, in Jesus name.

In the name of Jesus, everything added to our minds by evil spirits is now hereby removed; everything that was subtracted from our minds by them is now added back. We take back our Sovereignty forfeited and all ground given through an unrenewed or improper mind, misunderstanding Your truth, accepting suggestions, or the result of a blank or passive mind – and evict all occupied territory as our minds are renewed by Your revealing light of our **Positive Throne of Adam**, Dear Father.

Because we think for ourselves and resist every satanic lie, whether it be in the form of a thought, suggestion, imagination, or argument, Lucifer and his cohorts must NOW FLEE from us, in Jesus name; and we overthrow these lies, one-by-one, we formally believed – but now disbelieve, by the sprinkling of the blood of the sacrificed innocent Lamb, Jesus; and after which, the smudging of Your anointed oil of wisdom over our ear, thumb, and toe, as well as its pouring over our heads and minds, in Jesus name.

We thank You Father for the gift that is our children, born in our youth, which is to us a reward; We declare that they are our arrows that fill the quiver in our hands; when our accusers confront us at the city gates, we will not be put to shame, in Jesus name.

Ephesians 5:1 instructs us to imitate You, Father, as dear children; As imitating fathers, We declare we do not provoke our children to anger, but bring them up in the discipline and instructions of You Dear Lord, that they may dwell with us in joy and hunger for Your Word as we pray always over our children and grand-children, in Jesus name.

Father, we thank You for Your word in *Proverbs 18:22*; "*He that findeth a wife findeth a good thing, And obtains favor from the Lord.*"

We decree and declare that we will dwell with our wives with understanding, giving honor to her as the weaker vessel, as being heirs together of the grace of life that this and none of our prayers will be hindered, in Jesus name.

We decree and declare that we are compassionate, loving, tenderhearted and of one spirit with our wives, and we bind the enemy from having any further access to our oneness in marriage, in Jesus name.

We place Heaven and Earth on notice that: We are the husbands and fathers God wants us to be. We are led by the Holy Spirit in all decisions. We know how to really love our wives and children. We are delivered from negative behavior. We speak words that build up, and never destroy; Word Seeds that produce life and never death. We possess the desire to always pray for our wives and children. We will continue to grow spiritually, emotionally, and mentally, in Jesus name.

We decree and declare that in us, God has created a clean heart, a renewed mind, and a renewed right spirit, in Jesus name.

We decree and declare that we do not operate in anger, strife or contention, there is no confusion or breech in the spirit between us and our wives and children. We will be immediately convicted by the Holy Spirit of truth anytime we are unforgiving or do not operate as the head of our homes and family and immediately make the change, in Jesus name.

We decree that we love our wives just as Christ loves the church, and we declare that we will give our lives for them, in Jesus name.

In the name of Jesus, we announce and release in the atmosphere that our wives and children are strong in NOW-Faith, they continue to grow spiritually, the spend time in the Word of God, they have discernment and revelation, they are becoming mighty sons and daughters of God, they are a light to others, they know God's will for their lives and live in it daily.

We decree and declare; our wives and children have wisdom and understanding in all areas of business, banking, finance, real estate, insurance and their work, they posses in their hands the power to produce six and seven figure annual incomes so that our wives and daughters may diligently care for our homes and children effortlessly, as Proverbs 31: Women, in our absence, in Jesus name.

Lord, we effect and activate the **Sovereign Authority Dominion And Might** You have given us over all the power of the enemy, and we decree that **Sovereign Authority Dominion And Might** over the unseen spiritual enemy and his lies. We declare that he cannot twist the truth of God in our wives and children's minds another day in their life, in Jesus name.

By the **Sovereign Authority Dominion And Might** given to us, we declare that our wives and children are so solid in the Word of God and in truth that they can immediately identify a lie of the enemy, cast it aside, and listen only to the voice of Yahweh, in Jesus name.

We effect and enforce the mandate of Yahweh Sabaoth's mighty protection over our wives and children. We declare favor where favor is due and supernatural increase is chasing them down, overtaking them and providing abundant supply right NOW, in Jesus name.

In the name of Jesus, we declare that our every prayer asked of You is of one mind with Christ, in NOW-Faith; since we are not double-minded, we receive everything we ask of You because Jesus is right there interceding for us, right now, at Your right hand.

We decree and declare that the Body of Christ, which is us, is rising up together in revival, on one accord, in NOW-Faith, and love, as one glorious Church driven by the power of Jesus Himself, in Jesus name.

I thank You Father, Yahweh Shamma, that You always hear me. In the name of Jesus, I declare that these prayer points take on the characteristics of divine projectiles in the realm of the spirit; and hit their mark.

I bind any retaliation by Satan or any of his cohorts in heaven and earth, in Jesus name.

By the power and the blood, I seal this prayer and loose it in both heaven and earth, in Jesus name.

We ask You Father, El Roi, to fulfill Your Word and make Your purpose reign in our lives. We all have plans and goals that we are pursuing. We ask that You, Yahweh, establish whatever is from You – and cause to fade away whatever is not from You. We honor You as, El Elyon – our creator and as our loving Heavenly Father.

We affirm that it is You who work in us to will and to act according to Your good purposes as in Philippians 2:13. Renew our minds so that we may understand Your ways and Your plans more fully. We pray this in the name of Jesus, who said to Thomas & Andrew, "*I am the way, the truth, and the life, and no one comes to the Father except through me.*" (*John 14:6*)

5.) & 6.)
My Morning Accepted Evaluations, Declarations & I Accept's

"2026 is an incredible Year! Success, Excellent Spiritual and Mental Health, Exceptional Physical Shape, Prosperity, and Abundance in many different forms Blessing my life this year. I gratefully enjoy and accept their manifestations throughout 2026 and happily share these blessings of abundance with many others in order to bring happiness to their year as well."

"I'm Alert – I'm Alive – And I Feel Great!"
"I'm Alert – I'm Alive – And I Feel Great!"
"I'm Alert – I'm Alive – And I Feel Great!"
"My Best of My 43,100 Days are Still Out in Front of Me"
"I have a Bright Future"
"I Have Found the Second Adam"
"I Have the Favor of God"
"People Like Me"
"God, I Praise You Because You Have Made Me in an Amazing Way. What You Have Done is Wonderful – And For That Reason"
"I Accept:"
"That I Am a Victor, Not a Victim
That I Am Wonderful

That I Am Amazing

That I Am A Masterpiece

That I Am Happy

That I Am Healthy

That I Am Wealthy

That I Am Creative

That I Am Talented

That I Am Valuable

That I Am Secure

That I Am Worthy

That I Am Writer Of Favorable Contracts

That I Am Anointed

That I Am Positive

That I Am Blessed

That I Am Grateful

That I Am Strong

That I Am Beautiful

That I Am Fit

That I Am Confident

That I Am Mighty

That I Am Interceding Rock

That I Am Compelled To Compassion

That I Am No Longer A Wandering Son

That I Am Private Money Covenant Of Banking & Commerce

That I Am Rest-Ord

That I Am Courageous

That I Attract Money And Opportunities

That I Am Rich

That I Am Money Machine – Money Chases Me Down

That I Am Peace

That I Am Faithful To God

That I Am Blood Covenant Of Abraham, That's Mine Too

That My Wives And I Will Live 120 Years And Look 30

That I Am _____ Lbs And Fit With The Body Of A Tuned Athlete With 9% Or Less Body Fat

That I Am Healthy Eater

That All Food Eaten Is Healthy, Because I Bless It First

That I Am Wisdom

That I Am Just Like My Father – Love

That I Am A Man After God's Own Heart

That I Am Lender

That I Am The Head

That I Am Above Only
That I Am Established As Holy By God
That I Am Righteous
That I Am Leadership
That I Am Royalty
That I Am Excited About The Blessing That Is Today
That I Am The Standard God Is Raising Against The Flood Of Satan
That I Repeatedly Call Those Things That Be Not, As Though They Were; Until
They Are, With The NOW-Faith Of A Mustard Seed, In Jesus Name"
Amen!

7.)

And this same Jesus who taught His disciples, instructs us also to always pray this way:

Our Father
Who art in heaven, hallowed be thy name
Thy kingdom come, thy will be done
On earth, as it is in heaven
Give us this day, our daily bread
And forgive us our debts, as we forgive our debtors
And lead us not into temptation, but deliver us from evil
For thine is the kingdom, and the power, and the glory
Forever, and ever
Amen.

www.ingramcontent.com/pod-product-compliance
Lightning Source LLC
Chambersburg PA
CBHW070909130626
46555CB00001B/63